Advance Praise for *Increasing the Odds for High-Performance Teams—Lessons Learned*

▸ If you want to create "high performance teams," the lessons learned by Leholm and Vlasin will be invaluable to you. However, this book is not just about teams. It is a must read for all leaders who want to increase the engagement, commitment, and performance of their workforce.

Keith Ayers, President, Integro Leadership Institute

▸ This book is absolutely terrific. It contains rich, relevant content; formatted as a user-friendly resource for building high-performance teams—a realistic roadmap. Case studies are insightful and effectively translated into action plans for optimizing team performance and business results.

Catherine A. Kilstrom, Senior Vice President—Customer Care, Comcast

▸ This book gives corporations and organizations insights into how to create "high-performance teams." Techniques needed to change a workforce from average to excellent are laid out through case examples. The challenge in the United States today is not to find cheap labor, but to train leaders to empower workers and create "high performance."

Mary Ann Peters, Former Executive, Coastal Corporation

▸ A well researched and thoughtful guide to the role and power of team dynamics in enhancing organizational performance. It is essential reading for leaders, educators, and practitioners involved in utilizing teams to enhance performance.

Philip R. Smith, President and Executive Director, Midwest Universities Consortium for International Activities, Inc. (MUCIA)

Increasing the Odds
for High-Performance Teams

▶ **LESSONS LEARNED**

Arlen Leholm and Ray Vlasin

Michigan State University Press • *East Lansing*

Copyright © 2006 by Arlen Leholm and Ray Vlasin

♾ The paper used in this publication meets the minimum requirements of ANSI/NISO Z39.48-1992 (R 1997) (Permanence of Paper).

Michigan State University Press
East Lansing, Michigan 48823-5245
www.msupress.msu.edu

Printed and bound in the United States of America.

12 11 10 09 08 07 06   1 2 3 4 5 6 7 8 9 10

LIBRARY OF CONGRESS CATALOGING-IN-PUBLICATION DATA
Leholm, Arlen G.
Increasing the odds for high-performance teams : lessons learned / Arlen Leholm and Raymond D. Vlasin.
p. cm.
ISBN 0-87013-777-8 (pbk. : alk. paper)
1. Teams in the workplace. 2. Teams in the workplace—Management—Case studies. 3. Management—Employee participation—Case studies. 4. Performance—Case studies. 5. Organizational behavior—Case studies. I. Vlasin, Raymond, 1931– II. Title.
HD66.L447 2006
658.4'022—dc22
2005032534

Cover design by Heather Truelove Aiston
Book design by Sharp Des!gns, Inc., Lansing, MI

Michigan State University Press is a member of the Green Press Initiative and is committed to developing and encouraging ecologically responsible publishing practices. For more information about the Green Press Initiative and the use of recycled paper in book publishing, please visit *www.greenpressinitiative.com*.

CONTENTS

ACKNOWLEDGMENTS

We dedicate this work to our spouses, Betty and Claire, and to our children and extended families who have inspired us.

We thank our chapter co-authors and the many team members and other leaders who contributed their talents, ideas, and insights central to this book.

To Martha Bates and her colleagues at Michigan State University Press, a special thanks for their help and inspiration. We thank also, Michigan State University Extension and the University of Wisconsin Extension for their cooperation and their support.

We thank Ralph Levine, for system dynamics modeling assistance, and Rick Mills for graphics assistance.

Finally we thank our many reviewers with a special thanks to Jerry Hembd for his exceptional skill and contributions.

HOW TO USE THIS BOOK TO YOUR ADVANTAGE

We wrote this book for persons who are inquisitive but busy and who seek new lessons about high team performance but want them efficiently. For this reason, we are suggesting ways to make the best use of this book to your advantage. Our goal is to help you increase the odds that teams you form, manage, coach, or help develop will become high performing and will sustain that performance.

> Therefore, we suggest first a quick read of chapter 1. It will give you an overview of the book, the five cases analyzed, and the protocol used in gleaning the lessons learned from the analyses conducted.
> Next, we suggest a quick scan of chapter 2. It shares wisdom from masters in the field of team and organizational effectiveness. Their concepts and insights are directly relevant to the case study chapters that follow.
> Third, you can review the brief notations at the beginning of the five case chapters.
> If you are interested in *production and service teams,* these can be found in all five case-study chapters—chapters 3–7. If you are interested in *administrative support teams,* these can be found in chapters 3, 4, and 6.
> If you want to explore real teams with co-located members, they are described in chapters 3, 4, 5, and 7. If you want to explore real teams with geographically distributed members—that is, virtual teams—see chapter 6.
> Then, you can select the one or two cases that most interest you. Each carries a snapshot (overview) explaining the reasons that the case was included. It is followed by the organizational context, team perform-ance, dynamic considerations, and lessons learned. Lessons learned are highlighted so they can be found easily.
> A final chapter treats important lessons common to two or more teams that are more broadly applicable to team performance and organizational effectiveness.

While we hope that you find time to read the entire book, we hope these suggestions will enhance the book's benefits for you and col-leagues. Good fortune in your reading.

The Book, the Cases, the Protocol

▶ Arlen Leholm and Ray Vlasin

Why This Book

Have you ever wondered why some work teams greatly outperform others within the same organizational settings? Have you questioned whether work teams from very different sectors of the economy and society achieved their high performance by similar means? Have you considered what you or others might do to help teams increase their chances of becoming truly high performing? We have. And, it motivated us to perform our research on high-performing teams and to share the lessons we learned in this book.

Both of us have been members of work teams, leaders in such teams, and designers and organizers of teams as well as mentors, coaches, diagnosticians, and team educators. We have benefited from the valuable work of others—"the masters"—who have studied, worked with, and written about work teams and their organizations. We have joined those masters in concluding that you cannot design a work team from scratch to be high performing. You also cannot force a work team to be high performing and expect that performance to be sustainable. However, our experience from actually working with many teams has convinced us that *you can increase the odds that a team can become truly high performing and can sustain that performance.*

Increasing the Odds through Lessons Learned

Our goal was to find and select a handful of very high performing work teams from widely differing sectors of the economy and society and work with them to determine what caused them to perform so very well: What made them special? What made them stand out in the eyes of their team members, their team leaders, and others who knew about them? And most important, we wanted to learn from those directly involved what lessons could be drawn from their experiences and achievements and shared with others who want their teams to become high performing.

As a result, our book focuses on insights and lessons from the diverse cases that we analyzed. Though our analysis of the teams selected was detailed, we share here only the organizational and team details sufficient to provide a context for the lessons and insights learned. The book is condensed and in popular style. It is reader friendly, with a similar layout for each case. And it accommodates the busy reader by including a synopsis and a snapshot of each case. If you are between planes, you can decide what case to read first and what to read next, or you can jump to the last chapter and scan the lessons learned. We hope you enjoy the entire book and find it informative and useful.

What's in the Book?

▶ **Contributions from the Masters.** Fortunately, the field of work team performance is well served by an array of practitioners, writers, and scholars who have studied team performance and the organizations within which teams function. Since we have benefited greatly from them, we decided to recognize them and briefly to share concepts and ideas they have provided. We view these contributors as "the masters" in their field and are indebted to them for their contributions. We have devoted chapter 2 to their work and believe it will enrich the usefulness of the cases and lessons shared here.

▶ **Five Cases with Diverse Teams.** In the five case-study chapters, chapters 3–7, we give special attention to one or more teams and their organization plus lessons from the team experiences analyzed. Each chapter presents the organizational context, team characteristics, and key variables that influenced high performance. Each presents the views of team members and team leaders about what made the team special or unusual. Our treatment sets the stage for lessons to be learned from each individual case. While these lessons are specific to the high-performing team or teams involved, they may contribute to a larger set of lessons that apply more broadly to several of the high-performing teams from the five cases analyzed.

▶ **Both Administrative Support Teams and Production and Service Teams.** Self-directed real teams are recognized for their great value in producing products and services and in providing them to clientele. Self-directed teams also can bring major value to an organization by enhancing its internal administrative support services. The five case chapters explore examples of *product and service teams*—in food manufacturing, laboratory analysis of genomes, automotive product testing and development, education and technical assistance, and rural farm and community betterment (chapters 3 through 7). Three of the five chapters also include examples of administrative support teams—"a team at the top" in food manufacturing, a "team leaders group" in laboratory analysis of genomes, and a "regional administrative team" in Extension education and outreach (chapters 3, 4, and 6).

▶ **Both Co-located and Geographically Dispersed Teams.** The five case study chapters also provide an opportunity to explore teams whose members are located together and virtual teams whose members must work together across distances. Chapter 6 describes three virtual teams while the other case chapters describe teams with members at the same location.

▶ **Dynamics of Prominent Variables.** Also, for each of the five case chapters, our discussions will share key variables viewed by team members and team leaders as influencing high performance. These are typically both team variables and organizational variables. These variables are not static, and their influence changes over time. For each case, the increasing intensity of one key team variable illustrates the dynamic influence of that variable on team performance and on the team and organizational environment. The variable selected in each case was identified by organizational and team leaders as most prominent in their emergence as a high performing team.

▶ **Important Lessons Learned.** Each of the five case-study chapters provides lessons that were important to the team or teams in that case. We have deliberately retained each of the major lessons learned for each case, placed at the end of the case study chapters. Chapter 8 addresses the question "What lessons cut across two or more cases and might apply more broadly to enhance work team performance in other situations? Chapter 8 orders the lessons by those pertaining to (1) starting right—a key to performance enhancement, (2) investing in knowledge and skills for performance, (3) cautions in team formation and operation, (4) concepts that made a difference, and (5) administrative context and the huge difference it can make. Some twenty-one broader lessons are shared. These lessons provide ways to increase the odds that your team(s) can achieve high performance.

Five Cases—Deciding Which to Read

We have attempted to assist you in deciding which cases might be most immediately germane to your interests. For this reason, we have added here a very brief notation on each of the five case chapters. In addition, you will find a somewhat longer introductory statement called "Why the team story" at the beginning of case chapters 3–7. Furthermore, a "snapshot" provides a quick history and overview of the case without the detail on team performance or lessons learned.

The five case situations present "high-performance teams" from different sectors of the economy and society. They represent quite different organizational and team settings. Each case situation involves a special set of experiences, observations, and lessons. Readers may wish to focus first on the case or cases that most nearly match their interest and then explore the others. Listed for each case below are some highlights that may help readers select what to read first and what to read after that.

▶ **Chapter 3.** The Quaker Oats case shares how management and labor overcame an unsatisfactory manufacturing environment plus an extremely low-trust atmosphere. Through a trust-based partnership, they transformed an aging plant's work system into a highly productive, team-based, performance-driven, mutually gratifying environment for both labor and management. Trust, shared leadership, carefully crafted teaming and team education, and careful attention to team and organizational fundamentals propelled their successes. A "team at the top" energizes and enhances its sixty-four production and service teams. Important lessons learned are shared, starting with those from the mutual leadership achieved.

▶ **Chapter 4.** The self-directed teams of the Institute for Genomic Research (TIGR) demonstrate the productive power of deliberately seeking divergent thinking and approaches in this research-based laboratory environment. They also demonstrate unusual performance increases and staff retention improvements in moving to a shared-leadership and responsibility-based context for team operation. The teams demonstrate the performance gains possible from intense mutual accountability, highly complementary team members, and a focus on productivity measures and goals they help create. A "team leader group" guides and enhances its seven analytical, laboratory, and research and development teams. One key lesson is that by seeking diversity of applicable skills and knowledge and divergent approaches and thought, TIGR simultaneously has achieved great diversity of cultures and created a magnet for professionals.

► **Chapter 5.** The two teams of the Bosch Corporation demonstrate how midlevel management can enable a high-performance team to achieve unusual creativity. The case shows the importance of hiring persons who fit with the team. It also shows how professionals with differing technical knowledge and skills can meld into a very complementary high-performing team with trust and caring. Team creativity and outstanding performance can occur in harsh climatic conditions and challenging remote living situations. Camaraderie aids creative problem solving, and highly effective communication links the teams and customers and enhances customer trust.

► **Chapter 6.** At the heart of this case study is the importance of organizational support systems, including helpful administrative boundary conditions, and the roles they serve in enhancing high team performance. Short case narratives from two educational outreach entities, from Michigan State University (MSU) and Ohio State University (OSU), highlight geographically dispersed virtual teams. Within MSU Extension, two teams within a larger organizational venture show what can be achieved with shared leadership, self-directed team creation, a close partnership with clientele, and nurtured citizen financial and program support. A "regional administrative team" demonstrates how shared leadership in budgeting and in decisions about educational program coverage and staffing can result in major gains in team productivity and program impacts. Within OSU Extension, a virtual team demonstrates the value of directly linking university extension education programs with stakeholders to creatively advance mutual interests. In addition, this example shows how the active seeking of divergent views among cooperating scientists, educators, and stakeholders can lead to timely education actions that are highly beneficial to the nursery, landscape, and turf grass industries.

► **Chapter 7.** The Women's Interest Group from India shows how mutual caring, zeal to improve, and energized human spirits can lead to unusual performance. In a very low-resource environment, dedicated women undertook new and improved agricultural enterprises and increased family income. They used their newly created abilities and team strength to make other personal, family, and community improvements. The case shows how the women used their advancing skills to address other community problems and opportunities. As a major lesson, a "real team" can occur and achieve in a low-tech environment in which initial illiteracy and poverty were substantial—many village residents initially earned less than two U.S. dollars per day.

Taken together, the five cases provide a range of observations about the emergence and functioning of high-performance teams in both private and public sectors. The teams excel in creating and providing joint products and services in very different industry and organizational settings—whether for external clientele or for those within their own organization. The cases reaffirm the importance of supportive organizational conditions within which to operate. They also reaffirm the importance of team conditions that enhance team progress and performance and facilitate and encourage creativity and self-motivated performance. Last but not least, the five cases strongly reaffirm the tremendous value of the sound research-based works and applications highlighted in chapter 2.

Case-Study Protocol

A POOL OF HIGH-PERFORMING TEAMS

Our initial tasks included identifying a pool of "high-performing teams" from which to select individual teams and their organizations for interviews and analyses. We tried not to duplicate teams in case studies already covered in the popular and/or scholarly literature.

We deliberately sought teams from an array of situations—business and industry, private sector and public sector, high resource and low resource, high tech and moderate to low tech, research and education. We also deliberately sought to select teams that represented differing product and/or service outputs. We believe that teams can differ greatly by type of joint products and services they produce and still take actions that increase the odds that the teams can become high performing.

In our identification of high-performing teams, we relied heavily on the assessment of their contemporaries. We initially judged a team qualified for our selection if it appeared to have the attributes of a "real team," as per Katzenbach and Smith.[1] We required also that a team for the pool be recognized as performing at high levels by peers within the organization and by professionals beyond the organization who knew about the team.

OUR FIVE SELECTIONS

As a result, we selected five cases involving one or more teams for more intensive analysis. They were, as represented in chapters 3–7, the following types: (1) manufacturing teams producing food products, (2) genomic sequencing teams mapping organisms' DNA, (3) applied engineering testing teams improving automotive systems, (4) university extension-research teams for enhanced educational impacts, and (5) a low-income women's interest group producing agricultural enterprises.

OUR WORKING HYPOTHESES

We wanted to determine how teams could develop into high-performing units under an array of conditions. Our interest in teams operating in diverse circumstances comes in part from two working hypotheses we shared.

❶ *Interdependent work teams producing joint products or services can achieve high performance under an array of situations as long as the teams possess the empowering conditions and operating relationships that allow full expression of team creativity.* This view supports Katzenbach and Smith's excellent work concerning organizational basics, team basics, real teams, and high-performing teams (see chapter 2).

❷ *While one cannot deliberately command or direct an interdependent team into unusually high performance, the organization and its teams together can take a series of actions that will materially increase the odds that the teams will become very high performing.* We believe that this hypothesis applies whether the teams are public or private, high or low tech, or high or low resource and whether they are producing products, providing services, or both. The lessons learned, presented in chapter 8, respond to this hypothesis.

DEVELOPMENT OF DISCUSSION GUIDELINES

Drawing on the rich literature regarding teams, our research process included a comprehensive personal interview with each case study team, team leaders, and organization leaders. Our detailed interview process covered the following: (1) Formation of the team, and its operation over time, (2) The unusual or special nature of this team—traits, characteristics, (3) Features of the team and organization associated with high performance, (4) Variables influencing performance (the variables used in the case study explorations included eighteen organizational variables and twenty-two team variables; see chapter 2 for those variables identified by team and organizational leaders as most influential), (5) The team's possible influence on the rest of the organization, (6) Important lessons learned by team members, team leaders, and organization administrators.

ADDED ATTENTION TO LESSONS LEARNED

As a final part of our discussion we asked team members, team leaders, and administrators to think of any other lessons learned from observing the high-performing team or teams that they believed could be helpful in designing, operating, and supporting teams. We received their observations and blended them with those of our chapter coauthors and our observations for presentation in each of the case chapters. In our discussions we also encouraged participants to consider whether they believed some of the lessons they observed might have broader application—for example to teams they knew about elsewhere in their organizations or teams beyond their organizations. Their responses contributed to the selection and ordering of the lessons learned for chapter 8.

NOTE

1. J. R. Katzenbach, and D. K. Smith, *The Wisdom of Teams: Creating the High-Performance Organization* (New York: Harper Business, 2003).

2

Learning from the Masters of Team Performance

▶ Arlen Leholm and Ray Vlasin

This book focuses on high-performing teams. This chapter builds on the most relevant literature from the masters of team and organizational performance. Reading this chapter will help you integrate key concepts about team and organizational basics and other factors influencing organizational effectiveness. It addresses dynamics that propel a team to high performance, including the influence of leadership.

The use of self-directed teams has increased dramatically during the past twenty years. First the manufacturing sector and more recently a wide range of private, public, and nonprofit organizations have embraced the concept of self-directed teams. Why has there been such a rapid movement to teams? The answer is that teams perform! This is particularly true if attention is paid to key team and organizational basics—the building blocks for high team performance.

Self-directed teams, largely in control of their destinies, are far more than a passing fad. Self-directed work teams can foster an amazing amount of productivity if organizations nurture them appropriately. A major body of literature exists on how to form and operate effective self-directed teams and avoid many of the problems and pitfalls associated with their formation and operation.[1] Much less is known about very high performing teams.

History of Self-Directed Teams

During the 1950s, British coal miners were among the first to form teams based on the analysis of the technical and social requirements of their jobs.[2] Trist's research revealed clear indications of higher productivity and job satisfaction among coal miners who received more control over their work. Sweden's Volvo Corporation was among the first to experiment with teams of individuals responsible for putting whole cars together with limited supervision, resulting in major increases in productivity.

In the United States, self-directed teams emerged in the 1960s with an early corporate pioneer, Proctor and Gamble. A little later General Motors, General Electric, Ford, Cummins Engine, Caterpillar, and Boeing followed suit. However, not until the mid-1980s did self-directed teams become a major way of organizing for business.[3] Self-directed teams are now common in a wide range of government entities, service organizations, and nonprofit as well as private-sector corporations.

Concepts of Self-Directed Teams, Real Teams, and Single-Leader Units

The concept of self-directed teams evolved from a need to improve organizational performance in both the private and public sectors. Hierarchically structured, traditional organizations have been too slow in responding to competition and customer needs.[4] They have often lacked creativity, innovation, and enthusiasm in providing products and services because of the limitations of their organizational structure and operating arrangements.

Self-directed teams have emerged with decision-making and problem-solving authority in the hands of the persons closest to the product or service being created or provided.[5] Private-sector companies that have carefully designed, correctly applied, and properly supported self-directed teams have improved their products/services and markets, enhanced productivity, and increased customer satisfaction. Other performance benefits include better quality, cost reduction, improved timing, innovation, better use of employees' talents, and increased motivation.

What are self-directed teams? We use Kimball Fisher's definition from his highly acclaimed work, *Leading Self-Directed Work Teams:*

> **Self-directed team:** *A* group of employees who have day-to day responsibility for managing themselves and the work they do with a minimum of direct supervision. Members of self-directed teams typically handle job assignments, plan and schedule work, make production and/or service-related decisions, and take action on problems.[6]

Self-directed teams also bear joint responsibility for whole work processes, with individual team members performing multiple tasks. Self-directed teams have a common purpose: they are customer oriented and performance driven. All of this is accomplished with a minimum of direct management, control, and supervision.

Self-directed teams that function and achieve well are sometimes referred to as "real teams." Jon Katzenbach and D. K. Smith, in their seminal work, *The Wisdom of Teams,* define such a team:

> **Real team:** A small number of people with complementary skills who are equally committed to a common purpose, goals and working approach for which they hold themselves mutually accountable.[7]

In *Teams at the Top*, Katzenbach identifies three critical litmus tests as preconditions of a *real team:* (1) clear collective work products dependent on the joint application of multiperson skills, (2) shifting leadership roles to be filled by different people at different stages of the effort, and (3) mutual (as well as individual) accountability for the group's overall results.[8]

If these preconditions cannot be met, a self-directed team is not likely to succeed. Organizational leaders interested in forming teams must understand the difference between a *single-leader unit* and a *real team* and the conditions under which each should be used.

A *single-leader unit* is based on the classic managerial approach: one person is in charge, makes the key decisions, assigns individual tasks, and delegates responsibility. The single leader is accountable and chooses when and how to modify working approaches. If the sum of the individual contributions to a task can best meet the performance challenge, then a *single-leader unit* may well make the most sense.[9]

Neither the single-leader unit nor the real team is better than the other. The key for organizational leaders is to understand the performance challenges that are best addressed by one or the other approach. Choosing between the two approaches is not a one-time decision. The selection of a real team or a single-leader unit should be based on the performance challenges and changes in these challenges over time. *The Wisdom of Teams* is fundamental.[10] It provides the reader with an excellent background for understanding team basics, single-leader units, and how potential teams can become real teams.

A special application of the discipline of real teams is the case of virtual teams where the team members are distributed widely and are dependent on current and emerging communication technology. Jessica Lipnack and Jeffrey Stamps provide a comprehensive treatment of variables essential to virtual team operation in their book on virtual teams.[11] They describe the special challenges in the creation and operation of effective virtual teams. They conclude that "The best predictors of virtual team success are the clarity of its purpose and the group's participation in achieving it" and they add, "purpose is the camp fire around which virtual team members gather." "If *purpose* is the glue, trust is the grease. Purposes operate through trust—the source of legitimacy for and the vital spark of networks. Trust enables people to establish purposes that they articulate in detail and maintain over time. Trust enables people to construct *links*. It undergirds high-performing organizations with the profuse voluntary communications of fast, flexible, integrated responses."[12]

Organizational Basics

An important question for any organization is when or under what conditions it should use a self-directed team. Darcy Hitchcock and M. L. Willard do an excellent job of answering that question in their book, *Why Teams Can Fail and What to Do about It.* Their "Red Flag Assessment" of organizational readiness for teams is a useful starting point.[13] It helps to determine whether an organization's commitment is strong enough to effectively organize production or services around self-directed teams. A *no* to any of Hitchcock's six questions should cause serious reconsideration of the decision to create teams.

❶ Is top management/leadership committed to involving employees?

❷ Will top management be around long enough to see the implementation through (two to five years)?

❸ Are employees interdependent? Do they need to work together to complete a process, product, or project or to provide a service?

❹ Are self-directed teams a high enough priority that they will get the time and resources necessary to make them successful?

❺ Does the work or the work schedule allow employees time to think, meet, and discuss ideas?

❻ Are the employees technically competent in their work?

Our experiences prompt us to add several additional organizational questions to Hitchcock's list.

❼ Is the leadership of the organization prepared to share power and control and abide by this decision?

❽ After committing to empowering teams, is the leadership of the organization willing to avoid disempowering them later?

❾ Is the leadership of the organization prepared to recognize and deal with the consequences when a few teams become far superior to others?

⑩ Is the organization planning layoffs, or is it a likely merger target? (If so, creation of self-directed teams may need to be delayed.)

Organizational Variables

Fundamental to the success of teams is a set of organizational variables that increase the likelihood of positive team performance. Some organizational variables are internal and others are external to the organization, but all are external to the team. Organizational variables that proved to be very important in our high-performing case studies include:

> Upper or middle leadership's *commitment to performance achievement* for teams;
> Organizational *understanding of "team basics"* necessary for success;
> Organizational *alignment on purpose, values, vision, goals, procedures, and roles;*
> Development of *helpful boundary conditions* for the team to follow;
> Practiced *shared leadership and empowerment;*
> *Free flow and sharing of information;*
> Emphasis on *creativity and innovation;*
> *Resources* provided to support the team;
> Commitment to *knowledge and skill training;*
> Willingness to permit teams to be *entrepreneurial;*
> Positive approaches to the team's *risk taking with no blame for failure.*

Team Basics

In addition to organizational basics, there are team basics that cannot be ignored if teams are to succeed. No team is likely to emerge into a very high performing team unless both the organization and the team give careful attention to internal team characteristics.

Katzenbach and Smith list six team basics that are vital for teams to succeed in increasing performance beyond that possible by persons working individually or by single-leader units.

❶ *Size:* Is the team small enough to integrate work efforts effectively?

❷ *Complementary skills:* Does the team have adequate levels of complementary skills and skill potential in functional/technical, problem-solving, decision-making, and interpersonal categories?

❸ *Meaningful purpose:* Does the team have a broader, meaningful purpose to which all members aspire?

❹ *Specific goals:* Does the team have a set of performance goals on which all members have agreed?

❺ *Clear working approach:* Is the working approach clearly understood and commonly agreed upon?

❻ *Mutual accountability:* Do team members hold themselves individually and mutually accountable for the group's results?[14]

If one or more of these team basics are missing, an organization would have great difficulty in advancing performance using a self-directed team approach. If an organization has paid attention to organizational basics and if the team and its parent organization understand team basics, then conditions exist for a team to become a real team.

All the teams in the case studies in this book are real teams that have gone on to become very high performing teams. None of them started out as a high-performing team. They benefited in various degrees from organizational support and team functioning that provided the potential for them to achieve unusually high performance.

Team Variables Associated with High-Performing Teams

The literature on teams is rich with discussion of the organizational and team variables necessary for the development of real teams. Much less is known or understood about why some real teams become very high performing teams. Variables we have observed as important attributes of teams that have achieved very high performance include:

> A keen understanding about and demonstrated commitment to *performance objectives* to be achieved;

> Common *purpose, values, vision, goals, operating procedures, and roles* for the team and consistency with those facets of the larger organization;
> *High trust* among team members, between team members and team leaders, and between team members and the organization;
> *Shared leadership* within the team and with those to whom they are administratively responsible;
> Members *empowered to take leadership actions* and supported in such actions;
> *Clear and effective two-way communication* within and among teams, with leaders, administrators, customers, and stakeholders;
> Substantial *individual and mutual accountability and mutual responsibility for outcomes;*
> High *creativity and innovation* with exceptional performance within the organizational environment;
> *Conceptual breakthroughs* that recast the team's purpose, function, and identity or the definition of team performance;
> Commitment to *stretch thinking*, including seeking *divergent views* before converging on an issue, problem, or solution;
> *High level of caring* among team members for individual team members and for their families outside of team work;
> Substantial *zeal and spirited performance,* including ardent interest, and intense pursuit of team performance by the team members and leaders.

Very high levels of trust among team members and between the team and the organization, high levels of caring about team members and their families, and the emergence of optimism are present in very high performing teams at rather intense levels. These variables, along with zeal and energized team spirit, combine to provide an atmosphere where productivity is extremely high and burnout and turnover rates among team members are low. Members of high performing teams even describe feeling that their personal spirits have been energized.

The reader is encouraged to read the *One Minute Manager Builds High Performing Teams* by Ken Blanchard et al. for a listing of thirty-five team and organizational variables that influence team performance.[15] These variables group into the broad categories of purpose and values, empowerment, relationships and communication, flexibility, optimal performance, recognition and appreciation, and morale.

Learning from Masters of Organizational Effectiveness

Many authors have made major contributions to the literature on organizational effectiveness. We have chosen to highlight Jim Collins and Rob Lebow and Randy Spitzer, whose works provide special insights into high-performing organizations. Charles O'Reilly III and Jeffrey Pfeffer as well as Keith Ayers of the Integro Leadership Institute add a great deal of understanding to the role that trust and values play in high-performing organizations.

Collins's *Good to Great* is an excellent book that highlights six organizational variables influential in propelling good companies to great status.[16] Collins's search criteria involved identifying companies having a fifteen-year cumulative stock return at or below the general stock market, punctuated by a transition point, and then cumulative returns at least three times the market over the next fifteen years. Collins found that only 11 out of 1,435 Fortune 500 companies fit the criteria. The variables identified as most significant in propelling good companies to great status had to be present in 100 percent of the good-to-great companies and in less that 30 percent of the comparison companies during the pivotal years.

The significant explanatory variables are *two variables each involving disciplined people, disciplined thought, and disciplined action.* Disciplined people include *level 5 leadership,* a paradoxical blend of personal humility and professional will—more like Lincoln and Socrates than Patton and Caesar. Their ambition is first for the company, not themselves. The second disciplined-people variable is *first who, then what.* The good-to-great leaders first get the right people on the bus, the wrong people off the bus, and the right people in the right seats, and then they figure out where to drive it. This is precisely the opposite of much management theory, which posits vision and strategy first, then people.

Two variables involve disciplined thought. Good-to-great companies *confront the brutal facts* yet never lose faith. They create an environment where the truth is heard; where leaders lead with questions, not answers, and engage in dialogue, not coercion; and where autopsies on failures are conducted without blame. They institute red-flag mechanisms that turn information into information that cannot be ignored. Good-to-great companies also adhere to a disciplined thought variable called *the hedgehog concept.* They carefully identify what they can be the best in the world at, what they are passionate about, and what drives their economic engine. The overlap or intersection of these three "hedgehog" components enables the companies to focus on their comparative strengths and hence their "hedgehog."

The good-to-great companies have two variables that involve disciplined action. A *culture of discipline* is developed involving self-disciplined people who take disciplined action, fanatically consistent with the hedgehog concept. A duality exists with adherence to a consistent system, while freedom and responsibility are exercised within the system. The final variable is *technology accelerators.* Good-to-great companies avoid technology fads but are pioneers in the application of carefully selected technologies. They believe that technology accelerates but does not create momentum, according to Collins.

Good to Great does a nice job of demonstrating the dynamics of the six variables. The first three variables, *level 5 leadership, first who then what, and confront the brutal facts,* are associated with a buildup phase for the companies. The next three variables—*hedgehog concept, culture of discipline, and technology accelerators*—are associated with a breakthrough phase. Collins describes the dynamics of these variables acting as a flywheel—"There was no single defining action, no grand program, no one killer innovation, no solitary lucky break, and no wrenching revolution. Good-to-great comes about by a cumulative dynamic process—step by step, action by action, decision by decision, turn by turn of the flywheel—that adds up to sustained and spectacular results."

Collins concludes, "When you have disciplined people, you don't need hierarchy; when you have disciplined thought, you don't need bureaucracy; and, when you have disciplined action, you don't need excessive controls."

Lebow and Spitzer's *Accountability: Freedom and Responsibility without Control* describes the type of environment where creativity and innovation can flourish—an environment that builds a responsibility-based culture with a high level of trust as its foundation at all levels in the organization. It takes time and a change of mind-set for an organization to embrace a responsibility-based culture. Lebow bases his work on a shared-value process involving eight values: (1) treat others with uncompromising truth, (2) lavish trust on your associates, (3) mentor unselfishly, (4) be receptive to new ideas, regardless of origin, (5) take personal risks for the organization's sake, (6) give credit where it's due, (7) do not touch dishonest dollars, and (8) put others' interests before your own.[17]

In a responsibility-based culture, Lebow and Spitzer describe the leader's belief system about employees as "trusting the people to be great." Those who cannot be trusted must leave the organization. In a top-down-driven organization, leaders more typically trust the policies, not the people. In a responsibility-based culture, the leadership approach moves from that of a supervisor to that of a "wise counsel," who creates conditions in which employees can design their jobs and set their performance goals within administrative boundary conditions. A wise counsel never does anything for a team that the team can do for itself. The wise counsel waits to be asked. In a top-down environment, supervisors set the goals, delegate the work as they see fit, and ensure that policies are followed. In a responsibility-based culture, the approach to accountability is one of ownership by the workforce. People are willing to take ownership of their jobs and are accountable for their performance. In a top-down-driven culture, employees are accountable for following the rules, policies, and procedures.

In *The Integro Leadership Institute,* Keith Ayers suggests that trust is the foundation of a responsibility-based culture.[18] Ayers identifies four elements of trust, including congruence, openness, acceptance, and reliability. Ayers states, "Values are powerful motivators that drive behavior. To get employees committed to trust building behaviors it is important to identify, and gain commitment to, the values that drive those behaviors." The values behind each of the elements of trust are:

> Congruence
  straightforwardness: people knowing what is expected of them
  honesty: having high standards of honesty in everything we do;
> Openness
  receptivity: giving new ideas and methods a fair hearing
  disclosure: communicating openly one's ideas and opinions;
> Acceptance
  respect: people being valued for who they are
  recognition: people getting the recognition they deserve;
> Reliability
  seeks excellence: seeking excellence in everything we do
  keeps commitments: people following through on their responsibilities.

Ayers describes people who thrive in responsibility-based cultures as "self-directed" and compares them to people who are "other-directed." Self-directed people can thrive in an environment of personal responsibility and personal freedom. In an environment that permits autonomous actions, employees will be responsible to one another, accountable for their behavior, and accept the consequences of their actions.

To create a responsibility-based culture, leaders need to focus on building trust, facilitating problem solving, facilitating change, and satisfying needs. When trust is high, transaction costs are low. If trust is high, change in an organization is facilitated.

In *Hidden Value: How Great Companies Achieve Extraordinary Results with Ordinary People* O'Reilly and Pfeffer describe how eight high-performing companies have successfully tapped the hidden value in their workforces. Central to the success of the eight case-study companies is a values-based view of strategy. O'Reilly and Pfeffer's core ideas can be summarized as follows: "These companies began with a set of values that are energizing and capable of unlocking the human potential of their people. They then design management practices that reflect and embody these values. They use these values and management practices to build core capabilities. What these companies can do better than anyone else permits them to develop innovative strategies and approaches that outflank the competition. In this approach to management, strategy comes last, after values and practices are aligned and after the company produces capabilities that set it apart. Strategy is still vitally important but strategic decisions are secondary to living a set of values and creating alignment between values and people."[19]

The eight case studies, which range from Southwest Airlines to AES, a global energy company, describe the power of aligning company values with systems, structure, and strategy. It sounds simple to follow a values-based view of strategy. In reality, it takes a great deal of discipline to implement this strategy and to hold the course over time. That is also why such an approach is so hard for competitors to replicate. *Hidden Value* is a great read and has many lessons that can be applied by organizations that want to build high-performing companies and encourage high-performing teams inside of their organizations.

Leadership

The organization's approach to leadership is one of the most predictive factors in a team achieving high performance. We did not find a single high-performing team that reported directly to a command-and-control leader. In the five case studies analyzed in this book, teams succeeded with creativity, at least in part because of their shared leadership environment. Empowerment of teams is a necessary factor for high team performance.

Empowerment is fundamental to a high-performing team's achievement. Kimball Fisher describes empowerment as a function of four variables—authority, resources, information, and accountability.[20] If any of these variables is zero, empowerment does not exist. Organizational leaders who are willing to empower their workforces will have a much greater chance of developing real teams. Although organizations are unlikely to achieve development of real teams without empowering those involved, empowerment alone is not sufficient for the development of very high performing teams.

Figure 2.1 illustrates the approach of a *traditional leader* to each of the key elements of empowerment—resources, authority, accountability and information—versus the approach of a *facilitative/shared leader*. The facilitative/shared leader's approach to the empowerment elements increases the chances of a team performing very well, while the traditional leader's approach reduces the chances of a team performing at very high levels.

Principle-Centered Leadership

The work of many excellent authors on leadership could have contributed to this chapter. We have chosen to highlight Stephen Covey's *Principle-Centered Leadership* because it best exemplifies the role leadership can play in enhancing high-performing organizations and teams. Covey's seminal book describes a principle-centered leadership paradigm that involves four levels (personal, interpersonal, managerial, and organizational) with a key principle (trustworthiness, trust, empowerment, and alignment) for each level.[21]

Covey's paradigm is based on the effectiveness of people and holds that people are the highest value because they produce everything at the personal, interpersonal, managerial, and organizational levels. People represent the interpersonal level, and the key principle at this level is trust, which is fundamental for high team performance and is the foundation for all effective relationships. If an organization or team does not have a high level of trust, empowerment cannot be established or sustained. The

FIGURE 2.1. APPROACHES BY TRADITIONAL LEADERS AND SHARED LEADERS TO ELEMENTS OF EMPOWERMENT

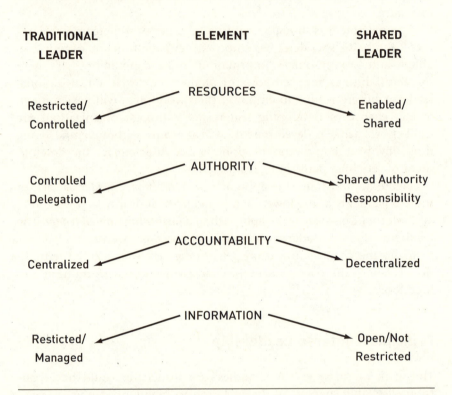

Supported by findings from K. Fisher, *Leading Self-Directed Work Teams: A Guide to Developing New Team Leadership Skills*, 2nd ed. (New York: McGraw-Hill, 2000) and from R. Schwarz, *The Skilled Facilitator: Practical Wisdom for Developing Effective Groups* (San Francisco: Jossey-Bass, 1994).

individual or self is at the personal level, where the key principle is trustworthiness. Covey states that "trustworthiness is a function of two things—character and competence." Character is vital but it is not sufficient for trustworthiness; an individual must also be competent. Change and improvement must begin with the self.

At the managerial level of the paradigm, the key principle is empowerment and style and skills are the focus. Covey claims that an empowerment management style creates more innovation, initiative, and commitment from employees. He describes a win-win agreement process with employees—where desired results and guidelines are clearly established, available resources are identified, and specifics of accountability and consequences are agreed upon. Many managers have not been willing to empower their workforces, but the reward for doing so can be very high because one can unleash the potential of people and capture the creativity and innovation that result from self supervision. Covey goes on to say that "skills such as team building, delegation, communication, negotiation, and self-management are fundamental to high performance."

At the organizational level, the key principle is alignment, and shared vision and principles, structure and systems, and strategy and streams are the focus. Creating a shared vision and mission through broad involvement of employees and based on principles provides a guiding compass around which all can rally. With a shared vision and mission in place, it is imperative for the organization to align its structures, systems, strategy, and streams with the principles embodied in the mission statement. Strategy should be flexible and congruent with the professed mission, with available resources, and with the relevant market conditions. Streams involve operational environments inside and outside the organization. They should be monitored frequently to make sure that strategy, shared vision, and systems align with external realities.

Covey also describes six conditions for empowerment in *Principle-Centered Leadership*. The first four are: (1) win-win agreement, (2) self supervision, (3) helpful structure and systems, and (4) accountability. At the center of these four conditions lie two additional conditions: (5) character and (6) skills. Covey states that "character" is what a person is, while "skills" are what a person can do. These are essentially the human competencies required to establish and maintain the other four conditions of empowerment.

Covey describes his principle-centered leadership paradigm as meeting the "whole person" or "spirit" needs of an individual. People want to have meaning in their work and to have work that is challenging and fulfilling. They want to be part of a mission that transcends their individual tasks. Covey's paradigm embraces the principles of fairness and kindness and makes better use of people's talents, resulting in increased efficiency. The paradigm also leads to what Covey describes as quantum leaps in personal and organizational effectiveness. Application of the concepts described in *Principle-Centered Leadership* can contribute to high team performance.

Leadership That Is Spirit Energizing
for Enhanced Performance

Three forms of leadership are crucial for a real team attempting to produce or provide products and/or services for its clientele. The first is that leadership provided by the executive level of the business, corporation, governmental unit, civic, or not-for-profit entity within which the team is situated. The second is the leadership that relates most directly to a team but is outside the team—as by a division head, shop foreman, labor steward, coordinator of programs, and coach to the team. The third is the leadership within the team as for specific projects, for specific product or service lines, for mentoring new members, or for the entire team as team leader(s) or team facilitator or team coordinator. At each of the three levels, the leadership provided can be spirit enhancing, spirit diminishing, or more or less neutral to the team's spirit.

In his book, *Leadership and Spirit,* Russ Moxley shows the importance of linking leadership at all levels with spirit to engage a workforce's total physical, mental, emotional, and spiritual energies. In *Spirited Leading and Learning,* Peter Vaill contends that organizational recognition of the spirit is vital to both leadership and the workforce. Both Moxley and Vaill show that without positive actions to enhance spirit, personnel cannot bring their full energies and personal values to the organization, its work, and their careers.[22]

Command-and-control-type leadership at any of the levels can be spirit diminishing, imposing decisions on the team and individual members. Such leadership does not engage team members or obtain the best they can bring to the job. Team members' analytical skills, creativity in problem solving, and ideas regarding new opportunities or ways of achieving them are underutilized. Further, team members' self-esteem and sense of self-worth are negatively affected. In short, the spirit of individual members and of the collective team is diminished. To a real team, it may matter little whether the command and control is systemic or episodic. Both forms of such leadership are disempowering and spirit diminishing.

It is possible to have preoccupied or indifferent leadership at one or more of the three levels. If such is the case, team members' engagement by leadership will be nil. Nearly all engagement regarding what the team produces and provides and how it functions would need to be initiated by the team. However, the organization stands to lose potential benefits by failing to capture the analytical capabilities, problem solving skills, and opportunity-achieving ideas that the team can bring to the rest of the organization. And, the team's performance will be less than its potential. The climate is simply not sufficient for the team spirit to be energized.

By contrast, assume that leadership at the three levels is dedicated to obtaining the best that can be achieved by the individual team members and the collective team. Also assume that leadership actively supports the team, engages it whenever other parts of the organization can benefit from the team's creativity. Assume further that the team and its members have a voice, can present ideas, and can present and pursue opportunities. Such a climate encourages creativity and risk taking for the benefit of the organization. It builds self-esteem and a sense of self-worth. It is empowering of the team and energizing of the team's spirit. The key here is that enlightened leadership exists at each level. The stage is set for very high performance.

The Five Disciplines for Enhancing Performance

A keen understanding and practice of the core disciplines, articulated by Peter Senge in his acclaimed work, *The Fifth Discipline, The Art and Practice of the Learning Organization,* are fundamental to organizations' success and to teams' performance impact. Systems thinking, as used by Senge, shows the importance and complementary nature of five disciplines or modes of action. He addresses the integration of four core disciplines—*personal mastery, team learning, mental models, and shared vision*—into a coherent body of theory and practice. This integration occurs through the application of *systems thinking,* which Senge presents as the fifth discipline.

Teams have become the basic unit for many organizations. The *team learning* discipline develops skills in teams that yield perspectives more powerful than individual perspectives alone. The team learning discipline starts with "dialogue"—team members' capacity to suspend assumptions and enter into a genuine "thinking together." We have called this dialogue "divergent thinking" in our case studies. Fundamental is the ability of a team proactively to seek divergent views before settling on a course of action. Building *shared vision* creates a picture of where the organization wants to be in the long run. *Systems thinking* anchors vision by understanding the forces that must be changed to make the vision a reality. *Mental models* give the openness needed to overcome the shortcomings in the present worldview. *Personal mastery* fosters the individual motivation to continually learn how actions influence the bigger picture. Together, the five disciplines are the basic tools for the learning organization. As an integrated set, they can help organizations discover how they can create their reality. If applied collectively, these five disciplines can materially enhance team performance, according to Senge.[23]

Dynamic View of Teams

Most often in the literature of teams, the dynamic nature of how a team progresses from infancy to a functioning team is viewed through a static framework. By moving from a static treatment of variables to a more dynamic treatment of team performance, key variables' relative importance, timing, intensity, and interrelationships help in understanding a real team's potential movement to a very high performing level.

In preparing to research the case studies, we used a modeling tool called system dynamics to focus on dynamic processes of the formation, growth, and achievement of very high-performance teams. We developed a theoretical model that identified key variables relevant to high-performance teams, the relationships among those variables, and their combined influence on performance.[24]

The system dynamics model provided a constructive and useful tool for organizing our thinking. It helped us think about (1) which variables are important in team performance, (2) when key variables and associated feedback loops likely have their greatest influence—that is, their dominance, (3) how the intensity of variables, singularly and in combination, dynamically influences the level of performance over time, and (4) what the configuration and intensity of variables might be at the highest levels of performance.

The system dynamics model also helped us think about the differences in the type and source of variables. This model helped us examine so-called hard, relatively easily measured variables, such as resource levels that influence performance, along with soft variables, such as trust, team zeal, and energized team spirit, which our experience indicates are vital in the very high performing teams. Further, the model helped us treat variables that originated from within the team and from the broader organization and beyond as well as those from within the team members' families or communities. System dynamics provided an initial theoretical framework to guide the gathering of empirical data on these high-performance teams.

Dynamic Nature of Variables Highlighted for Each Case Study

One approach to the theory is to develop a simplified dynamic model of the processes underlying team performance. In each of the five case studies in this book, we highlight a single variable that was very influential in propelling the team to high performance. The intensity of the variable is shown at three levels, and its influence on performance and environment are illustrated at three levels as well. This is obviously a simplification of the more complex system dynamics approach to analyzing the dynamic and combined influence of many variables; however, it illustrates the impact of the intensity of a single variable without the complexity of all other relevant variables. It demonstrates that key variables are not static and that their influence can not be understood by treating their influence as a constant. Figure 2.2 is an example of the framework we use in each of the cases and illustrates how three levels of intensity of a single variable advance the team to new performance heights. We use "shared leadership" as an example in this illustration.

INTEGRATING KEY CONCEPTS FROM THE MASTERS

High performance teams do not happen in a vacuum. Attention to team basics and organizational basics is fundamental to their success. Additionally, concepts from the masters of organizational effectiveness, such as the role of trust, leadership approaches, clarity of purpose, vision, values, strategy, goals and operating procedures, and communication protocols—particularly important for virtual teams—add understanding of team performance.

High performing teams do not operate in a static environment. Therefore, needed are systems thinking and an understanding of the dynamic nature of variables that enhance the team environment and propel it to high performance. We are indebted to the masters referenced in this chapter and their collective contribution to understanding high team performance.

FIGURE 2.2. DYNAMIC INFLUENCE OF A KEY VARIABLE (SHARED LEADERSHIP EXAMPLE)

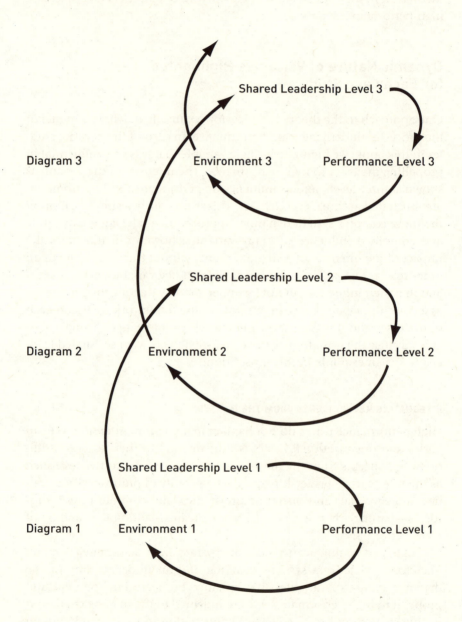

The masters show that many variables influence team performance and the environment within which teams function. Organizational and team variables can change in their importance and intensity over time. For example, as real teams progress the levels of trust, caring, and team spirit and zeal can become more and more intense and greatly influence high team performance.

Increasing the Odds Is Worth the Effort

Why is it important to understand the variables that influence the creation, development, or transformation of real teams into high-performing teams? Because high-performing teams produce products or services at unusually high levels. The team's creativity and innovation may soar, employee satisfaction may rise to new heights, and the level of enthusiasm may approach intense zeal. Outputs and profits plus customer satisfaction are positively enhanced. Work can be fun, and team members can be genuinely caring of one another and their families.

Can you set out to make a real team into a very high performing team? We are not willing to make that claim, but we do believe organizations that have successfully created real teams can increase their likelihood of having one or more very high performing teams. Even a small increase in the odds of having high-performing teams in an organization would be worth the effort because of the potential performance, financial rewards, and organizational benefits.

In this book we analyze a variety of very high performing teams in an effort to better understand the key variables that influenced their evolution. The more we know about what causes high-performing teams, the more we can do to create organizational and team environments in which they can emerge. We invite you to read each of the cases and to benefit from the lessons they provide.

NOTES

1. K. Fisher, *Leading Self-Directed Work Teams: A Guide to Developing New Team Leadership Skills*, 2nd ed. (New York: McGraw-Hill, 2000); J. Orsburn and L. Moran, *The New Self-Directed Work Teams* (New York: McGraw-Hill, 2000); Jon R. Katzenbach and D. K. Smith, *The Wisdom of Teams: Creating the High-Performance Organization* (New York:

Harper Business, 2003); J. R. Katzenbach, *Teams at the Top: Unleashing the Potential of Both Teams and Individual Leaders* (Boston: Harvard Business School Press, 1998); D. Deeprose, *The Team Coach* (New York: AMACOM, 1995); D. E. Hitchcock and M. L. Willard, *Why Teams Can Fail and What to Do about It* (Chicago: Irwin Professional, 1995); T. Quick, *Successful Team Building* (New York: AMACOM, 1992); R. S. Wellins, W. C. Byham, and J. M. Wilson, *Empowered Teams: Creating Self-Directed Work Groups That Improve Quality, Productivity, and Participation* (San Francisco: Jossey-Bass, 1991); Peter Senge, *The Fifth Discipline: The Art and Practice of the Learning Organization* (New York: Doubleday Currency, 1990).

2. E. Trist, *The Evolution of Socio-Technical Systems*, Occasional Paper no. 2 (Toronto: Quality of Working Life Centre, 1981).

3. Orsburn and Moran, *New Self-Directed Work Teams*, 11; Wellins, Byham, and Wilson, *Empowered Teams*.

4. Fisher, *Leading Self-Directed Work Teams*; Orsburn and Moran, *New Self-Directed Work Teams*; Deeprose, *Team Coach*.

5. Wellins, Byham, and Wilson, *Empowered Teams*; Orsburn and Moran, *New Self-Directed Work Teams*; Quick, *Successful Team Building*.

6. Fisher, *Leading Self-Directed Work Teams*, 17.

7. Katzenbach and Smith, *Wisdom of Teams*, 92.

8. Katzenbach, *Teams at the Top*, 70–71.

9. Katzenbach and Smith, *Wisdom of Teams*, xx–xxi.

10. Katzenbach and Smith, *Wisdom of Teams*.

11. J. Lipnack and J. Stamps, *Virtual Teams: People Working Across Boundaries with Technology* (New York: John Wiley and Sons, 2000).

12. Ibid., 142, 152, and 279.

13. Hitchcock and Willard, *Why Teams Can Fail*, 8.

14. Katzenbach and Smith, *Wisdom of Teams*, 61–64.

15. K. Blanchard, D. Carew, and E. Parisi-Carew, *The One Minute Manager Builds High Performing Teams* (New York: William Morrow, 2000), 12–13.

16. J. Collins, *Good to Great* (New York: HarperCollins, 2001).

17. R. Lebow and R. Spitzer, *Accountability: Freedom and Responsibility without Control* (San Francisco: Berrett-Koehler, 2002).

18. K. Ayers, *The Integro Leadership Institute* (West Chester, Pa.: Integro Learning[www.integrolearning.com], 2004).

19. C. A. O'Reilly III and J. Pfeffer, *Hidden Value: How Great Companies Achieve Extraordinary Results with Ordinary People* (Boston: Harvard Business School Press, 2000), 14–15.

20. Fisher, *Leading Self-Directed Work Teams*, 16.

21. S. Covey, *Principle-Centered Leadership* (New York: Simon and Schuster, 1991).

22. R. Moxley, *Leadership and Spirit: Breathing New Vitality and Energy into Individuals and*

Organizations (San Francisco: Jossey-Bass, 2000); P. Vaill, *Spirited Leading and Learning: Process Wisdom for a New Age* (San Francisco: Jossey-Bass, 1998).

23. Senge, *Fifth Discipline.*

24. J. Sterman, *Business Dynamics: Systems Thinking and Modeling for a Complex World* (Boston: Irwin McGraw-Hill, 2000). Dr. Ralph Levine, professor emeritus, Michigan State University, provided system dynamics modeling assistance.

3

Quaker Oats
A Team at the Top with Joint Management and Union Leadership

▸ Roger Vincent, Justin Shields, Terrance Stone,
  Arlen Leholm, and Ray Vlasin

Why the Quaker Oats Case

The Quaker Oats case study provides an excellent example of how management and labor can overcome an economically challenging manufacturing environment plus an extremely low trust atmosphere. Partnering together, they transformed an aging plant's entire work system and social system into a highly productive team-based and mutually gratifying environment for both labor and management. Initial diagnosis by the plant manager and union president revealed that trust building was the place to begin in reversing the declining plant's future.

Creation of a labor-management leadership team, innovative work agreements, and use of a skilled external consultant were important early actions. Preparation for teaming was comprehensive, and thorough and plantwide implementation and operation of teams was highly effective. The power of shared leadership, combined with careful attention to important team and organizational characteristics and team building, were fundamental to the successes achieved in the Quaker Oats case.

The Snapshot

Quaker Oats is a familiar name in the packaged-food and beverage industry. The Quaker Oats Corporation is a leading manufacturer of ready-to-eat cereals, hot cereals, pancake mixes, grain-based snacks, cornmeal, hominy grits, and value-added rice products. The Quaker plant in Cedar Rapids, Iowa, is the company's flagship plant, producing some two-fifths of the corporation's breakfast foods, including Quaker Oats (standard and instant), ready-to-eat cereals such as Cap'n Crunch and Life, Aunt Jemima Syrup, and other food and commercial products.

During the early 1980s and 1990s, the Quaker Oats company tried to transform its century-old flagship plant from a traditional to a high-performance environment. While the plant remained productive, the company's attempts to update its work systems were not successful.

The plant's production workforce has been represented by the Retail Wholesale and Department Store Union (RWDSU) since the 1940s. Throughout their history together, the union and the company have had a fairly traditional relationship without major strife or work disruptions—the lone exception being a three-day strike in 1987. According to union and management, however, relations had become increasingly strained beginning in the late 1980s and extending into the early 1990s. Both parties acknowledged the need for improvement.

When the company conducted an external search for a new plant manager in 1994, it sought someone who could redesign the plant's work systems and improve its labor relations. The company chose Roger Vincent, who hoped to implement a sociotechnical systems work redesign for the Cedar Rapids plant. Vincent realized that it would be impossible to reform the plant's work systems without the cooperation of the union.

The RWDSU president, Justin Shields, sensed that the Cedar Rapids plant was becoming outmoded when compared to plants of its competitors. Further, he feared that a continued decline could threaten the welfare of the union and its members. Therefore, Shields accepted Vincent's suggestion that the company and the union work as partners in running the plant and in implementing a system of self-managed work teams.

In 1996, efforts to improve the relationship between management and the RWDSU succeeded. The Quaker Oats Cedar Rapids management and RWDSU Local 110 entered into a partnership to improve productivity and enable the plant to respond to changing demands in the breakfast foods market while increasing wages and improving job security. With the help of a consultant, the union and the company rapidly developed their willingness and ability to cooperate. The partnership was the cornerstone of the redesigned work systems at the Cedar Rapids plant. It was a product of intensive effort and careful design by company and union officials and the respected and resourceful consultant. The partnership led to the design and implementation of a system of self-managed work teams that benefited both the company and the union.

Guiding the design and implementation was the Labor Management Leadership Team (LMLT), which consisted of the union bargaining committee and an equal number of management representatives. Besides the design and implementation roles, the LMLT provided overall direction, assisted teams, established plant objectives, and coordinated stakeholder interests.

The Quaker Oats case shares insights about the original partnership and the highly effective team at the top, with joint management and labor decision making vested in a sixteen-member labor-management team. The case provides insights about the effective communication and trust building and the dynamic influences they can have. It demonstrates the benefits from preplanning and knowledge investment before team creation and from continued team training and skill building as teams developed. Contrary to conventional theory, not one of the sixty-four production teams evidenced a drop in productivity during the initial formation, implementation, and team production stages. Since then, teams have substantially increased productivity.

Industry Context

THE CORPORATION, PLANT, AND UNION

The Quaker Oats Corporation, with its multibillion-dollar sales, is a major participant in the competitive packaged-foods industry. At the time of the team analysis, Quaker Oats was the fourth-largest manufacturer of ready-to-eat cereals and the fifth-largest manufacturer of branded dry pasta products.

The Cedar Rapids facility, which dates to 1873 (the oldest existing building dates to 1901), is the company's flagship. Hailed as the world's largest cereal mill (and one of the few with on-site milling capacity), the facility consists of what could be considered three plants—a ready-to-eat cereals plant, a hot cereals plant, and a regional grains plant. The facility supplied its parent corporation with approximately 40 percent of its breakfast foods production. At the time of the interviews in 2001, the Cedar Rapids plant's output (measured by cases produced) was 40 percent ready-to-eat cereals, 38 percent hot cereals, 8 percent syrup, 8 percent corn goods, and 6 percent industrial products.

To give some idea of the size of this facility, the plant is situated on twenty-five acres of land and had forty-five acres of floor space over twenty-two multistory buildings. Total grain storage capacity was ten million bushels. Housed within this plant were thirty-six packaging lines used to produce thirty million cases annually across 170 product codes.

The Cedar Rapids plant was unionized in the early 1940s. In 2001, Justin Shields was RWDSU local president. The union had some eight hundred core members, along with approximately one hundred seasonal employees (who worked about six months per year). Even though located in a right-to-work state, the plant's workforce was about 96 percent unionized. The RWDSU had joined the United Food and Commercial Workers Union, and was a member of the American Federation of Labor–Congress of Industrial Organizations (AFL-CIO). Although Local 110 always had a good relationship with its international union, the local has operated fairly independently because the international has few other work sites in the area. The local union has been strong over the past several decades. It takes credit for the fact that wages and benefits are high and that the Quaker Oats plant is considered a prime employer in the Cedar Rapids area.

Because union participation rates in local meetings had been fairly low, the officers and the union committee exercised a fair amount of autonomy. Still, union leaders were quick to point out they are held accountable by union members through elections and through flak from members. Union leaders indicated low rates of direct participation did not mean that the union was weak or that union leaders could act independent of membership.

Cedar Rapids, a city of some 109,000 people, was a healthy local economy with very low unemployment. The Cedar Rapids plant was the area's third-largest manufacturing employer (behind Rockwell International and Amana Refrigeration), and widely known as a good place to work. Quaker Oats was the employer of choice for most of its workforce, a reputation evidenced by the many workers who applied for available jobs and by the twenty-three-year average tenure of its workforce. The plant employed approximately thirteen hundred people, of whom approximately two hundred were salaried and some eleven hundred were production and technical-services workers. Men and women were fairly evenly represented in the predominantly white workforce. The average age of production employees was nearly forty-five.

EXTERNAL COMPETITIVE ENVIRONMENT

The ready-to-eat segment of the breakfast food industry was dominated by the "big four," consisting of (in order of market share) General Mills, Kellogg's, Kraft, and Quaker Oats. Quaker Oats has been a major player in the breakfast food industry since its founding, and the Cedar Rapids plant has been its most powerful production engine.

For decades, the ready-to-eat cereal industry was virtually immune to the increased competitive pressures facing the food industry in general. If grain costs increased, or if the company negotiated a new labor contract, it could pass cost increases on to consumers. During the 1970s and 1980s, cereal manufacturers regularly instituted price hikes. However, consumers began to cut purchases because of rising prices and refused to pay more than five dollars for a box of cereal. Thus, industry participants came under increased pressure to reduce costs.

Since the beginning of the 1990s, however, the ready-to-eat industry had undergone significant changes including price competition. Restructuring in the retail industry also pressured manufacturers to become more flexible and responsive. Consolidation in the grocery store industry enabled megaretailers to exert significant price pressure on manufacturers. In addition, Quaker Oats's customers used their increased purchasing power to demand added services, such as special packaging, bundling, and more frequent deliveries. The large retail chains were able to dictate terms to their suppliers.

EXTERNAL PRESSURE FOR INTERNAL CHANGE

The Quaker Oats Cedar Rapids plant needed to greatly increase flexibility and responsiveness. Unfortunately, the plant was not set up to meet the multiple new customer and industry demands occurring in the early 1990s. The perception was growing that the plant was diminishing in its ability to compete with other facilities both inside and outside the Quaker Oats Corporation.

The changing external environment was an impetus for internal change. Other companies were lowering their operating costs. They used downsizing, new technology, consolidating capacity, outsourcing, starting new greenfield plants in lower-cost regions, and acquiring, divesting, and merging divisions. A number of companies (for example, General Mills) were moving to higher performance work systems to build new capabilities.

In its attempt to maintain competitiveness, the Quaker Oats Corporation undertook corporate restructuring, consolidated production, and supply-chain management. While each of these factors affected the competitive position of the Cedar Rapids plant, supply-chain management created the greatest need for its work redesign.

Under its supply-chain management, the Cedar Rapids plant instituted a form of "just in time" production to reduce costs by operating with minimal levels of inventory. The plant would operate on a "pull" rather than "push" system actuated by user demand. However, "just in time" production required a capability to respond immediately as orders are received. This, in turn, necessitated efficient technical and human work systems that could adapt to continuously changing demands.

The Cedar Rapids plant was contributing $850 million per year to the corporation in the mid-1990s. However, the plant was perceived as slow to respond to demands of its corporation and its customers, in part because of its outmoded work systems and strained labor-management relations. While the industry was undergoing capital improvements as part of overall restructuring, the Quaker Oats Corporation had become reluctant to make major new investments in its Cedar Rapids plant, and the plant needed new investments to remain competitive.

Organizational Context at Quaker Oats Plant

In the mid-1990s, the Cedar Rapids plant's continued existence into the near future did not appear to be in doubt, but the long-term prognosis ended with a question mark. Would the plant be left to wither on the vine, or would it redesign its technical and human work systems to compete in the twenty-first century?

PRESSURES FOR NEW INVESTMENT

From the mid-1980s through the mid-1990s, competitive pressures and technological changes across the breakfast foods industry required companies to invest in new equipment and improve production techniques. Unfortunately for the Quaker Oats plant, the parent corporation had become reluctant to invest significant amounts of new capital into this older multistory plant. If corporate headquarters was going to make major capital investments in new and improved technology, it wanted the new technology and equipment to be operated in new and improved work systems. While the Cedar Rapids plant continued to contribute significantly to its parent corporation, its traditional work systems would not allow it to make optimal use of new capital investments. Further, its uneasy labor-management relations were troublesome.

LABOR-MANAGEMENT RELATIONS PRIOR TO 1995

Generally speaking, labor and management enjoyed good relations beginning with the plant's initial organization during the 1940s, although the relationship tended to be fairly adversarial and traditional. However, no major strikes, work disruptions, or other major instances of strife or conflict occurred. The 1984 collective bargaining agreement was very popular, and the rank and file approved the contract by a wide majority. About this time, however, labor-management relations across the country had taken a turn for the worse, and the situation at the Cedar Rapids plant and at other Quaker Oats plants seemed to follow the trend.

Union leaders sensed a change in management philosophy between 1985 and 1987. The grievance procedure had come under increasing strain because the union and the company could not resolve disputes without arbitration, and the union became bogged down in the volume of grievances. This experience did not set a good tone for the 1987 negotiations, and in February of that year, when the contract expired, the union went on strike, primarily over wage and seniority issues. The strike lasted three days, after which the union went back to work without receiving major concessions. It was not a good time for organized labor nationally, and the local union felt that it had to go back to work given the existing sentiment against unions.

Justin Shields was elected RWDSU president after the 1987 negotiations. One of Shields's early tasks was to examine the pile of unresolved grievances that plant employees had filed against the company. He noted that many of the grievances were not suitable for arbitration, and the volume of unresolved disputes indicated that the process had broken down.

The following year, the company hired a new plant manager, who unfortunately could not foster a cooperative relationship with the union. Labor and management did not meet on a regular basis except to resolve grievances. Union officials claimed that management had taken an antiunion position and was even attempting to weaken the union. Even if the union's interpretations of company actions were inaccurate, they reflected a level of distrust between the union and the company.[1]

Seeking to reverse their fortunes, the union and the company attempted an early start on negotiations for the 1993 contract. However, the resulting agreement was not popular. Despite the cold war between labor and management, the plant continued to operate profitably. However, the existing work system—sustained by inflexible work rules—was placing the Cedar Rapids plant at a competitive disadvantage to other facilities adopting flexible, high-performance work systems to meet the marketplace's new demands. The plant's work systems resulted from an often uneasy if not contentious relationship between management and Local 110 of the RWDSU, which represented most of the plant's production workers.

High Performance Organization, a Foundation

Things began to change in 1994, when the corporation brought in a new plant manager and charged him with improving labor relations and updating the plant's work systems. RWDSU leaders realized that the adversarial relationship between the union and the company was counterproductive for both sides and that the grievance process used was not the best way to advance union members' interests. The difficulties associated with an adversarial relationship were wearing on both sides.

SHARING THE DECISION MAKING

Roger Vincent, who became the new plant manager in 1994, describes the environment he faced as formidable. He believed the Cedar Rapids plant's only chance for survival was to get employees fully involved. He held that "To be successful in today's environment you must be competitive in time, cost, and quality." (Figure 3.1 represents the importance and intersection of the three prerequisites for high performance.)

Vincent added, "You couldn't have enough management on site to drive the thousands of decisions required, so we had to get our people involved. They didn't have information. We needed to provide it. We had to get them training and education on how to use that information so that they could make the decisions to run their piece of the business. Otherwise, I think we were doomed, and failure means ceasing to exist."

NEW PRODUCTION SYSTEM

Shortly after Vincent became plant manager, corporate headquarters began looking for a plant at which to try out a new production system. Cedar Rapids was not on the corporate radar screen as a site for this innovation. But Vincent asked Shields if the union would participate in pulling together a joint proposal to implement the new production system at Cedar Rapids, and Shields agreed.

Vincent related, "Part of the condition from corporate headquarters was, if Cedar Rapids turned out to be the best option, we would have to modernize our work systems to match the new production system. Based on our joint proposal, Cedar Rapids was chosen as the site for the new system. It took a leap of faith from both management and the union to proceed."

FIGURE 3.1. THE HIGH PERFORMANCE ORGANIZATION: TIME, COST, AND QUALITY

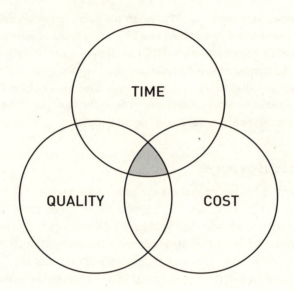

Building trust would be crucial if the parties were to proceed effectively on the joint proposal. Knowing that it takes more effort to build trust than to destroy it, the new plant manager's first task was to build trust and establish credibility with the union. Because he was an outside hire, he also had to build trust and credibility with his management staff and with corporate headquarters.

Building Trust

The process of building a trust-based relationship between Vincent, the Quaker Oats plant manager, and Shields, the RWDSU president, was fundamental to the successful implementation of a team-based system. The new plant manager made a conscious effort to build trust with the union and within management before undertaking the major changes involved in teaming. Trust was so low in 1994 that Vincent asked union officials to give him a chance to see if his actions matched his words. Shields also played a major role, and he and Vincent built "earned mutual trust" that played a central role in the plant's success.

OVERCOMING A LOW-TRUST ENVIRONMENT

Justin Shields described the years leading up to 1994 as "a disaster where we went six months at one point without even having a labor-management meeting. Management spoke of labor as a third party. Trust was very, very low in both directions." In 1994, Shields saw a plant that was in trouble: "Historically, we had good performance and good people who knew how to make cereal. But all you had to do was look at the numbers: we hadn't hired anyone between 1987 and 1994. Grievances had skyrocketed. We had used consultants for everything to try to get labor and management together, which all ended in failure. Then I had a chance to visit with Roger a little bit, and I could see he was a completely different individual than I was used to dealing with. My early impression of Roger opened the door for at least some beginning discussions where we could sit down and talk openly."

Vincent observed, "It was obvious that I could not start with the classic change process where you paint a vision of the future, decide your purpose and mission, your values, and the principles you are going to operate by. The situation here was that the whole thing hinged on trust. To go through that vision process again would have been a complete waste of time." He added, "Even in the first meeting that Justin and I had, we agreed on what values were important to us. We agreed that we were going to be open and honest—that I would share any information I had. We agreed we were not going to have any hidden agendas, even if we would disagree on matters being addressed. We both looked carefully at the data, and we came to a mutual conclusion that if we don't do something different, it's going to be harmful to 1,050 or more people at this site and to the whole community."

> "So we agreed on some values and the next step was to model those behaviors. Justin and I held a lot of town hall meetings. We had to show people by doing, by behaving as opposed to writing something on the wall." —Roger Vincent, Quaker Oats plant manager

TRIGGERING EVENT FOR TEAMING

As Vincent recalled, "The triggering event that convinced Justin and me to go with teaming was the opportunity to compete for a new fifteen million dollar state-of-the-art cereal production system. We knew we had to transform our work system if the new production system was to succeed. Corporate headquarters would never have selected the Cedar Rapids site if Justin and I could not have convinced the union to be a partner in this new teaming effort. Justin had a huge challenge from the union side with a very traditional union board. Board members were not inclined to try something new and were convinced [that] the union would get screwed!"

Shields added, "Roger and I discussed how to involve the union, and between the two of us we helped educate the union that maybe we do need to look at things differently. Now I had somebody from the management side saying, 'Look, you can trust me to be a part of this. I will be open and honest with you, and watch my actions and see if they match my words.' So Roger helped me a great deal early on. I could trust him. So that's really what led up to changing the work system."

Vincent observed, "The management group at the time didn't have any more trust than the union committee. But for management, it's easier since we're appointed. Management can mandate the group to work together, but that doesn't necessarily win over the person's heart and mind."

Creative Contracting and Partnering

> As the contract deadline approached, both sides realized that it would not be possible to come to a satisfactory agreement. Their interim solution was a nine-month contract enabling the two sides together to define the work redesign. Both signed a "Redesign Letter of Understanding" concerning the process, including creation of a Redesign Team, and agreed to return to the bargaining table after nine months to negotiate a new partnership agreement.

In 1995–96, both company management and the union were deliberating about whether to enter into a partnership to work together to redesign the plant's work systems. After years of traditional labor-management relations, deeply ingrained patterns of thought and habit governed views of how the plant should be run. For this reason, it would have been difficult and risky for either side to put its intentions into words and to put those words into an entirely novel but legally binding collective bargaining agreement.

The first milestone in the march toward redesigned work systems and a new partnership between the union and the company was reached in

February 1996. Vincent and the company wanted to use the contract negotiations to initiate work redesign. During the early phases of the negotiations, the parties attempted to lay the contractual groundwork that would permit an overhaul of the work systems at the plant. Both parties sought a contract that provided enough flexibility to permit a wide range of possible outcomes as well as the types of contractual guarantees that would comprise the main points of a collective bargaining agreement.

THE NINE-MONTH CONTRACT AND THE REDESIGN TEAM

The union and the company came to an interesting solution: a nine-month contract in which the two sides would together clarify the parameters for the work redesign. To this end, the union and the company signed a "Redesign Letter of Understanding" concerning the process, including creation of a Redesign Team. After the nine-month period, the parties would return to the bargaining table to negotiate a new partnership agreement.

While management wanted to push for a plantwide redesign including teaming, the union bargaining committee was split on this issue. A representative of the international union, Merle Householder, played an important role in convincing the union that it could benefit from a working partnership with the company. Householder provided a global vision, identifying places where this type of relationship could work while noting the things for which the union would have to watch out. His effort to convince the bargaining committee to foster a cooperative relationship with the company succeeded.

At the time, the workforce had seen enough change efforts fail so that the level of cynicism was high. Here, Shields's credibility with the union members was a key to getting this agreement (and the ensuing November 1996 agreement) approved. Shields had fought for the union for years (management described him as a "worthy adversary"). Therefore, when he suggested that the time had come to cooperate, sufficient numbers of union members were inclined to agree. It was only a nine-month contract, and the work changes were in only one area of the plant, the new cereal production area.[2] The rest of the plant received good wage and benefit increases. In the end, the contract was ratified, in part on the basis of these wage and benefit increases, and the union and the company commenced their redesign effort.

LABOR-MANAGEMENT STEERING COMMITTEE

> Redesign began with establishing a joint labor-management steering committee co-chaired by Vincent and Shields. The first act of the joint labor-management committee was to create a Redesign Team whose stated goal was to improve the plant's work systems by moving toward self-managed work teams.

The Redesign Team consisted of a cross-functional vertical slice of the workforce and was aided by a redesign consultant. A total of approximately 125 people, representing some 12 percent of the plant's employees, were selected for the Redesign Team. One reason for the team's large size was to create a critical mass of support for the change effort.

The redesign team was divided into two groups, which would alternate each week between redesign team responsibilities and normal work duties. The rotation kept the participants active in plant production and production processes in their units. The one-week-on and one-week-off strategy also served to maximize communication flows and information exchanges with the rest of the workforce.

REDESIGN TEAM RESPONSIBILITIES

The Redesign Team members were charged with learning workflow analysis, redesigning their functional areas, determining membership of the production teams, and devising a fair compensation system. The design changes sought to achieve flexibility in job assignment, to empower workers to make decisions as close to the point of production as possible, and to have team members take on certain traditional supervisory tasks (e.g., scheduling, overtime, quality tracking).

At the same time, the labor-management steering committee insisted that the Redesign Team establish targets for key performance indicators in each business area over the next three years and that the plant not slip from those goals. The Redesign Team was required to be cognizant of what other companies were doing and to perceive correctly the competitive pressures facing the plant. To this end, the team took several benchmarking trips to (among other places) other Quaker Oats facilities, the Saturn plant, and Corning Glass. After working for approximately twelve weeks, the Redesign Team proposed a design comprised of sixty-four natural work teams organized around the plant's business units. The team also devised some of the compensation systems that would raise pay for increased responsibility and allow employees to share in the gains brought by increased productivity. The labor-management negotiating teams attempted to incorporate the redesign proposals into the November 1996 contract and partnership agreement.

Supplemental Partnership Agreement (SPA)

The SPA's preamble recognized that the breakfast foods industry was going through a time of downsizing and restructuring while unions were facing declining membership. It declared, "The Union and the Company, as equal partners, are facing the competition head on."

The new partnership's stated goals were to increase employee influence over workplace issues, to create better jobs through higher skills, to increase worker control and responsibility over the workplace, and to increase workplace safety. The SPA retitled and formally created the LMLT and also created sixty-four self-managed work teams organized to serve as business units within the plant.

The parties negotiated a traditional agreement but supplemented it with a consensus statement that would constitute the framework for the partnership. The SPA became the charter for the new partnership. The SPA guided the day-to-day activities at the Cedar Rapids plant, while the traditional agreement served as a fail-safe for issues that could not be resolved through the partnership and its SPA.

MANAGEMENT AND UNION GOALS

The pilot redesign efforts under way inspired sufficient confidence for the union and the company to begin negotiating the contractual framework for their partnership and plantwide work redesign. Going into negotiations in November 1996, the company sought competitive advantages in time, cost, and quality and sought to be the low-cost producer for the company's products. These goals would require substantial changes in work organization, such as creating opportunities for employees to solve operating problems and upgrading employee technical and "soft" (team process) skills.

Vincent believed in the potential of the high-performing organization he was attempting to create and was convinced that it could be done at the Cedar Rapids plant. The plant had a strong workforce. Properly organized and empowered, it could increase productivity, lower costs, and increase flexibility and responsiveness. Vincent believed also in hiring good workers and giving them the knowledge, information, and power to make decisions. The new work system offered such promise.

The local union's primary goals were to increase wages and benefits, empower its members, and promote job security. The new contract included reasonable wage and benefit increases and tied these increases to the new teaming process. As for the quality of work life, the advice of the international union as well as several benchmarking trips had convinced the local union that the democratic processes of the new system, if properly implemented and supported by the workforce, would constitute a vast improvement over the plant's traditional ways.

MORE SECURE CONTRACT AND SUPPORT

The new contract improved job security by ending the long-standing policy of week-to-week layoffs as a result of changes in weekly production demand. Instead, the company offered job security to its core employees and began to hire "peak season" employees (who would be represented by the union). "Peak season" personnel would work for a maximum of six months in each calendar year. Core employees would no longer be subject to seasonal layoffs.

As in the February 1996 negotiations, the union committee did not unanimously support the partnership. Once again, Householder, the international representative, played an important role in working with the union committee to build consensus around the agreement and to assist in negotiations.

Vincent had found that corporate headquarters also was uneasy with some of the proposed contractual provisions. With the help of Russ Young, the senior vice president in charge of supply chain management, Vincent built support within the company to gain the flexibility he needed at Cedar Rapids to work with the union and implement the work redesign. With the assistance of Young and Householder, both the plant and the union mobilized the organizational support needed to proceed with the redesign effort.

ELEMENTS OF THE SPA

Realizing the difficulty of abandoning the familiar collective bargaining agreement and perhaps the wisdom of continuing such an agreement, the parties negotiated a traditional workplace contract. Attached to this contract, however, was the SPA, which would take the plant in a new direction while the traditional contract would serve as a fail-safe to handle matters that could not be resolved otherwise.

The SPA agreement set forth key elements crucial to the Cedar Rapids plant's work redesign, including: (1) joint leadership of the plant by the LMLT, (2) establishment of self-managed work teams, (3) employment stability for the unionized workforce, (4) roles and responsibilities for the team leadership triads, (5) mandatory training in the "Basic 5"—conflict resolution, communications, team problem solving, consensus decision making, and effective meetings as well as union history and leadership, (6) skill-based pay and pay for performance, (7) union security plus a strong company and a strong union, including union education, and off-site training for stewards, (8) union participation in hiring decisions, (9) handling of outsourcing and subcontracting issues.

The SPA was consistent with the ongoing efforts to transform the Cedar Rapids plant from an institution in which the parties operated according to a lengthy, detailed collective bargaining agreement to one in which labor and management jointly provided leadership for and operated the plant. This movement was advanced through two complementary actions, the formation and operation of the joint LMLT and the creation of the triad leadership arrangements for the sixty-four production teams.

Because of its central role in plant leadership and decision making, the LMLT is described here in some detail. Following the LMLT section, several other elements receive some limited additional elaboration because of their importance to the leadership and teaming functions of the Quaker Oats plant.

The LMLT[3]

The SPA retitled and formally created the joint LMLT. The sixteen-member LMLT, co-chaired by the plant manager and union president, consisted of equal numbers of members of senior management and of the union bargaining committee.

The LMLT functioned as an executive committee responsible for overseeing the plant's day-to-day operations. The SPA also created sixty-four self-managed work teams organized into business units within the plant. The work teams comprised the production and service workforce. The front-line leaders (supervisors) were incorporated into the teams, and the teams would determine what roles they would serve.

ORIGINS

The LMLT had its origins in the working partnership established by Vincent and Shields in 1994. Their trust-based working partnership between the plant manager and the RWDSU president led them to create a joint "labor-management steering committee" for the new team-based work system they hoped to create. Vincent and Shields served as co-chairs for the steering committee, whose first action was to create a Redesign Team to start planning for self-managed work teams across the entire plant operation.

The SPA in late 1996 renamed the steering committee and formalized it into the LMLT, which included the union bargaining committee and an equal number of management representatives. As Vincent pointed out, "For the most part, the steering committee and the LMLT that followed it have carried out the joint partnership with equal numbers. The numbers may vary a bit from meeting to meeting because of union business, vacations, bereavement, workers' compensation, or other pressing plant responsibilities, but we try to keep the LMLT as equal as possible."

ROLES AND RESPONSIBILITIES

Since its inception, the LMLT has assumed responsibilities for a number of broad areas, including:

> Strategic direction, including strong company, strong union;
> Work design, including self-managed work teams, and team leadership in a triad;
> Training and education, including intensive team training;
> Team development, including review and certification of teams' formation plans, skill-based pay, and pay for performance;
> Business information sharing;
> Interest-based approach to problem solving;
> Production workforce hiring;

> Internal public relations;
> Safety;
> Employment stability.

Following are brief explanations about strong company, strong union, self-managed work teams, team leadership in a triad, intensive team training, review and certification of teams' formation plans, skill-based pay, and pay for performance.

▶ **Strong Company, Strong Union.** The union-management partnership is premised on a strong company and a strong union. In addition to being a strategic objective consistent with the partnership commitment, it also has day-to-day considerations and applications. In the SPA, the company agreed to provide each employee with eight paid hours of union education on company time, plus eight hours of paid release time for off-site training for union stewards. The company and the union agreed also that signs and banners promoting the RWDSU and the Quaker Oats partnership would be visible throughout the facility. The SPA provided for union involvement in the hiring process and for presenting newly hired employees with union membership forms and copies of union literature, thus increasing the likelihood that new hires would join the company as union members.

▶ **Self-Managed Work Teams.** The redesigned Quaker Oats plant consisted of sixty-four self-managed work teams organized around business units covering the full range of plant functions. Under the previous system, a front-line leader who retained all of the prerogatives of a traditional supervisor or foreperson oversaw the activities of the plant's production workers. The workers were required to perform their posted duties—no more and no less. They had little autonomy to solve problems on the floor and would often have to take issues to supervisors for resolution. In short, a clear division of authority existed. The bosses bossed and the workers worked. The hierarchy was clear.

The redesigned work system made the relationship between bosses and workers more horizontal. In fact, the supervisors became team members, and each team defined the supervisor's role on that team. In addition to flattening the hierarchical relationship, the teams took over functions previously performed by supervisors, such as budgeting, scheduling, and allotting overtime and vacations. While these adjustments have broadened and somewhat increased the average employee's workload, they also represent increased team and individual empowerment and decreased dependence on management.

The combination of the key elements, including intensive training for the work redesign, joint and shared leadership, and empowerment of teams, reflects the careful attention to organizational support and team preparedness. These matters were so carefully planned and executed that not one of the self-managed work teams experienced a dip in performance during the planning and launch phases.

▶ **Team Leadership in a Triad.** A unique feature of the Quaker Oats–RWDSU system is in the structure of team leadership. Each team selected a team member to serve as team leader. The team leader, the supervisor (front-line leader), and union steward formed a triad that bore responsibility for internal team leadership and for representing a team in its interactions with other teams and with the LMLT.

Each member of a triad represented the plant's overlapping constituencies—the company, the union, and the teams themselves. Like the LMLT and the work teams, the triads arrived at decisions through consensus. In turn, they encouraged decisions through consensus within each of the teams. Shared leadership was practiced throughout the Quaker Oats plant.

▶ **Intensive Team Training.** To operate in a team-based environment, the workforce must train in a number of different operating skills and perform several "indirect functions." During the team formation process, each team determined which "technical" and "indirect" skills would be necessary to run its business unit and came up with staffing plans to meet those needs. Employees were expected to "skill up" by learning other posted jobs within their business units. In addition, employees were expected to add skills by learning and agreeing to take on a number of the indirect functions, which typically had previously been carried out by supervisors.

▶ **Team Formation Plans.** After appropriate training, teams created written team formation plans and submitted them to the LMLT for review and certification. While the team review and certification process challenged the LMLT, it completed actions for all sixty-four teams in

FIGURE 3.2. TRIAD LEADERSHIP STRUCTURE FOR EACH PRODUCTION
AND SERVICE TEAM

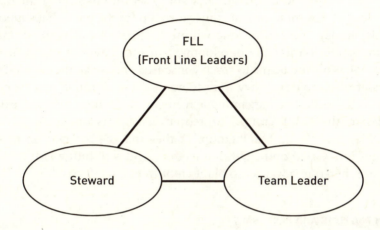

1997. With certification, team members became eligible for the skill-based pay increases. Further, the plans were designed to be revisited each year.

▶ **Skill-Based Pay.** The company structured pay increases based on attainment of competencies in three increasingly complex skill sets. Existing employees were not required to "skill up," but those who choose not to obtain additional skills did not qualify for skill-based pay increases (but remained eligible for general wage increases). New hires, however, were required to enter the pay-for-skill plan. One company goal was to have as many employees as possible trained at the highest skill levels.

▶ **Pay for Performance.** The SPA included a Redesign Team recommendation that employees should share in gains they produce for the company. Further, team pay should reflect team performance. As a way of aligning the interests of the company and those of the workforce, the SPA adopted a "pay-for-performance" model. If the plant achieved its goals on certain key performance indicators, the work teams became eligible for bonuses based on the performance of their business units.

REASSESSING LMLT TEAM ROLES

According to Vincent, "We continuously try to revisit what our roles are and what we should be doing. We want to set the strategy for the plant as a group. We want to provide the leadership for the plant that supports the day-to-day decision making within the plant. LMLT is the primary group responsible for the development of the sixty-four teams in the plant. We want the teams to reach consensus and make their own decisions. If they can't or if they want to go in a direction that may be contrary to the collective bargaining agreement, then that proposed action comes to the LMLT group." Moreover, "Problems or issues may be identified within the LMLT group, or they may be brought up to the group from a triad on behalf of a team. Agendas of future LMLT meetings are shared in advance, so plant employees are informed."

TEAM PROJECTS AND PROPOSALS

Another of the LMLT's roles involved reviewing proposed projects from the teams. An LMLT member reported, "There's a series of business-related projects that are designed to reduce costs. The projects that are advanced are reviewed at the LMLT meetings. Those submitting project proposals are helped so that the LMLT can more easily look at the proposals and evaluate them. I observed managers listening carefully for what concerns the union partners would have. If there was not enough information, the project would be sent back to those proposing it. Management was looking for alignment from the union partners and vice versa. It is a very clean process."

Another LMLT member observed, "Team proposals would come to us in all kinds of formats. So we had to develop a method, a format, telling teams the kind of information we are wanting, in this order, and this is how we will look at it. We have refined the process and format as time has passed. When we get the information, we won't act on it that day. We will be able to take it back to our work site, read it, digest it, and talk to each other. The whole team will address it at our next LMLT meeting."

Still another LMLT member shared, "At times we will hear a proposal that comes to us as unanimous from a team. At other times, a presentation comes from two factions within a team and they can't come to conclusion. In either case, we don't make a decision in front of the presenters. We discuss it among ourselves later. Sometimes the needed decision is obvious and we reach it quickly. Other times we have to discuss it a lot.

Then, we have a management/union pair, typically that is assigned to that area, go back and review with the team the outcome of the LMLT discussion—the decision."

The same LMLT member continued, "If the decision happens to deviate from the labor/management agreement that we have, we write a letter of understanding, which happens more times than not because the teams come up with very creative ideas—very innovative things that tend to have slight deviations from the agreement. Sometimes [the deviation] is more than slight. However, we will document that in a letter of understanding between labor and management. In the last five years we have written in excess of 150 such letters of understanding."

He went on, "Those are 150 deviations from some element in the existing labor-management agreement. I think it is astounding that we have had that many—many, many changes, some little and some that are major. So that is a part of our team process, and it has become fairly well ingrained. We probably slip out of that process now and then because we're human, but we try to live up to our process. And one thing I have seen, this group is not bashful in reminding each other where or when we slip out of something. And it doesn't matter whether it's management or a union person, there'll be some indication that we're not following procedure and that we are not doing something the way we should be doing it." Mutual accountability and mutual responsibility appeared very strong among members of the LMLT team.

TEAM DECISION-MAKING PROCESSES

The ground rules or principles under which the LMLT operated were jointly developed by labor and management representatives. The LMLT team, like the other sixty-four teams that followed it, went through the fourteen-step building-block process described later in this chapter. All teams must develop team guidelines, rules under which the team will operate. An LMLT member stated, "We felt that since we were a team and would be perceived as a team by the people in the organization, we needed to go though the same process that the other teams would follow."

In general, the LMLT would meet on a twice-weekly basis and used consensus decision making. When conflicts arose, the parties would use a conflict-resolution process to resolve the issue. They could resort to contract language if a conflict could not be resolved and could use the grievance procedure as the conflict-resolution method of last resort.

The LMLT's decision-making process has not been static. As one LMLT member observed, "I think there has been a progression in how decisions get made. Decision making by the team today in 2001 is different than how decisions were made back in 1996. I think there is a huge progression." There is much less concern about decisions being made by labor or management on their own. The decision process is more efficient and happens more quickly than in previous years. Also, through the triads, the teams bring items to the LMLT for review and decision in a well developed form.

▶ **Threefold Decision-Making Process.** When viewed overall, the LMLT employed a threefold decision-making process. The approach used depended on the issues to be addressed and decisions to be made as well as on whether either side perceived some potential negative impact and how crucial and possibly how emotional the issue was. LMLT members described the three approaches.

❶ For issues without substantial negative effects for either union or management, decisions usually were based on a sharing of facts, with all team members having an opportunity to express their views and concerns. Consensus typically was reached, and the LMLT acted quickly on issues.

❷ For other issues for which decisions might significantly influence unions or management, the LMLT had less latitude in acting. Team members would share points of view and concerns, even from a traditional approach, and then collectively reassess where they were. Then typically, they would use an interest-based format to try to develop options and try to find some common ground that did not violate union principles and/or the ability to manage the business. The LMLT's use of an interest-based approach and the team's desire to reach a consensus usually resulted in most issues reaching resolution.

❸ The LMLT members agreed that there would be matters for which they could not achieve a workable decision. As one member indicated, "We respected the fact that there comes a point in time that we've done everything that we could and there still may need to be a decision made, and we have a traditional process we may need to follow. You don't like to do that, but you get there because a decision does need to be made. But those instances are few and far between today, much less than they used to be in earlier times of the plant. Typically, we can find some middle ground to work toward a decision and at least walk out of the room and support it."

▶ **Increased Decision Efficiency and Effectiveness.** The LMLT has become more effective in decision making over the years. The team initially was very reluctant to do things or take actions that were not by the committee of the whole. Vincent pointed out, "We have found over the years that we couldn't operate that way. There were just too many things to be addressed. So what we typically did was determine the LMLT team members' area that the issue or problem affected and then ask those members to go off and 'prework the issue.' The members would come back with a recommendation to the entire group for discussion and action."

Continued Vincent, "We learned from this process and have gotten better, increasing our whole LMLT group's effectiveness. Over the years we have done a lot of the joint leadership team's work through prework and subcommittees of LMLT, but the members come into the whole group meeting, discuss and debate the issue or problem here, and 'talk it' until we arrive at consensus."

▶ **Implementation Team.** Shortly after its formation, the LMLT chartered an Implementation Team, drawing its sixteen members from the Redesign Team. The Implementation Team was charged with creating an overall implementation plan for teams. Included were the logistics of getting all of the teams through a structured development program, coordinating establishment of teams with production requirements, and maintaining communications between the LMLT and the plant. The Implementation Team was also asked to develop a means for evaluating the redesign process. Although the Implementation Team reported to the LMLT, it was led by Cornell University's Pat Semanek, who provided training and coaching and who assigned responsibilities to the team's members.[4]

▶ **Connecting with Triads.** Another LMLT action was to maintain close working connections with the triads. The LMLT received information and recommendations from all sixty-four triads, taking very seriously and acting efficiently on all of their ideas, issues, and proposals. The process resulted in implementing many creative ideas and innovations and in reaching workable solutions to many issues.

▶ **LMLT Leadership.** The LMLT was central to the plant's leadership structure, which is shown is figure 3.3. The LMLT continues to provide overall day-to-day plant leadership, with frequent input from the triads. The Training and Education Department (TED) provides ongoing training for the LMLT and for the production and service teams. All sixty-four work teams and their triads have continued along a high-performance trajectory.

The LMLT was instrumental in engaging the highly competent and skilled external consultant, at first part time and then later full time. The consultant was the initial owner of the process for moving the plant to a team-based technical/human work system. While the plant now has an in-house process owner, the LMLT and TED are central in the process, and the third-party consultant still provides input and facilitation assistance for the LMLT.

LMLT PERFORMANCE

As one LMLT member shared, "I have been with Quaker Oats for the last five years, all at this plant site. During that time, I have noticed significant progression in the team, among team members, and in individuals as well. From my perspective, this progression has been in maturity levels, in trust levels, and in understanding the business. It also has been in how we react to each other, the type of respect we show one another, and how we treat each other. Further, the progression is evident in what the teams are doing in the plant, what is happening with our production processing, and in the ultimate end product. I'm very happy to have been with this same team for over five years."

Another team member observed, "Over the last year this organization has experienced an incredible amount of change—the Quaker company, new products, new lines put in place. These could have caused a number of hurdles and roadblocks, particularly from the union or union concerns. And I was amazed about how much of that change was assimilated, and how the people [involved] were supported by this LMLT group."

FIGURE 3.3. LEADERSHIP STRUCTURE

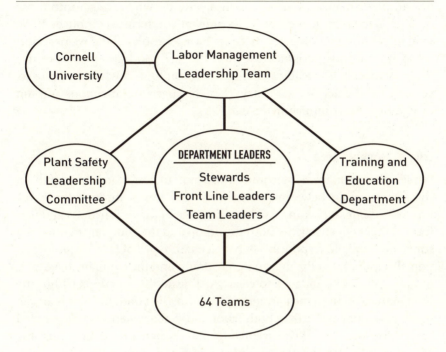

The team also conducted evaluations of its own performance. Every year, for at least one day, the LMLT met off-site to determine its future goals and assess its previous year's performance. Vincent, the plant manager, pointed out, "We determine the goals for our group for the next year and then we've gone back yearly and revisited how are we doing against those goals as sort of the prework for going into the next year. And again, that's been a process in which we used our consultant to facilitate. Sometimes we get caught up in the day-to-day activities and we lose track of how we are doing. Her role has been helping us understand, using some survey instruments and other means, how we think we are doing as a group. What are the areas we need to address? What kind of training and development needs do we have as a team? [The LMLT members] need to grow and develop. We need nurturing just as every other team does. So we look at how we are achieving our goals and perceptual things—how we as individuals feel we are doing as a group. Then typically we discuss it as a group and decide what we are going to do about it."

Still another member of the LMLT assessed the team's strong orientation to performance: "One of the things we do when we get into those off-sites is to go back and say, 'Look at what you have accomplished.' We tend to get hung up on every place we have a problem, and we beat ourselves up around the issues. We need to feel good about the positive things achieved. It is really amazing when you look at where we were six years ago and where we are today. There has been a tremendous amount of significant accomplishments here."

LMLT'S ENDURING ROLE

While labor-management councils are not uncommon, the depth of shared leadership between management and union through the LMLT was indeed rare. It encompassed a wide range of major functions and performed them effectively. Yet both the union and the company maintained some areas of sole responsibility (e.g., certain types of business information, discipline). For the most part, the union and the company have tried to draw helpful boundaries to clearly delineate the functions within the joint management of the partnership and those beyond the joint management arrangement. Further, both labor and management have attempted to develop the capacity to resolve disputes when they arise. Thus, the processes followed give strong evidence of being enduring.

One of the conclusions reached by Vincent and Shields and the other members of the LMLT was that if a system or a process to achieve that system were going to be developed, a "systems owner" would be needed. Semanek had at first served in that role, but in the summer of 2001, the LMLT identified and hired an experienced person to serve as the systems owner on a full-time basis for the company. Vincent pointed out, "We needed a systems owner full time because we needed to nurture the system on a continuing basis." That systems owner was invited to join the LMLT and works continuously with it, thereby boding well for the LMLT's endurance, role, and effectiveness.

What Made the LMLT Special?

One key aspect cited was the fact that the *joint labor and management approach has become a "living relationship" with an identity and increasing maturity of its own.* As one member of the LMLT team explained,

"Before, it was a group of individuals with their own interest—management interests and union interests. Those interests in many cases have now come together, and we live the relationship together versus as individuals or as individual groups. But we can still operate in our own spectrums at the same time, and the partnership will sustain that. So I see as one very important [reason that the LMLT is special is that] the relationship has continued to mature and still withstand our own sets of values."

Another reason given was the *partnership relationship is simultaneously prounion and procompany.* As Shields, the union president, pointed out, "One of the most important things we did in contract negotiations was to make a statement saying it's ok to be prounion. It's ok to be procompany. And both parties have to understand it, believe it, and live it. So if we constantly try to keep that in mind, it makes it easier to get to an answer for the really tough decisions. It is easier if you really understand what the true message should be and the results should be—protecting the union and protecting the company."

A third reason was the *level of understanding of boundaries—the areas in which there is joint union-management interest and the areas in which there are separate interests.* As Vincent related, "You can draw two overlapping circles to represent our relationship, one with union interests and one with company interests [figure 3.4]. You have an area in the center representing our joint interests. Outside that joint area (the overlapping area) you have things the union must do and things that the company must do. The area of joint interests has increased over time."

He went on, "For example, part of the collective bargaining agreement states the teams won't discipline their team members. If we get into a disciplinary issue, the company's responsibility is to deal with it. Likewise, the union is responsible for their elections, determining their bylaws, and taking actions in their relationship with their larger labor organization. There are areas where we proceed after consultation with each other. If we form ad hoc teams, union picks members and management picks members, but we do it with consultation—we don't do it unilaterally. This and many other actions are in the area representing the joint interests of the partnership."

Moreover, as Vincent explained, "It is particularly helpful to understand this relationship so that we don't get upset when the union is off doing stuff over here that's union business, or management is off over there doing stuff that is management business. We should understand these joint and separate interests so we don't get upset. So clarifying

FIGURE 3.4. INCREASING SHARED INTERESTS AND RESPONSIBILITIES

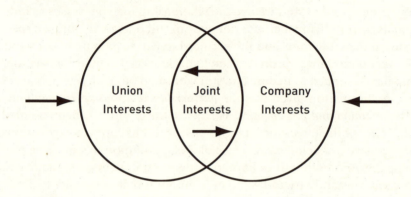

the boundaries is important, but only one reason" for the importance of the LMLT.

A fourth reason why the team was special, according to members, was *team members' respect for one another*. Team members report learning a great deal from one another. They respect one another for what they bring to the team, what they contribute. As one member observed, "I think there's a deep sense of respect and that drives a friendship, a feeling of fondness. These develop from the team functioning well as opposed to being something that you consciously work at achieving."

Still another reason given for the team's special nature was the *LMLT's resiliency, which allows members to continue to work together no matter how frustrating the challenges*. A team member explained, "There are things we're never going to agree on. That is OK. We understand that. We may get frustrated. We may get angry with each other. But resiliency brings us back, and we work through it the best we can. We've agreed that we can't agree on some things, and we move on. But it doesn't drive a wedge into our team. We can somehow get back and work on different issues jointly together. So we bounce back when we get set back."

A sixth reason cited for the team's special nature was the *team's ability to use conflict-resolution procedures and skills*. An LMLT member observed, "We have used interest-based conflict resolution—the process of getting to yes. It's hard to begin with, but we use it, and we rolled it out into the plant as interest-based conflict resolution. I think every one of our triads has been through it. Our team has been through it multiple times. If you get into positional arguments, you are in a win-lose situation. We keep trying to drive to a win-win situation. While it's hard, we have gotten better at it over the years. [The interest-based conflict-resolution process] allows us to arrive at consensus."

Still another reason cited was the fact that *no person, whether from the union or from management, is on his or her own.* People have help from other LMLT members. For example, on one important management issue in which the union had no specific interest, union members stepped forward and offered their assistance because they knew the matter was important to the company. As one member observed, "There isn't an issue that comes up, whether it's a specific company need or a union need, for which you are on your own, like we used to be in a traditional system. You can go and get some help from your union counterparts and vice versa—solicit thoughts, get recommendations. Then 'your' problem becomes 'our' problem. Having worked in the plant for fifteen years and seen both sides, that's most special to me. You're not out there on an island on your own."

An eighth reason given for the LMLT's special nature was the *stability and consistency that prevailed in the union and management leadership from the beginning.* As one member summarized, "A significant aspect of this team is we've had Justin [Shields] and Roger [Vincent] as our consistent leader pair through this entire thing. There's been continuity through all of that. And really, there's been fairly good stability as far as the membership on this team. If you take a look at the management members, we've pretty much had the same group for five years. For the union group, Justin has been through it right straight from the beginning. There has been a consistent [union] core that has helped provide stability."

The final reason given for the LMLT's special nature was *a combination of a high mutual trust level, a feeling of confidence in interacting with other members, the resulting ability to communicate early and clearly, and the comfort to explore sensitive labor or management conditions, even far-reaching strategic possibilities for the facility, without fear that such efforts will subsequently be used against you.* The expressions of this composite reason ran throughout the LMLT group. One member emphasized, "It is the trust factor—I mean, I can walk into anybody's office here and talk to them and feel that we can get something done that way. I don't have to play a game and go roundabout to get there. I've been in everybody's office at one time or another to say something that I've had on my mind.

And they will do the same. Yeah, there's a trust factor here. A lot more than there was [previously]." Another member observed, "You can't function without trust. Trust, honesty, and openness are very, very high on my part. I think that's crucial. If you don't have that, I don't think you can be a team. So I would rate it as an absolute necessity."

Regarding communication, a LMLT member commented, "The level of communication and interaction among this team's members is a lot higher than it was six years ago. I think a big part of it ties back to trust and respect. I think six years ago, when I came here, if you were having a discussion with a member of the union board, it was very, very guarded. You just wanted to make sure you didn't say something wrong that was going to come back and bite you. Today, I can sit down with counterparts and we can have a pretty open and honest discussion and it's comfortable. Because you're comfortable talking to each other, you talk to each other more. When it's an uncomfortable kind of sweaty situation where you're scared to death you're going to say the wrong thing, you try to avoid it."

Another member added, "A lot of things the LMLT has chartered are strategic in outlook—deal with what might be faced in the future. I think the trust level is such that we can have those discussions at the very early stage with the understanding that [the strategic event] may come to light or it may not. This is something we're looking at, and we all need to be thinking about it and discussing it. If it does come forward, how do we proceed with it? There are some issues that we look at that obviously would be real hot issues for the facility, and we've got to have that trust that everybody in this room can be on the same page and be thinking about options. When we have a hard topic, we may use the interest-based bargaining process to find the solution. So that's why I believe trust is paramount to the LMLT being successful."

Reemphasizing the role of trust, another team member said, "I think I could write a book on the other side that would indicate what happens when you don't have trust. We obviously hadn't had trust up to the point where Roger [Vincent] came to Quaker and was able to work with Justin [Shields]. And we failed in many earlier attempts on various teaming initiatives when the trust just wasn't there. Trust—it's the foundation for the team."

Implementing the SPA

A skilled labor-management consultant served a major role in the design of the team system at the plant. She brought expertise in industrial organization, with high credibility among company and union officials. She introduced interest-based bargaining, provided methods and techniques, and trained team leaders, stewards, and union and management leaders to function in a team-based environment. Roger Vincent described her as the "process owner," a role that proved crucial to Quaker Oats's success. He observed, "You need someone who is going to design and champion the process."

After the negotiations for work redesign were completed in 1996, the company and the union faced the challenging task of changing the work systems and culture that had developed over decades. During contract negotiations, both management and union had used a form of interest-based bargaining.[5] Semanek, from Cornell University's Programs for Employment and Workplace Systems, conducted two days of training sessions in interest-based bargaining for both union and management and facilitated some thirteen days of negotiations.

Impressed with her integrity and her expertise, the LMLT asked Semanek if she would assist the would-be partners with the development of their new relationship and implementation of self-managed work teams. After securing the company's and the union's promises not to sacrifice necessary steps in the name of expedience and determining they had sufficient budgetary and other resources to achieve the system redesign, Semanek agreed.

Semanek and the company faced considerable pressure to complete the changeover rapidly and without decreasing the plant's productivity. The union was pushing hard to fast-forward the transition to teaming. A significant portion of negotiated wage increases was tied to certification of the teams. Further, the union did not want members to wait three years to receive these increases. At the same time, the company insisted that the plant establish quantifiable goals for key performance indicators and that performance did not slip below those goals. While the company wanted to redesign the work systems in the plant, it could not afford a period of reduced or low productivity from its largest facility. The job had to be done fast, and it had to be done right.

Crucial Training, Education, and Team-Formation Roles

The phrase "work redesign" captures one major aspect of the change effort at the Cedar Rapids plant. In addition, the labor-management partnership attempted to change the culture, including interpersonal and group process skills of plant members. The skills and habits associated with the old, traditional organization and its reliance on authority were deeply ingrained, and inappropriate for a shared-leadership, team-based environment. On the advice of its consultant, the joint partnership designed training and leadership development programs to help those in the plant manage the ongoing change.

TRAINING AND EDUCATION

▶ **New Capacity for Team Development.** The TED had been created after the 1993 contract was completed. With Semanek's assistance, after 1996 TED created and delivered programs to facilitate team development and functioning. TED coordinated the workforce's training in team operating skills and technical skills. It was the only department in the plant run entirely by hourly employees.

▶ **Strong Early Emphasis on Training and Team Building.** One of the most impressive aspects of the Cedar Rapids plant's redesign was the strong emphasis on educating the workforce, both labor and management, in skills necessary to operate in a team-based environment. In the first year, managers, union leaders, stewards, and team leaders received up to 150 hours of training in the skills needed. The rest of the workforce received some 100 hours of technical and soft skills training, including team-building exercises. They provided each employee with the specific interpersonal and group process skills required to operate successfully in the new environment. The cooperating parties attempted to change the plant's culture.

▶ **Ongoing Training and Education.** The TED directed training and team-building sessions to provide the plant's workforce with the communication, facilitation, and conflict-resolution skills needed in the new work environment. (The plant manager noted that the entire workforce also was offered university-quality training in business.)

▶ **Institutionalizing Education and Training.** Recognizing the value of this training, plant management and the union made training in the "Five Basics" mandatory for all employees in the November 1999 collective bargaining contract and SPA:

> *Communication:* improve communications, ask effective questions, provide feedback;
> *Consensus decision making:* reach consensus in groups and teams and understand the process;
> *Effective meetings:* make meetings more efficient and productive;
> *Problem solving:* learn to differentiate between symptoms and root problems and to identify and implement solutions;
> *Conflict resolution:* resolve conflicts within teams and understand the use of feedback.

While the Five Basics help teams function, conflicts small and large are unavoidable in a work environment. Thus, the LMLT increased conflict-resolution skills throughout the plant. The TED offered the following programs:

> *Certified facilitator:* provides skills in facilitation, consensus, problem solving, and in enabling participants to lead team meetings and facilitate the achievement of consensus within groups;
> *Facilitation skills:* helps participants become effective at leading meetings;
> *Team leadership training:* identifies leadership skills, differentiates between a leader and a manager, prepares team leaders to function effectively within teams;
> *Team builder:* helps facilitate groups through team-building exercises and assessments and develops diagnostic skills to recognize where groups need reinforcement;
> *Interest-based bargaining:* understands and follows problem-solving processes when working through team, business unit, or individual issues;
> *Interest-based bargaining specialist:* facilitates groups through the interest-based bargaining process to help solve issues within or between groups.

▶ **Skill Diffusion.** With Semanek's assistance, union and management determined that it was important to disseminate these facilitation, team-building, interest-based bargaining, and conflict-resolution skills throughout the plant. Access to such capabilities would help ensure that teams functioned effectively, enabling them to resolve problems and issues that arose within teams, among teams, and between teams and management. Union and management wanted each business unit within the plant to have sufficient skills in facilitation, problem solving, and conflict resolution to deal with the many different issues that would arise.

▶ **Union History and Strength.** To maintain a strong union with informed members, Quaker Oats employees received eight hours of training in union history. In addition to participating in many of the leadership development training sessions, union stewards received training in their new roles in a team-based work environment. They received an additional eight hours of paid training leave each year, thereby reinforcing the strong union, strong company strategy.

TEAM-FORMATION PROCESS

▶ **Strong Foundation.** To enhance team members' ability to work together, with their triad, and with other teams, the Quaker Oats–RWDSU redesign required teams to lay a strong foundation for themselves. To this end, Semanek utilized a structured team-development process in which team members created consensus statements for each of fourteen "building blocks." The newly formed teams were allotted some twenty-five hours from March until June 1997 to complete the team-formation process and team-building exercises suggested by Semanek. The fourteen building blocks consist of:

> *Team mission statement:* each team developed a statement of its goals;
> *Team customers:* each team identified its "customers," including other teams within the plant, vendors, wholesalers and retailers, and the ultimate consumer;
> *Team responsibilities:* each team determined its responsibilities to its customers;

> *Team member expectations:* each team's members established expectations and ground rules;
> *Team guidelines:* each team transformed the expectations into operational guidelines;
> *Team member roles:* each team divided functional responsibilities among its members;
> *Team relationship with the front-line leader:* each team determined its leader's role;
> *Team relationship with other teams:* each team's members determined the nature of interteam relations;
> *Team information:* each team established means of receiving and disseminating information within the team, with other teams, and with the company;
> *Team training:* each team member received training in technical skills, indirect functions, soft skills, and union matters;
> *Team meeting strategy:* each team decided when and where to conduct its regular, mandatory meetings (on company time) and how those meetings would be conducted;
> *Team performance measures:* each team set forth performance measures that would enable it to track progress over time;
> *Team goals:* each team set goals;
> *Team assessment:* each team decided on its evaluation strategies and methods.

▶ **Team-Formation Plans.** At the end of the process, the teams presented their written team-formation plans to the LMLT for review and approval. The team-formation phase took between three and four months with an average of twenty-five hours (and a range of between twenty and forty hours) per team. The first team was certified in April 1997, while the final team received certification in November. While some employees wanted team-formation plans approved more quickly, all teams were in place and certified within one year, and workers became eligible for the skill-based pay increases.

▶ **Plan Review and Renewal.** Team-formation exercises were not a single-use process. Rather, they were designed to be revisited over time. Teams revisited their fourteen building blocks each year as a way to reassess and reorganize themselves. In addition, teams performed self-assessments twice each year, allowing the teams to understand their strengths and weaknesses, make adjustments, and create future team-development plans. These reassessments also provided opportunities for reflection. Teams compared their current status and functioning with the past, realizing what changes had occurred and what progress had occurred over time.

LEADERSHIP DEVELOPMENT

▶ **Expanding Leadership Responsibility.** The redesigned work environment expanded the number of individuals serving in formal leadership positions and changed the relationship between formal leaders and the rest of the plant. For this reason, Semanek provided more than 125 hours of leadership training to managers (at all levels), union leaders (committee members, stewards), and team leaders. This training was crucial because supervisors and middle managers can be a source of resistance when companies undertake team-based shared-leadership systems.

▶ **Creation and Dispersal of Team Builders.** One new role was that of "team builder." Despite efforts to enhance cooperation and reduce conflict, plant leaders (stewards, union leaders, supervisors, managers) and teams nevertheless found occasions to disagree, conditions that could disrupt teaming. Following the consultant's advice, management and union placed throughout the plant individuals trained in team building, including facilitation and conflict resolution. These team builders worked with the teams, often during periods of inactivity—e.g., when a line goes down—and facilitated meetings in which team members revisited their building blocks, performed self-assessments, and worked on problems and weaknesses. To deal with conflict, team builders and other individuals throughout the plant were trained in related facilitation skills.

▶ **Leadership Development Training.** Leadership development training was offered to deal with the intellectual and affective aspects of changing roles. One facet of this training involved asking plant leaders how much time they spent on routine daily tasks such as budgeting, scheduling, and problem solving as opposed to such higher-order responsibilities as strategic planning, innovation, union building, and relationship building. When the participants were asked what they would like this balance to be, a definite shift occurred in preferred time allocation from the former to the latter category.

This exercise had two goals: first, to help those serving in leadership roles envision the job-related benefits in shifting from traditional systems to joint labor-management team-based systems grounded in shared leadership; second, to prepare managers for their next task, redesigning their own jobs.

▶ **Help with Changing Relationships.** Semanek advised the company and the union to pay special attention to the consequences of power shifts within the organization and to help managers and supervisors deal with their changing relationship with others in the plant. Semanek conducted training sessions covering theories of relationships, motivation, and human needs, including what makes people feel significant (e.g., Maslow's hierarchy of human needs). She also covered establishing accountability and responsibility and transactional analysis (a model that suggests people have three ego states, parent, adult, and child). She created and delivered training programs to make plant leaders aware of these subtle shifts and to help them manage the profound effects that may be involved in moving to a shared-leadership, team-based system.

▶ **Cushioning Sense of Loss and Powerlessness.** Semanek also felt that it was important to address the sense of loss felt by people uncomfortable with the new system. The training covered the topics of power and powerlessness and how a traditional system reinforces the notion that people are powerless to take action. The leadership workshops included discussions about conversational styles that increase plant leaders' ability to listen effectively and respond appropriately.

▶ **New Problem-Solving Capacity.** Profound in the redesign was the substantial shift in problem-solving responsibilities from supervisory and managerial levels to teams. New leadership understanding was needed to help achieve this shift in problem-solving responsibility and to create new problem-solving capacity. Therefore, managers, stewards, and team leaders received leadership training in interpersonal process recall.[6] The training was designed to aid the transition from a system in which "somebody else" (i.e., supervisors and managers) solves problems to one in which team members solve their own problems with help and support from others. Supervisors' and managers' new role is to help the team to solve its own problems. As problem-solving facilitators, they help teams clarify and understand as much as they can about problems, frame the issue or issues involved, and proceed with identifying options and possible solutions.

▶ **Capacity to Deal with Change.** The leadership-development effort focused on possible changes caused by redesign of the work system. It addressed the challenges on both intellectual and emotional levels. Participants were asked to envision their new roles and styles. They were given a set of skills that would help them adapt well to their new functions. Also, they were encouraged to address the emotional aspects of the change process. As a result, no groundswell of interference arose from people who did not understand how the redesign changes would affect them or how to deal with the changes.

Taking Teams to the Next Level

In July 1998, the LMLT undertook further development of the team-based work system. To assist them, Semanek was brought on board full-time for one year. An array of actions followed that were implemented across the organization.

REASSESSMENT DIAGNOSTICS

▶ **Professional Assessment of Team Status.** As a first task, the LMLT asked Semanek to assess the status of the teams' development. The LMLT did so by analyzing team performance measures and off-line interviews with team members. Results showed that most of the teams were functioning appropriately. The teams that had problems were working through them and making plans to move forward. The diagnostic also showed that some other teams were confronting barriers that needed to be addressed.

▶ **Barriers to Team Functioning.** The teams not functioning well confronted a variety of different issues or barriers. Many of the problems were related to design issues and were complicated by the particular array of players and personalities. Perhaps the most common barrier to effective team functioning was the combination of unlike job skills and functions within a team (e.g., different seasonality, different types of work). Other barriers included issues of personality, structure, supervision, mental health, and working conditions (e.g., large amounts of overtime taking a toll on people). Although some issues relating to team design proved intractable, Semanek and plant leaders helped many of the teams identify and analyze their barriers, resolve their problems, and move ahead.

▶ **Team Self-Evaluation.** The next step was to have the teams evaluate themselves. The teams were asked to self-assess, review their building blocks, review past goals, and start setting goals for themselves for the next year. Teams often go through reassessment exercises—e.g., reviewing the fourteen building blocks—by simply "checking things off." This time, however, the teams were asked to review their work two years earlier and to assess the progress made. They were asked to take stock of how much things had actually changed. Most teams responded well to the self-evaluation exercise.

▶ **Broader Evaluations for Triads and Upper Managers.** Meetings were initiated with the triads and other leaders to address and implement a plan for their next steps. They received a variety of assessment instruments and instructions on how to use the instruments and analyze the results. Also covered were how to communicate results back to the teams and what to do based on that information (e.g., developing or improving performance measures). Upper managers were asked to reassess themselves as well. Their reassessment results showed a clear shift from the amount of time spent on supervisory and operational tasks to more long-term strategic and managerial tasks.

▶ **Development of a Focused Plan and Protocols.** Management and the teams worked to develop a focused plan to move the teams forward. For example, one problem experienced was lack of clarity about indirect functions. What was the nature of teams' responsibility for indirect functions? Could team members earn skill-based pay if they trained in indirect functions but then refused to perform them?

In January 1999, the LMLT commissioned a group to identify the common indirect functions and to set expectations about their performance. After interviewing and surveying all of the teams, identifying best practices, and developing a forum that would enable teams to communicate with each other, this special group developed a protocol for many of the indirect functions.

▶ **Institutionalizing the Consultant Function.** In January 1999, Semanek began to prepare for her exit from the plant. She sought to institutionalize her functions within the teams themselves. The creation and deployment across the plant of capabilities in team building, facilitation, and conflict resolution plus their infusion within teams helped make her departure possible and orderly.

▶ **Tracking of Performance.** In addition to having the teams and plant leaders conduct self-assessments, the Quaker Oats plant tracked the performance of its new work systems in several ways. One was by monitoring teams' attainment of their quantitative goals. Another was by assessing business units' performance on key indicators. A third was surveying team performance using external university researchers applying various metrics.

Union and Business Results from Successful Teams

One of the key characteristics of the redesign was attention to systemwide performance. As a consequence, actual performance never diminished throughout the process from 1996 to 2003.[7] The results of this attention to performance are summarized as follows:

UNION RESULTS

> No week-to-week layoffs occurred;
> Union membership increased by 11 percent;
> Employees achieved shift stability;
> Outside temporary workforce was eliminated;
> Employee education/training reached an all-time high, one hundred hours per year per employee;
> Significantly less grievance/arbitration activity occurred as a result of increased process effectiveness;

BUSINESS RESULTS

> Teams became self-sufficient business entities making real-time decisions affecting bottom-line business results;
> Average monthly "pay for performance" payouts increased by 200 percent;
> Annual case production volume increased 20 percent;
> Budget performance was significantly favorable;
> Costs were lower than in 1996.

Variables Influencing Performance

Our personal interviews with the plant manager and RWDSU local president, the LMLT members, and selected production teams confirmed that many organizational and team variables and conditions influenced performance by the teams and the broader team-based system at the Quaker Oats plant. These many organizational and team variables combined to keep performance stable during team introduction and to advance performance beyond that point.

ORGANIZATIONAL AND TEAM VARIABLES

The variables or conditions mentioned as important in advancing teams and enhancing team performance included:

> Creation of a trust-based union-management leadership partnership;
> Commitment to self-directed or self-managed teams and a team-based work system throughout the plant;
> Creation of shared management and labor leadership and the dispersal of shared leadership responsibility and accountability to teams;
> Encouragement of creative innovations, decisions, and actions, including support and facilitation of innovative actions and improvements at the team level;
> The organization's assistance in providing a format and process for submission of team project proposals, explanation of decisions rendered, and assistance in implementation;
> Team willingness and initiative in advancing projects, innovative ideas, and proposed improvements for review and approval plus their implementation;

> Education and training for employees' growth in skills and knowledge, both technical and process (soft skills), plus skills for indirect functions;
> Education and training of teams both prior to team creation and implementation and after teams began operating;
> The organization's commitment to freely providing information and to educating teams in its use;
> The organization's commitment to honest communication between management and union and with and among teams;
> Trust, respect, and professional caring within the LMLT;
> Communication within teams, with triads, and with the LMLT;
> Attention to performance within teams, triads, and the LMLT;
> The organization's commitment to self-assessment and renewal by all teams and time and support to make them possible;
> The organization's commitment and actions to advance strong union, strong company and to achieve the goals and objectives of both;
> Creation of new team process capabilities and their diffusion throughout the plant—conflict resolution, interest-based bargaining, team facilitation, and others;
> The organization's creation of team sharing in the production benefits achieved for their business unit and wage increases tied to team member skill enhancement and use.

Other variables or conditions were mentioned as having an influence on performance, but those listed here were reported in various ways and appeared to be among those most frequently mentioned. Collectively, they likely exerted an immense influence on performance. Not one of the sixty-four teams experienced a drop in productivity during the design and implementation of the team-based work system.

DYNAMIC NATURE OF VARIABLES

The relationships among the variables are dynamic, as are their individual and collective influences on performance. Also, a single variable may have different influences at different levels of team and organizational development. Further, the same variable can have increasing or diminishing influences as team development and organizational development proceed.

THE SPECIAL ROLE OF TRUST

We were particularly impressed with the fundamental and special role of "trust" and the manner in which it influenced performance at different stages in the transformation to a team-based work system at the Cedar Rapids Quaker Oats plant. Rather than chart here the combined influences of many variables, we display in simplified form our observations of the influences of trust in the achievement of management and union results.

Simplified diagrams 1, 2, and 3 in figure 3.5 represent three positive and connected dynamic loops that depict the changing role and influence of trust and its impact on organizational and team environment and on performance. Trust and resulting performance levels are both progressively greater in diagrams 2 and 3. In each case, the environment for team creation and team development is enhanced and a higher-order outcome results.

Diagram 1 illustrates the starting performance level at Quaker Oats in 1994. Trust level 1 reflects the initial positive influence of the trust established between Justin Shields and Roger Vincent. One outcome of this trust is the nine-month contract that established the initial positive environment for team creation and development.

Diagram 2 reflects a second order of trust and performance, with one outcome being a further enhancement of the environment through the SPA and creation of the LMLT and Design Team.

Diagram 3 reflects a third order of trust and performance, with outcomes including actions of the LMLT, and creation of the triads and the initial work teams. These further enhanced the environment for team development and plant performance, and the dynamic relationships go on beyond the level represented in diagram 3.

Lessons Learned[8]

When Vincent started the redesign process, his goal was to create a "learning organization"—one that would share ownership for the decisions and actions necessary to make the Quaker Oats plant flexible, responsive and high performing. The team-based shared-leadership system instituted jointly by management and union has helped the plant keep its "flag ship" role and remain responsive to changes in its external competitive environment. Its LMLT presents a powerful example for other industries to consider.

FIGURE 3.5. TRUST: DIAGRAMS 1, 2, AND 3

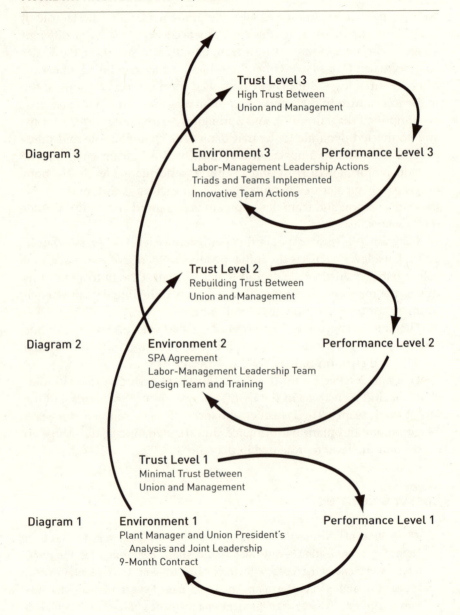

Diagram 3

Trust Level 3
High Trust Between
Union and Management

Environment 3
Labor-Management Leadership Actions
Triads and Teams Implemented
Innovative Team Actions

Performance Level 3

Diagram 2

Trust Level 2
Rebuilding Trust Between
Union and Management

Environment 2
SPA Agreement
Labor-Management Leadership Team
Design Team and Training

Performance Level 2

Diagram 1

Trust Level 1
Minimal Trust Between
Union and Management

Environment 1
Plant Manager and Union President's
    Analysis and Joint Leadership
9-Month Contract

Performance Level 1

The participants in the Quaker Oats plant redesign learned many lessons, which the interviewees kindly shared. The coauthors of the book have selected some that should not be lost in this sharing of the Quaker Oats story.

❶ *Be analytical first to determine the best place to begin in work system redesign.* This case study is an excellent endorsement of the importance of being analytical about the situation faced and of determining the best first steps the situation demands. In this case, the first step was one of building trust and then achieving organizational support from both management and union before undertaking work system redesign. While the lesson of creating trust is very important, not to be overlooked is the lesson of being analytical first.

❷ *A comprehensive structured process is necessary.* The challenges of transforming a work system are many and varied. In this case, great care was given to the processes required to design, prepare for, and implement the new team-based shared-leadership work system. This case study demonstrates how management and union joined together to approach the challenges. They created a partnership for new plant investment, a joint labor-management leadership steering committee, and supplemental agreements to enable the redesign to proceed. They formed a redesign team with members from across the plant and later an implementation team. They gave great attention to team preparation and organizational conditions, including involvement in and ownership of the change across the organization. They used a skilled consultant to serve as a process leader and educator, diffused new team process capabilities throughout the plant, and used the LMLT to advance and support the new work system and its sixty-four teams. The process was comprehensive, and the work redesign was successfully achieved.

❸ *The plant manager faces a special challenge when trust is very low.* Because of the careful diagnosis of the situation he was entering as the new plant manager, Roger Vincent knew he had to earn trust in the early months of his tenure, particularly with union leadership. He determined that starting with restatements of vision and mission would not work. He had to prove first that his actions matched his words, thereby building trust with the union and within management.

This approach built the foundation of trust, first with union president Shields and then with others, on which the rest of the system improvements could be developed.

❹ *Union and management leadership can benefit greatly from mutual decision making on team building and broader work system changes.* Their mutual decisions encompassed early and open communications on technical and social changes, shared-leadership changes, design of self-managed teams, and team implementation. Further, their mutual decision making allowed trust levels to rise high enough to make the leap of faith necessary to launch self-directed teams as a plantwide system. However, the case also demonstrates that clarity about decision boundaries is very important—being clear what things are joint between management and union and what things are separate interests of each and for which separate actions can be taken. The initial partnership and the effective joint leadership actions were crucial to the success of the Quaker Oats plant.

❺ *Trust is crucial.* It is imperative in creating team-based systems and achieving and sustaining high team performance. In this case, trust was viewed as the foundation for the creation of a well-functioning team at the top, the joint LMLT. Trust was central to the plant's revival and success. This case study provides a model for trust building between top union and company leaders. It shows that trust and a lack of hidden agendas can lead to greatly enhanced decisions and performance.

❻ *Champions and mentors can make a difference.* Those from corporate and national union headquarters can provide support, insights, and protection for the local organization and local union. This higher-level support can aid the open, honest, and timely dialogue necessary to proceed locally and can lead to more confident local planning and actions to undertake system changes—in this case, toward a shared-leadership team-based technical and social system.

❼ *Advanced training before team creation and continued training in technical and process skills can be crucial.* Such training greatly facilitated the creation of self-directed work teams and enhanced their initial and continuing performance. The training programs provided to team members, team leaders, midlevel managers and supervisors, and top management and union leaders offered clear benefits in planning, implementing, and operating a team-based system. The comprehensive training before, during, and after team introduction helped generate creative innovations by teams; higher team performance; and cost, time, and quality achievements for the Quaker Oats plant.

❽ *Self-directed teams can benefit from being certified and enhanced.* All of the sixty-four teams participated in a process of presenting their initial work system plans to the plant LMLT for certification. The LMLT reviewed the team plans, suggested improvements, and certified the plans after they had been accepted. Teams struggling with the transition to the new work system received special interventions. Teams wishing to adopt innovations, make changes, undertake new projects, reduce costs, or achieve other opportunities had a process for timely submission and expeditious review and approval of plans. The Quaker Oats case provides a workable example of team certification and enhancement.

❾ *Attention to performance metrics is vital.* In this case, assessment encompassed both team-level performance and broader work-system performance outcomes desired by both management and the union. Support and active team plans helped make team goals attainable. Union and management's strong partnership helped make the performance objectives for union and management visible and acceptable throughout the organization. The mutual commitment to "strong company, strong union" helped give recognition to each partner's goals and encourage cooperative actions for their achievement.

❿ *Periodic self-assessment and renewal are vital.* Management, the union, and the consultant agreed that after teams were established and functioning well, their success should not be taken for granted. Rather, the teams would need to periodically evaluate themselves and practice regular self-renewal. To this end, teams received training in goal setting and in self-assessment. They were charged with regularly conducting self-assessments and with revisiting their team-building exercises twice each year. Likewise, management and union leadership underwent regular training, evaluation, and self-examination.

The emphasis on evaluation enabled the teams and upper management to identify areas for improvement. It also provided a time for reflection, enabling teams to realize the progress they had made.

⓫ *A shared-leadership team-based work system, including team-based benefits, can create an environment where creativity and innovation flourish.* For Quaker Oats, the shared-leadership team-based system with team-based rewards for contributions to business units created a positive environment. Teams proposed many creative and innovative improvements. The LMLT group provided the process by which teams could advance creative ideas for action. When such ideas were reviewed and approved, LMLT would use letters of agreement and other means of support to assist teams in their implementation. In this case study, a shared-leadership approach with a team at the top plus empowered teams sharing in the benefits of their productivity provided an environment that fostered innovation, creativity, and high performance.

NOTES

1. As one example of mutual distrust, in 1989 management developed a plan to reform the plant's work systems and attempted to create union-management committees for implementation. Given labor-management relations at the time, the union told its people not to serve. In the end, the union did not actively resist the redesign but also did not give any support. The effort at workplace change never took hold. Those interviewed felt that other redesign attempts created an obstacle to later proposed changes by increasing cynicism among management, union leaders, and shop floor employees.

2. Indeed, people in the new area were very apprehensive about the change. Several people with seniority had bid out of the area, and some others were reluctant to bid in.

3. The authors are indebted to members of the LMLT who freely contributed their insights and comments: Roger Vincent, Justin Shields, Ian Bulliun, Chris Federlein, Al Hartl, Mike Hughes, Tom Kalopek, Don Chizek, Charles Lewis, Gregg Smith, and Dan Wombold.

4. Semanek, a labor management consultant at Cornell University's Programs for Employment and Workplace Systems, provided key counsel for the joint partnership between the company and the union. She provided valuable guidance and training in transitioning the plant to self-managed work teams.

5. Interest-based bargaining (IBB) represents a departure from traditional bargaining in that it encourages the parties to focus on interests rather than positions. Using IBB, both sides present their interests and attempt to find common ground. The IBB process begins with the identification of an issue and an elaboration of its underlying interests. Parties are encouraged to work collaboratively, through joint information discovery processes, to find options that can satisfy those interests and that are mutually rewarding. Traditional bargaining emphasizes the parties' relative power to force a desired outcome, even if it is at the expense of the parties' relationship. Conversely, IBB utilizes joint problem solving to arrive at a desired outcome and tends to result in a better understanding of each party's concerns or limitations. This allows the parties to achieve a more durable agreement, which can result in a more durable and stable relationship.

6. Interpersonal process recall is an intensive training to enhance interpersonal skills, particularly listening, framing issues, and asking helpful questions. Participants identify a real problem (outside of work) that affects them. Another participant then attempts to facilitate a solution to the problem. Their interactions are videotaped and played back with a third person, who acts as "inquirer," asking the facilitator questions that explore what was going on in her/his mind, what she/he thought the other person was thinking.

7. While the study period for this case was through 2001, performance changes were included from 1996 to 2003 to illustrate the impact of the attention paid to system-wide performance.

8. The text in this section is solely the responsibility of Arlen Leholm and Ray Vlasin.

4

The Teams of TIGR

▶ Tamara Feldblyum, William Nierman,
  Arlen Leholm, and Ray Vlasin

Why the Teams of TIGR

Three self-directed teams of the Institute for Genomic Research (TIGR) are the center of this case. They demonstrate the productive power that can be achieved from deliberately seeking divergent thinking and approaches, respecting them, and building on them. The teams experienced unusual performance increases when SEQCORE (the DNA sequencing facility) and its teams moved to a shared-leadership and responsibility-based environment within which the teams operated.

The case also shows the importance of leadership that created an environment in which responsibility and leadership are shared and in which leadership actions are encouraged. Leadership actions were undertaken at all levels, including by team members, subgroups, teams, and team leaders. Further, the case shows the effective use of boundary conditions and their material enhancement of performance.

As the teams advanced, their achievements helped spur even greater performance. Their high performance was accompanied by intense mutual accountability and responsibility, by diverse and highly competent team members, and by a strong focus on productivity measures and goals that the teams helped to establish.

While seeking diversity of applicable professional skills and knowledge, problem solving was enhanced. Team members' ownership of problems and solutions increased. Closure of genomes was accelerated. Employee retention was greatly improved. The dedication to diverse thinking and approaches created great diversity of cultures. The TIGR environment became a magnet for professionals.

The Snapshot[1]

ADVANCING GENOMIC SCIENCE AND APPLICATION

TIGR is a not-for-profit research institute founded in 1992. It performs structural, functional, and comparative analyses of genomes and gene products from a wide variety of organisms in its large DNA sequencing facility and office complex located in Rockville, Maryland. TIGR has modern facilities for bioinformatics, biochemistry, and molecular biology and is credited with major contributions in genomic science. It makes its analytical findings and scientific contributions available to the scientific community and to the public.

TIGR materially advanced the identification of genes in the human genome. In 1990, a pioneering strategy developed by Dr. J. Craig Venter to generate expressed sequence tags (ESTs) greatly accelerated gene identification. By 1994, scientists at TIGR had used this new technique to identify more than half the genes in the human genome. Fewer than three thousand human genes had been identified before the EST approach was created. In 1995, TIGR researchers published the first complete sequence of a free living organism, *Haemophilus influenza*, a bacterium causing respiratory infections in children. This project was accomplished using whole genome shotgun sequencing, a pioneering technique developed by Dr. Venter and Dr. Hamilton Smith. This method was applied to sequencing of other medically important and environmentally significant microbial, protozoan parasite, and plant genomes. TIGR's studies of functional genomics are helping to define the minimal set of genes required for a free-living organism and genes that are shared among species. TIGR's bioinformatics research involves the annotation and comparative analysis of small and large genomes and the identification of gene families.[2]

TIGR has a major commitment to continued expansion of sequence data and to their application in medicine, agriculture, and basic biological research. It has employed the latest scientific knowledge and analytical procedures in genomic research and has recruited the brightest and most capable employees and empowered them to achieve. TIGR has captured the creativity of administrators, researchers, and professional staffers. Its performance reflects both effectiveness and efficiency. It has received numerous large public-sector grants because of its capabilities and proven record. TIGR has sponsored a wide variety of programs to promote public scientific knowledge as well as to advance the scientific profession related to genomics. It has encouraged scientific careers and provided professional research and training opportunities.

A major component of TIGR is its institutional core DNA sequencing facility, known as SEQCORE. At the time of the interviews, it comprised seven operational teams and one leadership team, which included the leaders of the operational teams and the SEQCORE director. The work of the seven operational teams was highly interdependent. Success of the two closure teams, which worked on the final stages of the sequencing process, depended on successful performance of each of the prior functions, the responsibility of the five other operational teams. The entire sequencing group performed at a very high level despite the challenges of extremely high interdependence.

While this case chapter focuses on three teams within SEQCORE, it also examines the rapid changes in TIGR from its origin and initial operation to its restructuring and continued operation. It includes the context within which TIGR was created, its adjustments over time, and its empowerment of operating teams and team leaders and their functioning. We report on three very successful teams operating with a high integration of process and product and high clarity of purpose and procedure.

TIGR benefited from a restructuring and new leadership in 1998. Dr. Claire Fraser, who had been a key officer and one of the scientific leaders of TIGR from its creation, was appointed president. Under her leadership, TIGR recruited and appointed a new SEQCORE director. Both the purposes and processes of TIGR and its SEQCORE unit were clarified. Team arrangements that had been in place were restructured and materially strengthened. Together, the director of SEQCORE and the president established functional boundaries and set new processes for the working relationships between the research faculty and the laboratory teams, which resolved some earlier difficulties.

The president and the SEQCORE director shared authority and responsibility with the operating teams and team leaders. The president and the director supported and empowered team actions, recruited highly skilled staffers who were committed to team approaches, and materially reduced personnel turnover. Team relationships became more functional. Diversity among cultures, knowledge, experiences, skills, and capabilities was sought and secured. Alternative and diverse views within teams were encouraged, respected, and used. Mutual respect, trust, and responsibility within and among teams increased. Optimism also increased. The teams, their leaders, and the SEQCORE director developed and monitored performance metrics.

In the new organizational environment, the empowered teams achieved continuous improvements in productivity. The enhanced team relations plus team creativity, zeal, and spirit contributed to the increased performance. Based on their performance metrics, the teams' combined outputs doubled and redoubled. The three teams reported in this case study benefited from the enhanced environment and support and truly became very high performing.

Challenging Context[3]

CONDITIONS SURROUNDING TIGR'S CREATION

> Probably the key event that led to the creation of TIGR was the 1991 publi-
> cation in *Science* of a paper that established a new paradigm in gene analy-
> sis.[4] Authors Venter, Mark Adams, and their colleagues, then at the
> National Institutes of Health (NIH), described new methods for rapid
> identification of the part of the human genome that codes for proteins, the
> major structural and functional components of the living cell. The *Science*
> paper attracted much attention for two reasons: the potential in terms of
> scientific processes and implications for genomics and the fact that NIH
> filed a patent on the 347 genes described in the publication.

Until this point, it had been very difficult to find genes in the human
genome. Using the new method to generate ESTs, Venter, Adams, and
colleagues identified 347 human genes in just months, whereas previous
processes had required as long as years to find a single human gene. The
new process, with its successful application, proved to be one key factor
in TIGR's formation in 1992.

Also important among the conditions surrounding TIGR's creation was
a companion development in the pharmaceutical industry. A major pharmaceutical corporation had brought to market two gene-based therapeutic
products that yielded a billion dollars a year in revenue. That success generated much excitement among venture capitalists, who began to think
about biotech and genomics and about the possibility of a lot more
nuggets in the human genome than were represented by these two mar-
ketable products.

Various venture capital (VC) groups approached Venter, hoping to interest him in establishing a new company to use the EST method for mining
in the human genome. The typical VC offering included between eighteen
months and three years of funding amounting to between two and three
million dollars. Such offers provided no research advantage over the laboratories and continuing support Venter and colleagues received from NIH.

One day, while Venter was visiting with the president of a VC firm
investing in health care opportunities, he was asked what it would take for
him to leave NIH. Venter indicated that if the VC firm wished to engage
in serious discussions, it would have to be willing to create a separate
research institute and to provide at least ten years of significant funding.
When asked to define "significant," Venter indicated approximately

seventy million dollars over ten years. The president of the VC firm announced that they had a deal.

The VC firm clearly was not going to give Venter and colleagues seventy million dollars to do basic research. Therefore, the parties tried to structure an arrangement that made sense to both the VC firm and to Venter and his colleagues. They founded TIGR as a not-for-profit research institute and established an entity called Human Genome Sciences (HGS). The venture funds would go to HGS and from it to TIGR. In exchange for the stream of funds, the intellectual property generated at TIGR would flow back to HGS for possible commercialization.

All the early plans defined HGS as being a very small company with no laboratory facilities of its own. It would be working with all the initial projects coming from research performed at TIGR, and these initial projects would be based on the EST method to conduct very large-scale screening of the human genome. Given the planned level of support, TIGR could conduct large-scale screening that would not be possible at NIH and could do so with planned support for ten years. The arrangement seemed very exciting to those involved.

Venter and colleagues and Fraser and colleagues closed their laboratories at NIH and moved to a rental building in Gaithersburg, Maryland, in August 1992. According to the initial plan, both groups would stop the work they had been doing for some time at NIH and everyone on board would concentrate on using the EST method to catalog the human genome. Thus, TIGR was formed.

EARLY COMMITMENT TO TEAMING

At the start, a shift occurred in the kind of work that the newly formed TIGR group was going to perform. Venter and Fraser brought from their NIH labs ten Ph.Ds who had been conducting their own research. Right from the beginning, the TIGR group was set up to be a single team. Members of the group were quite excited, understanding the potential of applying the EST approach. For as many years as would be necessary, the team was going to work together on this single project, the cataloging of the human genome. The common goal of applying the EST methodology plus the self-selection by those joining TIGR increased the initial team's commitment and compatibility.

From the beginning, one of TIGR's goals was to operate as an academic institution and make all of the information it developed available to the scientific community. It would publish findings without little if any delay; however, if there was something important on which HGS wanted to file a patent or if HGS wanted further to commercialize something, the TIGR team would allow HGS some time to do so.

During these early years, the bulk of the TIGR's funding came from HGS, thereby limiting what individual scientists could do. TIGR moved along a path that in large part represented Venter's vision of the organization and how it should develop. TIGR's early growth was accompanied by a directive management style. During this initial period of rapid growth, stress was sometimes high. TIGR staffers were both empowered and disempowered at various times. For these and other reasons, personnel turnover became substantial.

The TIGR group achieved great success in its work on the human genome. Working out of its temporary facilities, TIGR researchers and staffers used the EST method to discover many thousands of new genes. In 1995, the scientific journal *Nature* created a special supplement describing the ESTs used to identify more than half of the then estimated sixty to eighty thousand genes in the human genome. Further, newly identified genes were being associated with specific diseases, such as colon cancer and Alzheimer's disease, creating opportunities for better and earlier diagnoses and more effective treatment.[5] In addition, TIGR scientists applied the concepts, techniques, and software developed for human gene sequencing to microbial genomes. After its success with *Haemophilus influenza*, TIGR sequenced other medically and environmentally important organisms. Sequencing of these complete microbial genomes was characterized as revolutionary in microbiology.[6]

TIGR completed the DNA sequence of the first three microbial genomes in history. By the end of 1998, TIGR had completed seven microbial genomes, half of the world total, and had twenty-six more partial and full genomes in progress. It completed the genomes of the pathogens that cause stomach ulcers, Lyme disease, and syphilis. In process at the time were the genomes that cause tuberculosis, cholera, malaria, and streptococcal pneumonia, an organism that causes many hospital infections. TIGR's contributions to the scientific, medical, and health communities clearly were enormous.[7]

Since its beginning, the TIGR group has been highly productive in its laboratory work and in its scientific publications and other informational outlets. However, this extraordinary productivity generated a problem. Both the TIGR group and HGS, which was responsible for possible commercialization, were overwhelmed by the amount of data generated. Thus, HGS began to ask TIGR to delay releasing data while HGS figured out what to do with it. In addition, HGS had entered into an agreement with a major pharmaceutical company, thus increasing the incentive for holding up TIGR's release of information. The concern was that TIGR would release important information into the public domain and competitors might take advantage of it, resulting in lost opportunities to HGS. Tension between HGS and TIGR consequently started to build, and both institutions decided that they had matured enough that they no longer were absolutely dependent on one another for success. After the idea of separate futures was brought forward, a rather quick parting of the ways occurred.

PARTING OF THE WAYS

Possibly the greatest change in the external environment surrounding TIGR occurred in 1997 when TIGR split with HGS. This split occurred about halfway through the original ten-year plan. TIGR had not received its entire seventy million dollar funding commitment up front, so the termination of agreement between TIGR and HGS cost TIGR the opportunity to secure the remaining thirty-eight million dollars.

At the time of the separation, TIGR had grown to some 120 employees. Payroll costs alone caused TIGR leaders deep concerns about continuing support. A few grants of limited size and duration were in hand, but crisis loomed in twelve to fifteen months.

TIGR's researchers and leaders shifted into a grant-writing mode. A flurry in grant development and submissions yielded positive results, with the total value of grants doubling for several years in a row. The TIGR group has progressed well since the separation from HGS. However, a successful transformation was not guaranteed.

> TIGR's leaders viewed this severing of relationships with HGS as the greatest change in the external environment in its early years. Further, it viewed the shift to a grants mode of support and TIGR's success in grants acquisition as its greatest response to that external environment. TIGR continued to rely on multiple grants—performance grants for specific genomic analyses.

New Context for the Teams[8]

NEW LEADERSHIP

In September 1998,Fraser was named TIGR's president. She had been with TIGR from its formation and had served as vice president for research and director of the Department of Microbial Genomics. She brought a range of competencies spanning biology, pharmacology, neurobiology, and computer and information technology plus scientific recognition and an extensive scientific publication record. Fraser brought to her position a philosophy of shared leadership, a belief in the delegation of authority and responsibility, and a commitment to the empowerment of TIGR's professional staff. She believed strongly that professional staff should be rewarded for their achievement without having to take on managerial roles to earn substantial salary increases.

Some uncertainty also accompanied the change. Venter, TIGR's founder and first president, left in 1998 and partnered with a corporation to form Celera Genomics, which was committed to producing a substantially complete sequence of the human genome in three years. Staff members at TIGR questioned what Venter's departure and the creation of Celera Genomics would mean for TIGR's future. Some wondered if TIGR could survive. Others wondered how things would change with Fraser taking over.

FLEXIBILITY AND COLLECTIVE WORK

People outside of TIGR often asked Fraser, "What have you done to make TIGR so successful?" The key reason she gave was that the organization has been flexible—it lacked both physical and organizational barriers. From its earliest days, the organization functioned like a large team. It has not grouped people by their expertise or interests when coming into the organization, as one might group persons in academic departments of a university. Instead, TIGR has mixed its faculty and kept them working together. This process was initially somewhat accidental.

When TIGR moved into its first space, a short-term rental, it did not want to spend any more money in renovating the space than necessary. To organize its functions in the large open warehouse, it placed only one wall down the center of the building, permitting easy access from side to side. On one side of the wall was the sequencing operation. On the other were all the other laboratory functions. So faculty and staff with very different backgrounds all shared a common open space. Although the arrangement was temporary, this early experience with a common large shared open space facilitated teaming, which is what the group wanted going forward. Fraser believed that this reason accounts for TIGR's phenomenal success.

The orientation to total group and to teaming continued. TIGR faculty and staffers realized that all the projects at TIGR essentially were team projects. New faculty members were told that they are expected to develop individual areas of expertise, but they also must be energized about the idea of working as part of a team. Further, they were told that if they were not energized by the idea of team efforts, that TIGR is probably the wrong place for them, according to president Fraser.

DIFFERENT MANAGEMENT AND TEAM ARRANGEMENTS

President Fraser observed that in the early stages, TIGR was small enough that management did not worry about team structure. TIGR managed its efforts without setting up specific teams with specific functions or tasks. SEQCORE was managed on a part-time basis by a member of the TIGR research faculty, who along with a number of others, had been with TIGR from its earliest days. TIGR's employees apparently hesitated to admit that procedures and approaches that had been acceptable when TIGR was at 50 professionals in size could not be continued when TIGR grew to 250 professionals.

By 1998, some prior arrangements appeared to be unworkable because of TIGR's growth. The company enlisted a consulting firm with capabilities in organization and management to evaluate how well TIGR was functioning. Through individual and group interviews, the consulting firm determined that communication within SEQCORE and between it and the research faculty was seriously inadequate. No operating procedures were in place for SEQCORE or for its relations with the research faculty. Some of the more aggressive faculty would make deals with research associates in SEQCORE to get their own work moved up in priority. Morale was low in SEQCORE. Confusion abounded. Quality control received insufficient attention. And operating efficiency was being adversely influenced. President Fraser concluded that such conditions were a recipe for disaster within TIGR.

SEQCORE's new director came to TIGR having been hired to oversee sequence production control and staff in the SEQCORE facility. The day she arrived she was told that the part-time director of SEQCORE was leaving and that she would now be taking over the entire operation of the sequencing core facility. The president delegated full authority and responsibility for SEQCORE to the new director.

> The new director soon realized that she had inherited a very dysfunctional operation and that it was her job to fix it. She focused attention on the structure and operation of the functional teams in SEQCORE and did so through a shared-leadership approach with the leaders of the functional teams. One of her first actions was to formalize the team structure for the functional teams. She established helpful boundary conditions for the relationship between SEQCORE and the rest of the organization, particularly with the research faculty.

SEQCORE members learned early on that they no longer had the option of making individual arrangements with research faculty. They were instructed to respond to faculty requests as politely as possible but as forcefully as necessary, telling them that SEQCORE would not operate as in the past. Some SEQCORE research associates felt that their jobs would be in jeopardy because faculty members were viewed as more senior. Some research faculty members were stunned at not being able to get things done as quickly as they wished. However, once it was clear to all that operations would function under new procedures, both faculty and staff settled in and played by the new arrangements. A very successful SEQCORE operation resulted, demonstrating that clarified team structures and procedures for interacting with faculty (boundary conditions) were very important and could work effectively.

The president invited the consulting firm to return and conduct a second round of interviews after the restructuring was completed and in operation for about two years. The consulting firm learned the operation could not be more efficiently run. In short, it heard effusive praise for the teams, SEQCORE, and its new director. SEQCORE's operation was viewed as the way other units of TIGR should be run. President Fraser credits the director of SEQCORE, Tamara Feldblyum, with turning the operation around.

CONTINUOUS CHANGE

According to Fraser, "The field of genomics has changed so rapidly that it is really difficult to predict out even a year or eighteen months with any certainty. TIGR likely always will have some sequencing operations under way. Therefore, some number of the teams will look very much like the teams in TIGR today."

She continued, "But faculty members are moving into new research areas, and opportunity will be there for new interests and pursuits. Professionals interested in staying at TIGR as a career and not going on to graduate school to retrain and get into entirely new fields should find new opportunities within the organization. It is likely TIGR will even evolve the way it conducts its sequencing. New faculty and new professional staff are told when they join TIGR that the only thing they can be sure of is things are going to change. Continuous change is part of the normal way that business is conducted at TIGR, being an organization in the forefront of genomics."

Moreover, said Fraser, "Recruiting of faculty and professionals for TIGR is undertaken with the clear indication that those entering TIGR must expect change. Further, TIGR seeks those who are intellectually interested in what the SEQCORE professionals and others are doing. Then professionals, even those who perform rather routine tasks, are given the opportunity to be intellectually engaged and challenged. Effort is made to help professional staff on teams and elsewhere know why the work is being performed and understand its scientific importance. The adoption of this developmental approach has had a very positive effect on staff morale."

"Further," explained Fraser, "TIGR is making sure there are effective lines of communication, things are done through efficient processes, and performance is consistent with standard operating procedures. However, within those constraints or boundary conditions, each team can operate in a way that is most appropriate to that group. There may be different ways for teams to get to the final product, and TIGR's continuous recognition of this possibility has contributed to its success."

Fraser concluded, "Finally, teams may form and reform depending on the opportunities that come along for TIGR. Where new professional opportunities emerge, TIGR will likely give those opportunities to the more senior employees first as part of its career development for them. However, it is difficult to say with much certainty where the teams will be in two to three years."

The Teams and Their Status[9]

TEAM OPERATIONS IN 1998

SEQCORE's *team leader group* was in place in May 1998, when the new director arrived. The team leader group had limited leadership and coordination roles. Team leaders expressed dissatisfaction with their ability to make independent decisions and lacked an advocate within the TIGR organization who took their concerns seriously and made requested changes.

In addition, SEQCORE contained *six functional sequencing teams* covering the full range of laboratory functions and procedures. The range extended from generating random clones from genomic DNA of an organism before random shotgun sequencing begins to the final assembly of the resulting sequences—grouping and ordering those sequences to reconstitute the genome sequence for the organism.

Shortly after arriving, the SEQCORE director, with support of the team leaders, wanted to increase the facility's production, improve its success rates, and cut costs. These leaders realized that if the sequencing facility was to remain competitive, teams must achieve higher levels of sequencing and closure (genome finishing) production, enhance the quality of processes and outcomes, and reduce the per-unit cost of a sequence read. They remained aware that genomics was a young and rapidly developing scientific field. New equipment, chemistries, and processes were emerging and being rapidly integrated into the sequencing process. To keep abreast of such developments, SEQCORE needed some persons, possibly a team, dedicated to essential process-improvement goals so that TIGR's sequencing could remain competitive.

One way to move SEQCORE toward its improvement goals held particular promise: creation of a new team—a seventh functional team—within the sequencing facility and dedicated to quality control and related research and development. Being internal to SEQCORE, such a team could communicate easily with other teams, observe problems when they arose, and anticipate potential problems. The new team could serve as a resource for other teams, respond to their questions, and engender clear and timely communication and cooperation. Those on existing production teams were fully engaged. Thus, a new group would be required to perform the innovations in production, processes, and cost reductions needed by the sequencing facility. This approach to quality control and research and development would be consistent with the objective of effective team building and team operation within SEQCORE.

TIGR rejected the creation of a totally autonomous quality control unit outside SEQCORE that would come in to assess quality, report findings, and call for improvements. Such an external team would be far less timely for the operation of the sequencing facility. Also, an external team would run the risk of creating an adversarial climate and generating hostility.

The team to be created would be somewhat independent of the other teams within SEQCORE. It would monitor quality and quickly identify and solve problems that occurred. Further, it would promptly perform maintenance, restore quality processes, and do so with a minimum of delay, enabling efficient and quality functioning of the sequencing facility. Downtime in the various laboratory processes would be minimized.

QUALITY-CONTROL RESEARCH AND DEVELOPMENT TEAM

Well before installing the new team, the TIGR sequencing facility was run much like a research laboratory. People talked easily with one another in the lab. When they confronted a problem, they just talked to each another about it. The more relaxed atmosphere was appropriate when the lab was small, but as the lab and its workload grew, quality control and communication about it required a more deliberate process and structure.

Thus, creation and implementation of the new quality-control group ran somewhat contrary to TIGR's existing corporate culture. Some initial stress resulted. When introduced, the new quality-control and research and development team structure, called the *R & D team*, was not well received by some members of the other teams. For example, they did not like having someone else checking their processes. Creation of the new group also involved a learning process—figuring out what would work best, finding the right quality-control persons, and forging positive relations with the production staff.

R & D TEAM'S EXPANDING CAPABILITIES

As the new R & D team proceeded, it needed to address the considerable amount of repetitive lab work performed by hand. More automation was needed. As new robotics appeared on the market, this team evaluated them for possible use in the laboratory, along with adaptations to make them even more functional for SEQCORE's teams.

While the initial approach to quality control proved effective, the new team's role and capacity quickly expanded. The team brought in new equipment, wrote new programs, and monitored innovations. Further, as SEQCORE adopted more robotics in its processes, persons adept in running and repairing robots were needed. Over time, the R & D team embodied a substantial core function in robotics and automation.

Also developed over time were positive working relationships between this unit and SEQCORE's other functional teams. Other teams became accustomed to having quality-control persons around their operations and would ask questions and request help. Relationships between the R & D team and members of other teams became much friendlier and more proactive. Members of other teams came to view the R & D team as helping rather than as looking over their shoulders. The R & D team shared responsibility for problems that occurred and ownership of the solutions.

TEAMS SELECTED FOR CASE STUDY

Three teams were selected: (1) the *team leader group*, (2) the "prokaryotic closure team" or simply *closure team*, and (3) the newly formed *R & D team*, with its automation and robotics competency. While all of SEQCORE's teams were very productive and performed at high levels, TIGR leaders selected these three teams as appropriate for our case study of high-performing teams.

The Environment for SEQCORE Teams[10]

Special in this case are the organizational conditions, including the boundary conditions, created for the teams in SEQCORE and enhancing their performance. This group included conditions for team operations, empowering support, shared leadership and new team responsibilities, promotions based on skill attainment, recruitment for skills and team fit, diversity in experiences and culture, a training program for team members, and valuing differences in views and approaches. Included also were conditions encouraging creativity plus performance metrics to measure progress. Collectively, these conditions enabled a new working environment. The conditions are described here because of their major positive influence on performance.

BOUNDARY CONDITIONS

Teams within SEQCORE received substantial freedom in deciding how they would operate on a day-to-day basis. For example, a team determined for itself what team members would perform specific parts of jobs within the team's responsibility. The team determined its members' rotations in work assignments, how long they would last, and what needed to be done. For these reasons, trust and respect of the team leader was very important, as were mutual responsibility and trust among team members, the team leader, and the SEQCORE director.

> Within the new environment, SEQCORE's teams were highly self-managed. The director of the DNA sequencing facility characterized her role as "just overseeing the operation, being more of an adviser to team leaders, but definitely not a 'micromanager' of the teams or team leaders." The director did not run laboratory production or interfere with the daily work of teams. However, she provided substantial technical assistance that contributed materially to the range of SEQCORE functions and processes.

To enhance SEQCORE's management, the director set performance goals in cooperation with the team leaders. She also might set criteria for deciding on new equipment, new instruments, or new chemistry in cooperation with team leaders, but she would leave the research and analysis on these matters to the teams. The director worked closely with the R & D team regarding technical matters within the laboratory facility and in monitoring the optimization processes. However, the director trusted each team leader to know the team's part of the process better than she did. Therefore, she did not attempt to tell the teams how to do their jobs.

If team leaders wanted to make major changes in their teams' operation or performance, they were expected to present their ideas or proposal to the director and team leader group for exploration and discussion. When confronted by a major personnel matter within a team, its leader was expected to interact with the director before attempting any official remedial action.

Requirements for effective communication and interaction constituted additional helpful conditions. The genome sequencing projects were complex undertakings because of the large number of components in the process and the large quantity of data generated. The process was divided into various steps requiring teams to interact internally and with each other to optimize the successive steps. In earlier times, significant mishaps had occurred in the processes because of miscommunication, thus highlighting the need for enhanced communication and interaction.

The need for effective and accurate communication was further amplified because the laboratory had day and night shifts. Interaction between shifts had previously constituted a problem but had improved substantially as a consequence of deliberate efforts at better communication. The director and team leaders stressed the need for thorough, timely, and accurate communication among those responsible for the different parts of the complex process both within and across teams. For SEQCORE, required communication and interaction constituted a key boundary condition.

Procedures existed also for rectifying the "bad days," although they occurred only occasionally because of the greater consistency in laboratory processes. For example, if the success rate for any specific sequence run fell below 70 percent, the matter was to be reported promptly to the director so that she could become involved as needed in remedial efforts. When significant problems occurred that were specific to one project and represented more than a single day's bad quality statistics, the director and the project's principal investigator joined with the particular team or teams involved to formulate the best solution.

EMPOWERING SUPPORT

Soon after taking over, the new SEQCORE director sought observations from the team leaders and teams. Team leaders in particular indicated that when they previously had ideas and wanted to change something, no one seemed to listen. Team leaders and team members wanted very much to make inputs about processes and to change them in ways that would, it was hoped, enhance performance. Therefore, the director listened to the team leaders, determined with them which of their ideas were usable, and gave them the chance to make a difference. It was the beginning of providing team leaders and teams an effective voice in SEQCORE and of empowering them to help implement actions they judged to be needed.

With this new level of organizational involvement and support, team leaders and members generated a wealth of new ideas. They provided technical and managerial suggestions, including ones for organizing and operating team functions, because they were performing and observing the laboratory processes every day. When team members saw problems, they were empowered to undertake responsive actions. These actions, in turn, generated more ideas and more success.

Other means for brainstorming and follow-up were used. If the R & D team was working on a technical issue and got stuck, persons with relevant experience, including team leaders, were pulled from other teams to give a hand. Key persons also could focus on issues during "transition periods" between projects. For example, one process employed by a team proved very marginal because of its excessive costs, and production for the team consequently was stopped temporarily between projects. Some members of the team were temporarily loaned to other teams, while a small core group from the team and its leader worked full time on the problem, with meeting minutes and follow-up actions for each step of the process. The vice president for research participated actively, serving as a technical adviser and leader of the small group. The problem process was remedied, and the full team resumed its operation.

SHARED LEADERSHIP AND NEW RESPONSIBILITIES

Before SEQCORE's new director joined TIGR, a traditional division of responsibilities existed between the "random teams," which performed only random sequencing, and the "closure teams," which performed only genome closure. The random sequencing processes were routine, repetitious, and viewed as low-end tasks, while closure analyses were varied and viewed as high-end tasks. Those on the random teams had no opportunity to learn the high-end tasks. To advance in skills and experience, they would need to move to other teams or change jobs. The functions, as organized, constrained staff development and eroded team stability.

The new director restructured the functions among the two random sequencing and two closure teams. Each of the four teams received the opportunity to learn and perform the highest tasks. The reorganization of functions enhanced team members' responsibilities and skills and provided team members with new opportunities that had not been available under the previous traditional division of responsibilities.

The reorganization of functions was complemented by an improved set of career paths leading to new opportunities for promotion. Both laboratory technicians and research associates were provided with new career steps. Thus, longer career ladders with added steps were put in place for the full range of SEQCORE staff. Opportunities for new skills and responsibilities were matched with recognitions and salary awards for achieving them.

PROMOTIONS BASED ON SKILL ATTAINMENT

Prior to 1998, if a staff member in SEQCORE was employed for a year, the person could request promotion. After two years, promotion was likely. The problem was that many staff left TIGR before they had completed two years, and complaints about the existing promotion system were common. Promotion based on time in the organization was proving unsatisfactory.

The team leader group and the new director responded by addressing the skills employees needed to perform effectively, regardless of length of employment. As a start, one team leader created a description of the specific skills required to perform functions within her team—the closure team selected for this case study. The director reviewed the achievement and concluded that it represented an excellent improvement to the promotion system, with potential applications to all of SEQCORE. She brought the team leaders together and they transformed what had been prepared into a generic set of skills applicable across the teams.[11] The result was a set of skill requirements for each type of SEQCORE position, complementing the position descriptions that TIGR had in place.

The SEQCORE group set forth skill requirements for all of its employees, from first-level laboratory technicians to fourth-level research associates. The skill requirements encompassed the generic skills the employee must possess in her/his current job plus the skills that must be mastered for the employee to be promoted to the next step. The skill requirements were documented and available to all SEQCORE staff. The development and implementation of the skill-based promotion system largely eliminated complaints about the promotion process. In addition, it diminished staff turnover throughout SEQCORE.

RECRUITMENT FOR SKILLS AND TEAM FIT

Considerable change in team leadership occurred prior to the new director's arrival. Most of those leaving were hired away. As a result, new team leaders were recruited into SEQCORE. The new director began her recruitment by focusing largely on applicants' technical skills but discovered the limitations of this approach when one newly hired team leader with high technical skills proved incapable of functioning in the team leader role.

The SEQCORE director modified her recruitment of team leaders. While she still sought persons with technical skills, she placed more emphasis on their fit as a team leader. She reported that trust was the first requirement—that is, she looked for people whom she could trust with the job, a particularly important requirement because team leaders are asked to take on large challenges and tasks. She also looked for people whom team members, other team leaders, and she could respect because mutual respect goes along with trust. The director sought people who were diligent and who possessed the leadership abilities or potential to lead teams and manage large processes. The director needed to be able to give responsibility and authority to team leaders and their team members and have confidence that they would perform without being micromanaged.

The director sought team leaders who were capable of interacting well with others and willing to explore problems and answer questions. The SEQCORE director looked for people with the personality and ability to help team members and others and to serve as a mentor and a trainer for them. And she looked for people with applicable technical experience and skills, which also were fundamental to performance output and on which trust and respect build.

This more comprehensive assessment of potential team leaders proved beneficial to SEQCORE. At the time of our interviews, all team leaders were considered to be highly capable and effective. They were diligent, evoked trust and respect, and possessed both team leadership and technical skills. All accepted and met the challenges of large processes and projects and worked well with other team leaders, the director, and others. Even when pressed by a colleague in the TIGR leadership, the SEQCORE director could not decide which of the team leaders she would need less than the others—all performed at a high level and made strong contributions to SEQCORE's overall efforts.

DIVERSITY IN EXPERIENCES AND CULTURE

The teams and team leader group represented a richness of diverse human capabilities. As one team leader observed, "There are many dissimilar educational and professional backgrounds, varied ages and experiences, and even different ethnic backgrounds represented in the teams and team leaders. This diversity brings with it a wide array of views on approaches and processes and on problems and opportunities. The more diverse and creative the views brought to a situation, the greater the possibility that the resulting agreement and action will be appropriate and functional."

TRAINING PROGRAMS

TIGR personnel designed and offered a multidimensional training program for new and continuing employees. The training focused largely on the technical content and processes of random sequencing and closure. The offerings included a two-week training program on the "closure process" for new employees who would be working in closure, a two-week course on "random sequencing" for new and current staffers working in SEQCORE, and three- and two-day courses on "sequencing and closure," mainly for people at TIGR outside of SEQCORE. The training covered TIGR's history and goals, its organization, genomics projects, introduction to shotgun sequencing, library construction processes, computer systems and databases, laboratory processes and robotics, sequencers and sequence analysis, various standard operating procedures and applications, and troubleshooting. While SEQCORE's teams received a variety of solid training opportunities, they centered on scientific and technical content and processes. One important exception was the training TIGR offered on valuing differences among staff members and their divergent views and approaches.

More recently, time has been given to team concepts, team processes, and team building and strengthening. TIGR's training team and representatives from two closure teams engaged in a two-day training design process known as Developing a Curriculum (DACUM).[12] DACUM encompassed the general areas of competency, the tasks and skills required to perform random sequencing and closure, and the knowledge and skills necessary to enable staff members to function in effective teams. The training team group used the DACUM findings to redesign offerings within TIGR, including components of team functioning.

VALUING DIFFERENCES

TIGR's staff-member training included a component on divergent views and approaches. Outside resource persons taught staff about the benefits of encouraging different points of view. Staff learned that people see things and approach situations differently and that various people are motivated by different things. Grasping this knowledge and understanding its implications was not difficult, but the uninformed saw such understanding as not intuitive.

Some staff members taking the training indicated they had not previously thought extensively about these differences or their importance. Some considered the training among the most useful they had received, a very effective use of their time. TIGR instituted this training as a part of normal business. Conducted on-site for new and advanced employees, the training helped to promote an appreciation of the dynamics of working with individuals who come to a team with different experiences and different cues and triggers for motivation and action. TIGR leaders believe that an appreciation of differences is critical when working as part of a team.

SEQCORE and other TIGR staff members were highly responsive to such training. In a staff survey and in companion interviews, staff members were asked whether TIGR valued or encouraged different views and different approaches. They responded unanimously that TIGR valued and encouraged such differences.

ENCOURAGING CREATIVITY AND ENHANCED PERFORMANCE

A relationship—likely a close one at TIGR—existed among valuing and encouraging differences, growth in creativity, and enhanced performance. Fraser reported, "When one looks back some five years [from 2001], TIGR's attention was not given to valuing differences or to enhancement of creativity. Those then at TIGR were very busy cranking through sequences. They did not take time out to address such matters, believing it would detract from productivity. But nothing could be further from the truth. Once people realize attention to these matters actually enhances performance, they make time for them. They see that by making time available for quality training on valuing diversity and divergent views and approaches, the net result is much more efficiency, a much happier staff, and much more productivity."

PERFORMANCE METRICS

Under the leadership of the new SEQCORE director, laboratory production parameters and standards were instituted on a formal basis. In addition, the new director established a data tracking system to measure performance for SEQCORE. This tracking system provided data on (1) number of projects being served, (2) number of sequences performed, (3) number of good sequences that resulted, (4) success rates, and (5) data quality. In addition, the tracking system provided information on the number of useful DNA bases in each sequence—the average edited "read length" and "direct costs per sequence read." The measurements were readily accessible to those within the sequencing lab and others in TIGR, who could monitor performance on a daily, monthly, and annual basis for individual projects and for all projects served.

A review of TIGR's performance data at TIGR between 1997 and 2001 shows that the facility's annual production increased from 741,000 sequences with a 65.9 percent rate of success to 3,400,000 sequences with an 81 percent success rate.[13] Thus, total annual productivity more than tripled while the success rate jumped by nearly one-fifth. Performance data for the year 2002 indicated continued increases in both productivity and success rates.

Equally important for TIGR is its experience in cost reduction. In August 1997, the laboratory's direct cost per sequence read was close to $5.40. By the end of 2001, the direct cost was approaching $1.20 per read—about one-quarter of its 1997 level. Because TIGR relies heavily on grants from government agencies to perform genome sequencing, this reduced cost of sequencing serves it well in competing for grant awards.

> The existence of SEQCORE goals for increased production, improved success rates, and reduced costs combine to provide one incentive for effective team functioning. A second incentive is provided by the performance tracking system readily available to all teams and team leaders and to the director. These two features appeared fundamental to the high regard for performance shown in the three teams analyzed. Further, these features appeared to reinforce the shared responsibility for enhanced production and success rates that was evident at all levels.

High Interdependence

GENOME SEQUENCING[14]

The genome of an organism is comprised of DNA, a linear polymeric molecule assembled from four monomeric components, which are termed bases and are symbolized by the letters A, T, G, and C. A DNA sequence is represented by a string of these letters, such as GGGACT-GTTC. The genome of a bacterium, for example, contains on the order of two to ten million of these bases. Determining the complete genome sequence of a bacterium involves establishing the sequence of all of these units with an error rate of less than one in ten thousand.

DNA sequence is determined by analyzing the products of a DNA sequencing reaction on an automated DNA sequencing machine. The analysis of one sequencing reaction provides sequence lengths of about 650 bases with 2001 technology. TIGR's sequencing laboratory analyzes the products of about eight thousand sequencing reactions each day from about thirty-five projects at any one time, amounting to some 11.7 million DNA bases each day. The complexity of the DNA sequencing process and the large amount of data generated require simultaneous management of people, machines, and data.

HIGHLY INTERRELATED NATURE OF PROJECTS

The complex process of sequencing a genome is accomplished in four interrelated phases. The final phase in this process depends on the scientific accuracy with which all of the previous interdependent phases have been performed. Thus, the final products represent a very advanced form of joint work product.

The first phase is library construction, in which genomic DNA from the organism to be sequenced is fragmented into pieces for subsequent propagation and amplification. The second phase is random sequencing, in which every portion of the genome is sequenced a number of times for high accuracy of the consensus sequence obtained. The third is called the closure phase, in which sequences obtained are sorted into their order in the genome using assembly software programs and gaps in the sequence of the genome are closed through direct sequencing techniques. During the fourth phase, genome annotation, the boundaries and identities of the genes are assigned by comparison to the sequence of similar genes in the universe of other sequenced genes.[15]

MUTUAL RESPONSIBILITY

The nature of these interrelated phases, their complexity, and the resulting joint work products place special demands on the teams. Team members and the team leader must be capable of working together to ensure that the work is done accurately and on time. They must anticipate and thereby avoid problems, address any problems that occur, and communicate fully any matters that should be shared. Further, people must stand ready to solicit views from others to help resolve possible difficulties that arise or foster necessary improvements.

The complex, multistep process and successive phases of the work performed by teams necessitate a very high level of mutual responsibility both within and among teams. Teams must be able to depend on one another for completion of the many steps and to trust that work is performed at a high technical standard. The SEQCORE director, team leaders, and team members recognize, practice, and encourage this mutual responsibility.

As an example of this mutual responsibility, one team member said, "I am in charge of the first two steps in the process. I know if my first step does not go well, then my second step can't go well, and the next team that depends on us can't perform well. It will translate into difficulty all the way down the line. So if I don't make a good library to start with, others are going to have a horrible time closing the genome. Everything we do affects people in the year down the road, and that is really important." The director indicated that the flow of analyses, data, and findings throughout the sequencing process might be thought of as a lifeline, a concept that helps capture the intensity and importance of the interdependence involved. All parts of the lifeline, from beginning to end, demand the highest mutual responsibility.

NECESSARY GUIDELINES

The thirty-five or more individual genomic sequencing projects on which SEQCORE works at any one time required careful attention to the scheduling and progress of work. SEQCORE's teams were responsible for performing the sequencing steps required and meeting target deadlines. Thus, the complex processes, the numerous projects, and the sizable workload necessitated guidelines for laboratory operation. These guidelines encompassed such matters as maintaining quality in process and product, reporting and remedying problems, and proposing changes in laboratory operations. The volume and deadlines also required clear

guidelines for managing the interactions between the laboratory personnel—technicians and research associates—and the faculty investigators
who provided scientific leadership for the projects.

ENVIRONMENT OF CARING

We also probed the level of caring about one another—by the director,
team leaders, and team members—and about their families. Those interviewed distinguished between caring for one another and their families
and interacting frequently on a social level, emphasizing the former
rather than the latter. As one person observed, "If anything happens to
one of the people here, the rest would care a lot and be there—to help
and support that person." Another team member told of other work
environments where people were reluctant to ask how fellow employees
or their families were: in contrast, "Here, within the SEQCORE group
people ask, 'Well, how is it going?' 'Do you want to talk?' They initiate
such comment, inviting others to share their situation and receive team
support."

Another team member told of a recent incident when a person who
had been employed for less than six months became ill and was hospi-
talized. "TIGR could have terminated her employment but did not. Her
employment was continued, and persons with whom she had worked
came to visit her. People wrote and stayed in touch until she was able to
return to work. Later she was accepted into a graduate program and left
TIGR. She wrote letters back to the president and director, thanking them
for the unusual support she had received. She also created a plaque for
TIGR, recognizing all the support she received from fellow employees
and the director during her illness. The plaque is kept at TIGR. It is but
one of many instances demonstrating that an environment of caring and
personal support exists." Before moving to the individual teams in this
case study, a general observation can be made about the context in which
the teams function.

> SEQCORE and its parent, TIGR, have a special clarity—clarity of purpose
> and clarity of process. This dual clarity and the participation and shared
> leadership for their achievement help focus the creativity and energies of
> the director, team leaders, and their teams.

Team Leader Group[16]

CHANGES

The team leader group operated for several years before the creation of Celera Genomics. In the spring of 1998, three team leaders plus other team members left to join Celera Genomics. Their departure had both negative and positive impacts. On the negative side was the loss of key bioinformatics personnel, including the three team leaders, who had helped TIGR and SEQCORE advance. On the positive side, the loss of team leaders provided an opportunity for a new start, a chance to re-create the team leader group within a new organizational context.

The 1998 survey and analysis of how well TIGR was functioning also proved beneficial. Something had to be done to fix the serious communication problems identified within SEQCORE and between it and the research faculty. According to one of the team leaders present at the time, the combination of the survey findings and the departure of some of the team leaders and others served as incentives for action.

An important change influencing the team leader group was the change in SEQCORE's leadership. The new director replaced a person with less management experience who served only part time in the position. The new director brought both technical and management experience to her new position and gave it her total energies as a shared and empowering leader. She also brought a disposition to seek and use the ideas of team leaders about laboratory and team matters, both technical and managerial. The team leader group saw the change as very important. One group member characterized it as "a big difference, the main difference."

Also significant in the organizational context for "teamness" was the fact that the new director had no project of her own, as had been the case with the prior director. In the new director's eyes, all projects were equal and all project work with all faculty principal investigators was important. Thus, she and the team leaders had no tendency to favor one project over others or to give the impression that one group was better or more important than another. This change helped to eliminate the legacy of divisiveness that the new director had inherited and created an environment within which all teams and team leaders had the opportunity to cooperate and perform well.

The departure of team leaders in 1998 and the new appointments that followed substantially changed the composition of the team leader group.

One team leader believed that the group changed totally, becoming more positive and more effective. Others concurred. Members of the team leader group believed that the group's nature, composition, and functioning were evolving and would continue to evolve in a positive manner.

ROLES AND COMMITMENT

At the time of the interviews, the group comprised eight persons—leaders of the production teams plus the R & D team leader. SEQCORE's director met with the team leader group members and functioned much as one of the group members.

The team leader group served in a leadership and coordinating role for SEQCORE's team operations and provided a mechanism and place where all manner of issues and questions pertaining to the sequencing facility or one or more teams within it could be addressed and explored. The team leader group members interacted beneficially on a variety of technical, managerial, and team operating matters.

The team leader group was very much oriented toward performance. Rather than focusing on mission, the group spoke about specific goals—for example, number of sequences per week, costs, and number of closed genomes. When asked if the group had a vision and what might it be, one team leader said, "To sequence the genomes as best you can." Another replied, "To be the best in the world." A third responded, "To beat them all. Since mid-1998, the group has met each goal it established. It has never missed a goal."[17]

These quantitative performance goals are adjusted upward at least once a year as they are achieved and as permitted by other circumstances such as number of grants and amount of money to support the production process. The higher goals—particularly those regarding efficiency, costs, and success rates—are driven in large part by the external competitive environment for contracts and grants. The goals are also in part self-imposed by the team leaders and the director. The team leaders participate in, understand, and support the higher goals but are also clearly challenged by them. However, the team leader group evidenced a high zeal about its role and responsibilities and appeared to take the greater challenges in stride. Furthermore, the team is self-motivated and evidenced a high level of team commitment. Team members are proud of TIGR and SEQCORE and hear of the high regard for their unit from other TIGR employees. Complementing these attributes is a sense of optimism. As one team member remarked, "Everybody feels that they can reach their goals. Nothing really is impossible." Another team member added, "I was once asked what TIGR would do if it couldn't close a genome. My answer was, 'I don't know. Never have we not closed a genome.'" Team members reported that they work on a genome until they find a solution: one took five years to complete. They also indicated that there is a very strong feeling of job security among the team members and at TIGR, which reinforces the sense of optimism.

> In performing its role, the team leader group followed one informal operating guideline—that is, that everyone's opinion is important. The team leaders were chosen in part because they are open-minded, willing to seek out others' views, and willing to try new approaches. The group members felt quite free to go to any source within SEQCORE, within the broader TIGR organization, and beyond to get the information they needed. They were willing to do whatever was necessary to achieve their goals.

The team leader group believed its strength was in its members' diversity and their willingness to share and be supportive. Members brought widely varying knowledge bases, experiences, cultural values, and capabilities to the group's deliberations. Any team leader could approach any other member or the entire leader group for assistance. All they needed to do was ask and give reasons to receive valuable insights or remedial suggestions from the other team leaders or the sequencing facility director.

The group's central commitment was to make the sequencing facility work. The team leader group wanted to keep laboratory processes and machines running, produce the data necessary, and finish the genomes on time. How the group achieved these objectives largely was decided among the members and the SEQCORE director. Though the group met and usually had an agenda to make its deliberations efficient and effective, it had no hard and fast guidelines about meetings, minutes, and team leader group operations.

ENHANCED TEAM FUNCTIONING

Members of the team leader group cited effective communication and increased interaction as major improvements since early 1998. As one team leader reported, "The level of communication definitely was an addition to team functioning that wasn't there before." Members prized opportunities to talk freely about the full range of matters—what was going on in their teams, in other teams, and beyond. Sometimes they obtained important insights about their teams' operations from other leaders who supplemented information from within the team.

Team leaders who sought to determine what was happening about some matter in another team could easily just ask. In addition, what was communicated within the team leader group was positive. Gone were the prior references to which team was better than others, which team was not doing what it should, who should and should not get the next employee, and similar negatives. Instead, the team members focused their communication on such matters as needs of the sequencing laboratory, needs of teams, where new employees were needed most, why particular needs prevailed, and what positive actions could be taken.

The team leader group also brainstormed and provided suggestions for consideration and action. At the end of each regular team leaders' meeting, time was allotted in which any team leader could put forth ideas or proposed changes in such areas as managerial or technical issues involving laboratory processes or team operations. The team leaders discussed each idea and explored its merit. As one member observed, "Ideas are discussed before anything is done. If we offer an idea, we are likely to be able to try it. Further, it is acceptable for us to express how we feel about things." Another observed, "The creativity is not freewheeling. Rather, it is creativity with precision. The team can be creative about the ways to organize or ways to streamline laboratory processes. However, once the discussions are completed and decisions are made, a production process is set. That production process is carried out with standard operating procedures, and it is performed with precision."

Team leaders reported that the creativity and production are tempered by the reality that the closing of genomes is so new in the world that there is little history concerning the time required or complications for the new genomes undertaken. The history is limited to the genomes that have been completed, and each new genome appears to differ in the requirements for achieving completion. Thus, production processes can differ substantially from one genome to another, making it difficult to set time goals for achieving genome closure.

One of team leaders' major roles involved interviewing candidates for employment as new team leaders. The director usually interviewed each candidate first, accompanied by the outgoing team leader. Then, top candidates received a second interview with members of the team leader group. The director was not present at this meeting, permitting members to ask any questions they desired. Next, the director and the team leader group discussed the top candidates, shared observations, and proceeded toward a mutual decision.

Another major change was strengthening team leaders' role in dealing with matters of staff development and promotion. Through close cooperation with the SEQCORE director, jobs were redesigned, shifting some staff from factory-style work to assignments that were 50 percent creative and 50 percent technical but still necessary. Team leaders helped design professional development opportunities for advancement through technical and management tracks, including determining the skill levels needed to advance along each track. The improvements helped team leaders make decisions about development and promotions of their staff and newcomers.

Team leaders also fostered staff development in other ways. As one leader reported, "My view of managing my team members has changed since becoming a team leader. It went from, 'How do I use the people that I have to accomplish the goals that we have?' to 'How can I develop the people so that they don't need me?'" Such profound attitudinal changes and related actions supplemented the organizational changes made for career development.

Members of the team leader group portrayed a distinctly supportive attitude toward one another and the SEQCORE director. They stood ready to assist one another in gaining insights, clarifying issues, analyzing problems, and suggesting appropriate and functional solutions. In addition, they viewed the director of SEQCORE as very supportive of their role as members of the team leader group and as leaders of individual teams.

Another helpful change was the sharing of personnel. Members of the team leader group stood ready to lend staffers to other groups when emergencies or special team needs arose. For example, a closure team might send a person to help the template and library construction team with a special need or might obtain a person from the research and development team to assist with quality control or automation. As evidence of this strong sense of sharing and cooperation, team leaders reported that they can request and obtain personnel from another team with minimal effort and sometimes with a single e-mail.

Team leaders reported a sense of real joy when in 2000 they received special recognition in SEQCORE—specifically, for increases in sequencing output, increases in success rates, and reductions in costs. Team members indicated that the recognition came at a time when SEQCORE's problems had been fixed, everything was coming together, and there was a sense of well-being and accomplishment. Their recognition was accompanied by the award of an additional day off, to be used at their discretion.

The combination of these mutually supportive conditions gave team leaders a sense of empowerment. They felt strongly connected to and backed up by one another and by the SEQCORE director. As one team leader remarked, "I feel totally empowered and I believe that the other members of the team leader group feel the same way."

WHAT MADE THE TEAM SPECIAL?

Members of the team leader group and the SEQCORE director were asked what made this team so unusual or special. One reason they cited was the *composition of the team, which included dedicated achievers.* Each of the members was a high achiever—superachievers, according to the director. They believed in what they did. They were not afraid to make mistakes. They viewed themselves as dedicated TIGR and SEQCORE workers, type-A personalities.

Another reason the team believed it was special was the *very diverse nature of its members.* They encompassed a wide range of scientific knowledge competencies, including animal science, microbiology and molecular biology, chemistry and biochemistry, DNA technology, genetics, molecular genetics and genetic toxicology, forensic science, immunology and virology, laboratory and medical technology, and research methodology. They brought new technology applications, robotics and automation, and machine redesign and maintenance plus computer and software design and applications. They also possessed skills in communication, leadership, organization, evaluation, quality control, problem solving, training, and mentoring. As one leader remarked, "Everybody brings something special, whether from school and learning or other jobs. These contribute to the different views and creative suggestions and outcomes."

Other group members contended that the team was special because of its *use of the group as a place to sound out ideas and to learn techniques and approaches for managing situations and dealing with problems.* Some team leaders came to their positions with little prior management experience and consequently learned team leadership, interpersonal, and management skills on the job. Team leaders proved valuable in helping one another with these skills. A high premium was placed on being able to talk freely with other team leaders and to explore responses to situations that a team leader had not experienced or handled in the past.

Still another reason cited for being special was the *supportive way the group handled attempted innovations and occasional failures.* According to team members, within the group as well as more broadly in SEQCORE, they felt free to try new and different things to improve processes. As one longtime group member pointed out, "We aren't afraid to make mistakes. The team has tried a number of different methods of doing things within the lab, trying to get what's going to work the best. Sometimes an attempted method has been a failure. The team leader group and director allow this to happen and accept the fact that failures can and do occur."

Closely associated with this condition was the team's *positive disposition toward change.* As a result of conditions within SEQCORE and new developments beyond SEQCORE, team leaders were continuously adding new things and training people in new methods and in new uses of software. The team leader group members viewed themselves as being very able to accept and respond to change rather than being resistant to it.

Another factor cited as a reason for being special was the group's *strong customer-like orientation and a related sense of mutual responsibility.* As one person explained, "In the past, some of the team leaders let their ego move into the situation and create barriers to good work. However, this group realized there is a complex sequencing job to be achieved and that each team leader has a part in it. Each has a responsibility to the other team leaders as well as to TIGR research faculty involved in the process—as customers for the output. The team leader group treats the director of SEQCORE as its most frequent customer."

As another member pointed out, "This customer-like orientation and sense of mutual responsibility are very different from exercising one's power or withholding one's help—actions counter to effective functioning of teams. Instead of telling others that you are not going to do something, the customer orientation is more likely to result in the statement, 'Well, ok, how can I change my way of doing it to help you?'" Still another indicated, "The principal investigators [faculty members] are customers. Rather than viewing them as holding an axe over our heads, treating them as customers yields more effective results."

Another reason cited for being special was the *team's desire to keep up TIGR's and SEQCORE's cutting-edge reputations.* The team indicated that TIGR has been at the forefront of genomics for so long that it has moved well beyond what many other research entities are doing, having moved on to the next level or to other things. In addition, other people expect TIGR to perform high-quality work. It is constantly competing for grants to extend its achievements. It had the reputation as being the first company in the world to publish genomic analyses, and team leaders did not want to lose that special reputation.

As one team member observed, "Many companies look to us to see what new work we are doing and what we are testing. When at a professional meeting, people who meet us exclaim, 'Oh, you work for TIGR! How are you doing so and so?' They come to read the TIGR posters with a notebook, to find out and record what we are doing. Given our positive reputation, we feel obligated to keep a certain high standard, because this is what we have done before." Another group member added, "Other scientific labs and institutions may do really well once or twice, but TIGR's success keeps going and going."

Also cited as special was the *positive support and cooperation of others in the TIGR organization.* Team members valued the faculty's understanding of the importance of the teams' work, increased team understanding of the faculty's work, and increased ease of interacting with faculty. As a result, faculty and team members interacted on the same level—no hierarchy, with everyone working with each other. Furthermore, the SEQCORE director was a major contributor to the success of the team leader group. Team members indicated their reasoned requests received positive support. Also cited was support for computer and bioinformatics systems fundamental to the work of teams.

In addition, the director of SEQCORE received strong upper-level support from TIGR's president that was crucial for fulfilling requests from the team leaders and the director. Without top-level support, many of the director's changes would not have been possible. This support reflected the shared and facilitative leadership that both the president and the director practiced and modeled.

ORGANIZATIONAL AND TEAM VARIABLES AFFECTING PERFORMANCE

Members of the team leader group were asked to indicate the importance of various organizational and team variables in the team's achievement of high performance. Team members from the leader group indicated that the *most important organizational variables* in achieving team performance were (1) commitment to creativity and innovation throughout the organization and (2) the organization's commitment to this team's success. Also of high importance were (3) the organization's willingness to encourage and help this team be entrepreneurial, (4) the organization's commitment to employee growth in skills and knowledge, (5) the organization's commitment to this team's creativity and innovation, and (6) the organization's commitment to team approaches and team success.

According to the team leader group, the *most important team variables* for the group's successful performance were (1) trust between team members and the SEQCORE director, (2) trust among team members, (3) a commitment to team success by team members and the director, and (4) the complementary nature of the team, both among the members and with the director. Also very important were (5) the team's commitment to stretching thinking and searching for new ideas and approaches, (6) the team's commitment to creativity and innovation, (7) mutual respect among team members and for the director, and (8) self-motivation of the team members and the director. Next in importance were (9) willingness to take risks to achieve success by the team members and the director, and (10) optimism among team members and the director.

The Prokaryotic Closure Team[18]

ROLE[19]

The Prokaryotic Closure Team was one of two closure teams within the sequencing facility. The closure team received the sequences of the bacterial genomes generated during the random (or shotgun) sequencing phase and used TIGR software tools to group those sequences, creating assemblies based on sequence similarities.

As the leader of the team shared, "The role of the closure team is to link those assemblies and order them correctly to reconstitute the complete genome. Reconstituting the genome is similar to assembling a very complex jigsaw puzzle without having the puzzle picture available. The assemblies may have some missing sequences among them. These are called gaps, thus the word 'closure'—closing the gaps. The team fills in the gaps using a variety of molecular biology techniques and the total genomic DNA extracted from the microorganism. Some gaps prove easy to close, while others present a major challenge."[20]

At the time of the interview, the team included eighteen persons. Each of the team's fifteen research associates and molecular biologists worked on at least two genomes at a time. Between two and five persons and usually three or four worked together with the team leader and the TIGR faculty principal investigator to close a given genome. The number of persons in the subgroup depended on the size of the genome, and each subgroup was named after the particular genome being closed. The size of the overall closure team varied from time to time because it comprised both persons under the supervision of the team leader and persons from other teams, including the night team, performing closure functions.

The closure team served a crucial role in the sequencing facility, working very closely with the TIGR faculty principal investigator on a particular genome and with TIGR's Bioinformatics Department. The team could analyze a total of sixteen or more genomes at different stages of closure at any one time. A team goal was to streamline closure by using powerful software and robotics to decrease the costs and the labor involved in this process. The team also sought to stay up to date with the literature to improve SEQCORE's functioning and the molecular biology processes used. The closure team's efforts were highly complementary to those of the R & D team, which also helped to create greater efficiencies and quality enhancements.

FUNCTIONING

The team was assisted by a creative and capable leader, Hoda Khouri, with a rich and varied background in science and with management experience. Her background included a bachelor of science degree in agriculture and a master of science degree in animal sciences as well as previous work experience in immunology, virology, genetic toxicology, and microbiology. After becoming a molecular biologist, Khouri joined TIGR in April 1998 as a member of SEQCORE's molecular biology core group. She worked with a team of molecular biologists hired as troubleshooters to help train others in new techniques in microbiology and DNA technology. Her professional contributions to TIGR led to her July 1999 appointment as a team leader with the closure team, a position that required both her scientific and her management skills.

The team appeared to feature an especially good fit between its members and its functions. The observations of colleague Jyoti reflect that fit.

Jyoti earned an undergraduate degree in India before moving to the United States, where she obtained a second degree emphasizing microbiology. After serving in microbiology labs she joined SEQCORE in 1998 and was present during the rapid changes and the introduction of automation to advance sequencing, which permitted her to devote her energies full time to closure.

Within the closure team, Jyoti operated in a subgroup of three to four persons working on an average of two to three closure projects at a time. She found working on multiple projects simultaneously to be beneficial. She learned from each of the unique genomes. Trouble experienced with one genome often contributed valuable insights to work with other genomes. Communication was close within her subgroups and with the larger team. She reported, "The subgroups and team had a wealth of information and ideas. Someone may say, 'Oh, I did this for one genome. Try this on your problem.'" Furthermore, she said, "That's the wonderful thing about TIGR. You can go to anyone, anytime, discuss problems, and everyone comes up with such great ideas. The team leader sets the agenda, and we have the freedom to do certain things, try certain things our way. That kind of freedom really motivates us to do more."

The newest addition to the closure team, Heather, provided equally valuable insights. She came from a private school devoted to science, providing students with the opportunity to conduct research on their own. She joined TIGR already possessing skills in research and laboratory methods, communication, and multitasking. According to Heather "I felt like I quickly slid into place with TIGR. One reason was the nature of the closure team—the larger team and the subgroups for each genome. In a subgroup, you can talk about and negotiate what you want to do with the project and help each other with ideas. The others in the subgroup know exactly what is going on with the same project." She pointed out that the subgroup meets with the larger team to report on project status. Her smaller group had just resolved a trouble spot in a genome and shared it with the larger team. Heather also said, "The team is friendly and personal, and it's not competitive against individuals. It's not like a team where everybody has their [cubicle] and it's a race against the person in the next cube. There is a group of three or four persons that want to finish a project as badly as you do." She added, "Sometimes you have a problem and sit on it. Then someone else asks, 'Have you tried this?' Suddenly you're enlightened, and that sparks an idea for other things. But you have to be good at organization, multitasking, and communication. You can't be competitive, and you can't seclude yourself, or you're not going to learn and pick up the new ideas you need."

Heather related that she could not have guessed that in one year she could learn so much and put together so many things. She could not imagine being allowed to do something, get the results, and decide what to do next. At the time of the interviews, she was working on three projects simultaneously and closing so many gaps she thought it amazing. "You always have room to think, with your small group and larger team—sharing ideas about what works and what doesn't. There are always new ideas coming in—so many people come from so many different backgrounds with so many different ideas they share freely. Nobody laughs at you or looks down on you for your idea. You try your idea. If it works, that's great. If it doesn't, you move on. Because of advances in processes and communication, the output is amazing."

Jyoti and Heather's observations leave little doubt that the freedom provided to the closure team and its subgroups marks them as part of a real self-directed team. Creativity, a strong sense of trust, and clear mutual respect were evident, as was support for trying one's ideas—support for taking risks to complete the genome closing and to advance the total team's knowledge base. The enthusiasm and drive demonstrated left little doubt that the team members possessed real and substantial zeal for their work and achievements.

WHAT MADE THE TEAM SPECIAL?

High on the list of conditions that made the closure team special was *communication among team members and with the team leader.* As one team member observed, "We communicate a lot. and we help each other a lot, so we are always learning from somebody else. In some labs elsewhere, it's competitive, and no one talks to anyone else. Here we are always communicating, and that is very important for our research." Another team member reported, "When we are having a project team meeting, if someone else overhears, they jump in and share ideas." Still another observed, "I can go to anyone, anytime, for their ideas."

Also contributing to the closure team's special nature *were the team members' interpersonal skills.* While respectful of one another, they joked and conveyed a sense of humor about problems and challenges. They shared responsibility for problems and remedial actions and shared information across the team. They readily assisted one another. As one team member observed, "If you are not busy one day, it's not uncommon to help somebody else with their project just because they have a lot to do."

The closure team *represented one of TIGR's most diverse arrays of knowledge, human talents, and experiences.* In addition, the closure team represented the *broadest cultural diversity* of any team in SEQCORE, where diversity is the norm, not the exception. Of the eighteen team members on board at the time of the interviews, fifteen came from country backgrounds other than the United States, creating a truly multinational team. The leader and team members prized this diversity of knowledge, experiences, skills, and culture as a major strength and contributor to the closure team's recognized creativity and high performance. These diverse capabilities served the team well, and it was viewed as one of TIGR's most productive teams.

The team was also special because its *members were highly motivated.* Team members were eager to be involved in more than one project at a time even though they were not required to do so. They actively sought multitask responsibility. The team leader indicated that she sometimes held persons back because they wanted so many projects. Part of this eagerness stemmed from complementarities among genome projects and the possible learning involved. Part stemmed from the subgroups' desire to show achievement on a second or third project when they confront a problem and their progress on a first project is delayed by such factors as waiting for receipt of a reagent on order.

Also seen as special was the *close interaction among members within and among subgroups, which benefited the entire team and its production.* The leader of the closure team was managing eighteen team members in the closure of sixteen genomes. When asked why she chose not to place one person on each genome and allow that person to concentrate on it, she shared her belief that such an arrangement would not work as well as having a subgroup responsible for each genome. She believed that under a one-person, one-genome arrangement, some genomes would never get finished because of personal isolation.

The team leader knew the team members well and worked carefully to establish subgroups based on overall team needs and interests and members' abilities. A person might serve as a member of three different subgroups for three different genomes. As a result, more diverse interaction occurred, providing opportunities for more good ideas or suggestions to be raised and used. She was convinced that the intensive and continuous communication and interaction provided by the subgroups were essential for rapid progress on genome closings.

Team members had *respect for one another, thereby helping the subgroup and team processes function well.* According to the team leader, the key to establishing the best subgroups was explaining what was needed and why rather than dictating who goes where. She reported that team members immediately responded to such explanations. She indicated that some team members have very strong personalities, and they do occasionally clash. But because there is respect among team members, they can and do work together effectively.

Team members also prized the *flexibility their work permitted.* They were responsible for certain outcomes—completing closure of two or three genomes. How team members within a subgroup organized their daily efforts was up to them. As one team member stated, "I am a working mom, and I want and need the flexibility that the team provides. If I have to attend a parent-teacher meeting or go to see my daughter, it's always flexible here. You can come in later and make up the hours over the weekend. The flexibility provided is very important, and I like it."

ORGANIZATIONAL AND TEAM VARIABLES AFFECTING PERFORMANCE

Members of the closure team also were asked what influential organizational variables and team variables were most important in determining this team's success. The *organizational variables* they cited as very important were (1) the organization's commitment to team approaches and team success, (2) the organization's commitment to creativity and innovation, (3) the organization's commitment to growth of employee skills and knowledge, (4) the organization-wide commitment to sharing information, (5) the organization's commitment to this team's success, and (6) the two-way communication and interaction between the team and the organization. Also considered quite important were (7) the organization's commitment to this team's creativity and innovation.

Team variables cited by the closure team as being very important to its achievement were (1) the existence of a team mission and goals and the team's commitment to them, (2) the team members and leader's commitment to the team's success, (3) the team's commitment to stretching thinking and searching for new ideas and approaches, and (4) mutual respect among team members and the team leader. Also considered quite important or very important were (5) the complementary nature of the team members and leader, (6) the team's commitment to creativity and innovation, (7) team members' commitment to education and training, (8) members' willingness to take risks to achieve team success, and (9) trust among team members and with the team leader and the organization. The variables dealing with the team's self-motivation, common vision, recognition of members, optimism, and spirit also were cited as quite important.

Research and Development Team[21]

ROLE[22]

The R & D team operated within TIGR's sequencing facility as a small and flexible group. It performed multiple functions, utilizing its own expertise plus personnel from other SEQCORE teams. This team was devoted to quality control, automation and research, and development. It worked to achieve enhancements for the production and closure phases of the genome sequencing process. Seven persons constituted the core of the R & D team at the time of the interviews, although it has subsequently grown.

Quality control was led by a quality-control specialist and a laboratory technician who bore responsibility for creating and managing the standard operating procedures and other documentation necessary to help ensure quality operations. They also tested reagents before release to production teams and followed trends and results within the sequencing facility.

Automation efforts were lead by an automation specialist, who supervised two team members who would set up, troubleshoot, and maintain critical automation equipment employed in laboratory processes. The R & D team leader was responsible for reporting the status of the team efforts to the SEQCORE director and for reviewing and evaluating new technology for possible incorporation into the TIGR sequencing pipeline.

The R & D team's goals were reducing costs, streamlining sequencing processes, introducing automation where appropriate, and increasing the quantity and quality of data outputs. These goals and efforts toward their achievement remained in constant flux as a result of changes in technologies and project requirements. To meet these goals, strong emphasis was placed on interaction within the team and across teams, particularly with TIGR's software engineers.

The R & D team explored options and took a variety of actions to help reduce operating costs in the sequencing lab. Actions ranged from evaluating possible reductions in use of expensive bulk reagents and plastics to the use of robotics and other forms of automation. The team introduced automation at various points in laboratory processes, decreasing the hands-on time required by lab personnel and the repetitive tasks they performed. The time saved permitted lab personnel to devote extra time to other duties. Together, the reductions in manual, repetitive tasks and the savings in time improved job quality and reduced employee turnover.

The team helped to maintain a sense of stability and order in the sequencing lab. The R & D team considered making changes to the sequence production process only when doing so would meet or exceed the existing sequencing standards and process achievements. Furthermore, experience had shown that no successful process change could be made without effective interactions within and across teams, without appropriate technical training for those involved, and without educating users about why a change in process was needed.

FUNCTIONING

The R & D team functioned across SEQCORE, operating in a highly integrated manner with the other SEQCORE teams. The R & D team assisted other teams with detecting and correcting problems as they occurred and worked to anticipate others, particularly those that might be overlooked and might subsequently become major issues. The R & D team helped improve processes and enhance quality, efficiency, precision, and clarity. While all of these responsibilities were important, the director pointed out that because SEQCORE had so many different projects at any one time, without clarity of process, the sequencing facility would be lost.

The R & D team's leader, John Gill, brought an array of knowledge and skills to his role. His background included a bachelor of science degree in biology with a concentration in anatomy and physiology plus a master of science degree focused on new technology, biotechnology, and molecular biology. He became involved in genomics, focusing on large-scale biology—that is, looking at all the genes in an organism. He was influenced by Dr. Venter and the scale of biology conducted at TIGR and joined TIGR in March 1998 as part of its molecular biology core group in SEQCORE. Gill became R & D team leader in May 1999, applying his research, mentoring, and teaching skills. His strengths included visualization of large-scale systems and analyzing and solving problems.

The R & D team has a broad array of responsibilities and has identified and hired staffers with diverse knowledge and skills. The team has been mindful of the need for a creative disposition in each of its staff and has focused not on degrees but on experiences and skills that collectively give the R & D team capabilities in quality control, automation, and robotics in a manner that fulfills the team's research and development and problem-solving responsibilities.

This approach to securing creative talent for the R & D team is best exemplified by Steve, a team member. Building on early education in engineering, science, and mathematics, Steve moved on to product development at a motorcycle racing apparel company, where he designed motorcycle racing equipment and was put in charge of a motorcycle race team. According to Steve, making a motorcycle compete optimally on a racetrack—that is, taking into account turns, surfaces, elevations, gravity, and other factors—is almost as difficult as making sequencing reactions perform optimally.

Steve brought his problem-solving and design skills to his new position in SEQCORE. As he related, "Initially I worked in the laboratory, surrounded by knowledgeable people in a system that was largely manually operated. It seemed like an incredible waste of resources to have highly educated persons doing manual tasks." The frustration motivated him to automate the process. Machines previously acquired to help automate processes had been set aside because they did not work when first tested. Steve determined how to keep them clean and performing correctly, eliminating the reasons they had been abandoned. Staff members were thrilled.

Steve also visualized the possibility of performing the quantification of DNA using a robot instead of two persons performing the operation. Starting in May 1999, he and colleagues brought in companies that could design or create such an automated system. He visited all team leaders to determine what they would want the new system to do. Then he and colleagues visited with ten companies to determine what each really could do. After gathering information, Steve and his coworkers designed the first fully automated laboratory system, which was delivered in October 1999. A robotic system was instituted to assist with picking colonies in

November 1999. A new software system to handle the vast quantity of data generated was brought on line in January 2000. Steve and his colleagues went on to create other robotic applications and automations, enhancing both laboratory performance and quality.

Systems built for the laboratory may not work the way companies claim or may otherwise need to be customized to SEQCORE's specifications. Steve reported that the team leader, Steve, and two other team members participated actively in customization, giving the team solid capability in this skill area as well. The team reported that for a recent week their production was 300 percent higher than what had been the case two years earlier. They judged the payoff from their team efforts in robotics and customization alone to be substantial for SEQCORE and TIGR.

Another key function of the team was quality control. A good match existed between the interests and creativity of those responsible and the tasks to be performed. For example, Jennifer joined TIGR in 1999. She started on a closure team and then moved to the R & D team when it had an opening. She took the opportunity to work on quality control and saw a dual challenge: solving problems after they arose and looking at data to figure out what could go wrong before it happened. She said, "I liked the work because I could have a hands-on experience for every aspect of SEQCORE's operation. And I enjoyed the challenge of thinking on my feet, having new problems to solve, and preventing problems."

Within SEQCORE, the R & D team members sought suggestions or ideas they could use to advance quality or reduce costs of sequencing processes. As the team leader shared, "If there is an idea out there—for example, to improve production speed or closing speed—it will be shared somehow with the R & D team. The team will consider whether it should become an R & D project leading to possible implementation. No standard steps must be taken to get an R & D project on its way. The suggestions can come to the R & D team directly, or to the team leader group, or to the SEQCORE director. This allows for greater flexibility in getting good ideas to the R & D team for consideration."

Of SEQCORE's teams, the R & D team had the most opportunity to be entrepreneurial and to act on that opportunity. The team leader talked to a wide range of private and public sources in an effort to identify and bring in new technology and approaches and then to apply them in SEQCORE processes. For example, the R & D team had determined ways to save money in the use of reagents by implementing a different process.

According to the SEQCORE director, that improvement alone had saved TIGR an incredible amount of money over the past year.

WHAT MADE THE TEAM SPECIAL?

One condition that made the R & D team special was "its *vast knowledge base of different types of systems,*" according to one member. The diversity of the automation subteam alone allowed it to look at any aspect of automation for use in SEQCORE. Another member observed, "The automation subteam wasn't always so special and high performing. At first, some people did not like the idea of a machine doing their job, possibly taking away some responsibility and reducing staff. Also, in TIGR, we didn't know exactly how to make the robots and automation work cleanly. But as a team, we discussed what sort of changes we wanted to see. We really paid attention to what worked for us in development of automation and what didn't. Our diverse group is really working well together and with others."

Also important in making the team special was the *high level of communication among the team members.* As one team member pointed out, "Even though I am on quality control, I know everything that the automation and robotics subteam is doing. We keep each other informed of exactly what is going on every day. There are good reasons. For example, if something goes wrong with one of our robots, the sequences are going to look bad the next day, and we need to have an explanation to deal with the reduced quality that will result."

Others in SEQCORE indicated that the *R & D team operated with a great deal of zeal for what they do.* The team leader confirmed that his team members had a very high level of enthusiasm. They were intense about performing their work well. The level of zeal that the R & D team members demonstrated in their work was so high that the team leader believed it might scare some persons from wanting to join the team.

Closely associated was *team members' high levels of motivation.* The team leader indicated that because his team had the opportunity to use new technology and equipment to improve SEQCORE processes, motivation was very easy. Another member pointed out, "Team members who were here when I joined were friendly and excited about their work. There was a lot of communication and interaction, and they were helping each other. You quickly fit in and you quickly feel motivated to be a part of the team."

ORGANIZATIONAL AND TEAM VARIABLES AFFECTING PERFORMANCE

The R & D team representatives interviewed reported on the importance of organizational and team variables in the team's achievement of high performance. The *organizational variables* judged to be very important were (1) the organization's overall commitment to team approaches and team success, (2) the organization's commitment to shared leadership and shared control, (3) the organization's nondollar support, and (4) the commitment to creativity and innovation throughout the organization, within teams, and for this particular team. Other organizational variables considered to be quite important or very important to this team's achievements were (5) the organization's commitment to employee's growth in skills and knowledge, (6) the organization's commitment to education and training of teams, (7) the organization's commitment to providing time for the education and training and covering costs, (8) the organization's commitment to sharing information, (9) the organization's support for risk taking by the team to achieve successful team performance, and (10) recognitions and awards given by the organization to this team for its achievements.

The *team variables* that team members judged to be very important in fostering their achievements were (1) members and the leaders' commitment to team success, (2) the team's commitment to team creativity and innovation, (3) trust among team members and team leader, (4) mutual respect among team members and with their leader, (5) level of caring among team members and their leader, and (6) the zeal about team performance by the team members and team leader. Additional team variables judged to be quite important or very important were (7) the team's commitment to stretching thinking and searching for new ideas and approaches, (8) the existence of a common team vision and commitment by the team to it, (9) the team's commitment to members' education and training, and (10) the team's willingness to take risks to achieve team success.

Growth in Team Spirit among the Three Teams

Team members, the team leader group, and the director reported a performance-enhancing condition beyond empowerment—that is, a growth in team spirit and individual spirit. Recognition of both a team spirit and an individual spirit occurred in each of the three teams featured in this case study. Furthermore, all three teams reported that growth in team and individual spirit had positively influenced performance and productivity.

Members of the *team leader group* indicated that they often use the term *team spirit*, viewing it as a composite comprised of many dimensions. It embodied positive communication, open sharing of information, interacting, caring about each other, being able to go to others with problems, and feeling comfortable that strong support exists. Team spirit also embodied feeling good about what you do, joy and inspiration of the work, not wanting to work anyplace else, trusting relationships with others, creativity, thinking about how to improve work even when away from the job, fulfillment, and a passion for work. The concept also included working well with others, being excited about the achievements of others, and being energized by others. In short, team spirit represented a tangible, multifaceted condition that was experienced collectively but interpreted somewhat differently by each individual. Moreover, reports show that team spirit definitely has grown over time and has influenced individual performance.

Members of the *closure team* also recognized *team spirit* as an important force. As one team member exclaimed, "Does team spirit definitely exist? Oh my goodness, yes!" Others chimed in, indicating that both team and individual spirit definitely existed. Furthermore, the team leader shared that the growth in the team spirit had been gradual and that it had grown to quite a high level as a result of a number of external factors as well as some internal team conditions and operations. For the closure team, the sense of team spirit had many of the same dimensions as was the case for the team leader group. In addition, some team members indicated that while team spirit had grown gradually to a high level, individual spirit had experienced rapid growth and strongly influenced team and individual performance.

The *R & D team* members also believed that *team spirit* exists. One of the most technically oriented team members admitted, "I think that team spirit is such a corny expression, but it is there." This team also saw team spirit as multidimensional. Among the conditions it embodied were good feelings that resulted from generating ideas and taking action to make things happen, pulling together when resistance to an improvement arose, drawing on a good teamwide sense of humor, and excellent communication among team members. Also involved was the team's realization that its actions reduced work, burnout, and staff turnover.

The three teams reported that team spirit represented a multidimensional condition that emerged and strengthened over time rather than blossomed suddenly. Team spirit and individual spirit had grown and appeared to be at high levels but were not uniformly high all the time. Team spirit began to grow for the three teams at the time when TIGR and SEQCORE leadership became shared and facilitative, the team leader group was reconstituted, and the benefits of automation began to be experienced. The continued growth of team spirit resulted from a combination of internal and external conditions, the latter appearing to be more influential. Team members, team leaders, and the SEQCORE director observed that the spirit of teams and of individual members were viewed as enhancing team performance and productivity.

Divergent Approaches

As in chapter 3, instead of attempting to show the dynamics of the many influences, we display in simplified form the influences of one variable—the influence of divergent approaches used by the three teams. We also illustrate the influences of divergent approaches on two conditions, performance levels and environmental levels. Performance refers to the various outputs achieved, both quantity and quality, by the sequencing facility. The environment refers to that set of circumstances that the teams helped to create for themselves and within which they operated.

Simplified diagrams 1, 2, and 3 in figure 4.1 represent three positive and connected dynamic loops that depict the changing status and influence of divergent approaches. As the teams' understanding of divergent approaches and their skillful use of them increased, levels of performance increased, and the environment within which the teams worked improved, becoming more conducive to greater creativity and still higher performance.

Diagram 1 illustrates the starting level of creativity in the use of divergent approaches among the teams. Creativity level 1 reflects the limited use of divergent approaches that existed at the time the new director of the sequencing facility arrived at TIGR. The initial performance is reflected in performance level 1. As the facility director, the team leaders, and members of the teams progressed, they began to take a series of actions that strengthened their working environment, represented by environment 1. Initial team approaches were enhanced, team capabilities were broadened, and the TIGR organization as well as its sequencing facility director, team leaders, and teams began functioning as shared leaders. The use of divergent approaches in information sharing, problem solving, and solution development was growing, leading to creativity level 2.

Diagram 2 illustrates an increased level of creativity, creativity level 2, that in turn enhanced the sequencing facility performance, represented by performance level 2. Divergent thinking about Sequencing Facility processes, problems, and solutions grew, with increases in the skill and effectiveness of its use. Subgroups were created and used to enhance divergent thinking and creative solutions. R & D team members joined with the closure team and other teams in anticipating and solving problems. Accompanying this emphasis on divergent thinking were growth in mutual responsibility and trust, added creative use of robotics and computerization of processes, greater attention to quality enhancement, and greater clarity and commitment to performance objectives, leading to creativity level 3.

Diagram 3 illustrates the higher level of creativity throughout the sequencing facility, creativity level 3, and the resulting higher level of performance. Performance in all indexes increased, represented here by performance level 3. Growth in team capabilities continued and was recognized and rewarded. As successes in divergent approaches increased, mutual trust and mutual responsibility within and among teams also increased. Creative problem solving advanced, with enhanced ownership for problems and solutions throughout the sequencing facility. Divergent approaches became more widely regarded and proactively used, and these conditions were accompanied by creation of increasingly high performance objectives and tracking of their achievement by all in the sequencing laboratory. These conditions together are represented by environment 3. The information shared by those interviewed indicated that these positive relationships could continue to grow beyond level 3.

Special Insights

The three teams of SEQCORE, TIGR's DNA sequencing facility, featured in this case study provide a series of insights worthy of sharing. The insights listed here and the lessons learned that follow should be of value to others who wish to create teams or to improve existing teams on the way to high performance.

FIGURE 4.1. DIVERGENT APPROACHES IN CREATIVITY: DIAGRAMS 1, 2, AND 3

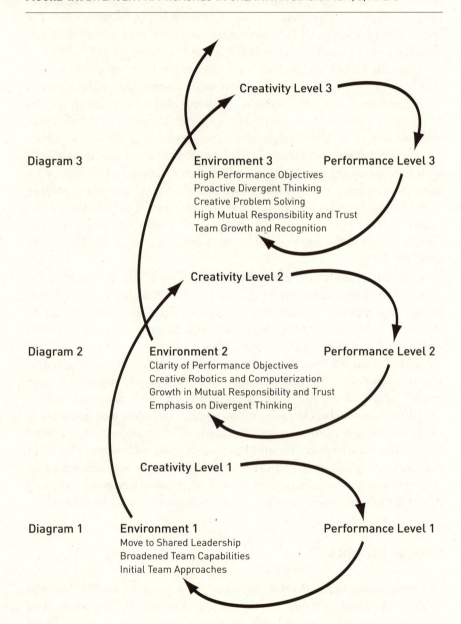

❶ *Team members performed more effectively because they had an intellectual connection with what was being done in the organization.* The president of TIGR observed that the most important insight for the culture of TIGR—and likely elsewhere—is that an intellectual connection must exist to what the people on the teams are doing. At the time of TIGR's 1998 restructuring and the appointment of the new facility director, some in TIGR saw SEQCORE's staff members as second-class citizens. The president and the new director never held this perception. The faculty did not anticipate that staff needed to be stimulated intellectually. In response, the director provided new intellectual opportunities to teams burdened with "low-end" tasks. Across SEQCORE, robotics and computer applications made routine and repetitive tasks less burdensome, freeing team members' time for other creative and intellectually stimulating activities. Guidelines for proper working relationships between the faculty and the research associates and others in SEQCORE were created. These and other actions increased team members' intellectual connection.

❷ *The Sequencing Facility gained from matching knowledge, specialties, unique skills, and disposition toward teaming of individuals with requirements of the teams.* While this represents a very basic concept, failure to be attentive to the match can result in team difficulties. As one team leader shared, "In the early days, we had a whole group of persons in our team who were big-picture oriented and only one who was detail oriented. When we lost the detail-oriented person, it was a huge problem for our team. So one should figure out characteristics needed on the team and look for the people that possess them." Another shared, "We need to look for people that fit the team." Efforts were made to avoid hiring or placing on teams persons who could not or would not be team players.

❸ *Empowerment of teams was vital and was made more functional by being set within helpful boundary conditions.* Both the TIGR president and SEQCORE director held that to empower teams, an organization should truly listen to feedback from its employees. Both leaders viewed feedback from teams, both volunteered and solicited, as a major and vital source for learning in SEQCORE and the broader TIGR organization. Further, TIGR leaders were very analytical about the need to have clear and functional operating procedures for its sequencing facility. It is unlikely that SEQCORE could have achieved a doubling and redoubling of its laboratory performance in just three years without development of clear and functional operating procedures, including helpful boundary conditions, in which team leaders were involved.

❹ *Team leaders needed both technical and interpersonal skills to perform well as leaders.* Technical skills alone proved insufficient for the team leadership required. Sought in team leaders were ability to interact with others and willingness to explore and answer questions plus ability to help, mentor, and train team members and others. Also sought were abilities to manage large processes, evoke trust, demonstrate trustworthiness, and garner respect from team members and others. Members of the team leader group possessed these various interpersonal attributes and employed them to advance their teams' performance.

❺ *Creativity and high performance were significantly influenced at the team level by actions of the team leader and team members.* According to the SEQCORE team leaders, the climate for creativity at the team level can be enhanced. It requires attention to divergent views, valuation of new ideas, and encouragement of team members to try new ideas and approaches. It also requires supporting risk taking within the team, developing a feeling of security, and fostering trust among team members and with the team leader. Among these, divergent thinking and approaches and providing encouragement were viewed as two of the most important determinants of team creativity.

❻ *The sequencing facility and its teams benefited from supporting risk taking and enabling persons to try and test out innovations without fear of blame if they did not work.* In SEQCORE, if a new approach worked, those involved received credit; if it did not work, those involved were not blamed because they had acted to benefit SEQCORE. TIGR leaders were willing to take risks and accept the reality that things sometimes fail. This attitude and related empowering support were essential for TIGR's efforts to define the forefront of genomics. As Fraser, TIGR's president, pointed out, "One can be sure that if you don't take risks and innovate, you are going to do things tomorrow with yesterday's approaches, and that's the way you get left behind."

❼ *Performance was enhanced by career development opportunities and by recognition of staff and team achievements.* SEQCORE demonstrated that staff must have opportunities to learn new things, be rewarded for their growth, and advance their careers as needs and positions evolve. New career development opportunities were instituted and proved beneficial to teams, enhancing their morale and performance, and strengthening retention.

With the president's support, the SEQCORE director established a promotion system with two professional tracks—for those seeking advancement through technical skills and those seeking it through leadership roles. Achievements were recognized with title changes and pay increases. Promotions were based on skill attainment, not length of service, within the five levels of seniority in SEQCORE. Informal recognition also was provided to teams and groups by the SEQCORE director via group lunches, social gatherings, time off, and other means.

❽ *Interventions into team matters worked beneficially because they were anticipated, performed logically, and avoided disempowering the teams.* While the closure team and other DNA sequencing facility teams were clearly self-managed, they were subject to intervention by the R & D team with its quality-control, automation, and robotics responsibilities. The R & D team, as an internal SEQCORE team, earned the trust and confidence of the other teams, sharing owner-ship of problems and solutions. Over time, other teams came to view the presence of the R & D team members as very helpful, fully antic-ipating their interventions. Team actions were viewed as logically performed. And interventions were empowering rather than disem-powering to those assisted.

❾ *Financial support of teams and SEQCORE proved fundamental in the high performance achieved by the three teams and others.* Our experi-ences with other organizations show that organizational support, particularly financial support for teams, often is cited as being very important. Those interviewed typically did not rate financial support highly among factors causing very high performance. Since resource support to teams was well provided in this case, team members did not view financial support either as a factor limiting performance or as a very important factor. However, if financial resources had not been available to implement automation, fund new career paths and staff promotions, employ needed staff, and permit adoption of creative changes, lack of financial resources likely would have been cited as a very important factor inhibiting high productivity.

⑩ *The sequencing facility was clear about the composition of employee turnover and the type of turnover to remedy.* Prior to mid-1998, a time when turnover rates were substantially higher than they are at present, much of the turnover in SEQCORE was comprised of persons dissatisfied with their jobs, situations, or salaries. Initial adjustments had as one objective diminishing such turnover. Under the shared-leadership environment and creative changes fostered by the president of TIGR and the SEQCORE director, such turnover diminished greatly. Given the changed environment, the turnover came to be comprised mainly of young persons going back to college for advanced education, persons moving because of their spouse or family situation, and persons making a career change or achieving a new career opportunity. Some of the turnover also resulted from persons taking positions elsewhere at TIGR. The composition of current turnover was seen as reflecting the new professional environment and creative challenges provided by SEQCORE.

⑪ *The DNA Sequencing Facility provided the rest of the organization with substantial benefits beyond high productivity.* SEQCORE and its teams addressed and enhanced the analytical, production, and support processes they used, including SEQCORE's relations with the research faculty and other components of TIGR, such as bioinformatics. While clarifying and improving such processes for themselves, the director and team leaders helped to clarify and improve processes and approaches for others in TIGR. SEQCORE served as a useful reference when others explored ways to improve and to enhance performance. And SEQCORE's expanded productivity has placed greater expectations on other units in TIGR.

⑫ *The sequencing facility overcame some limitations in teaming capabilities because of other attributes.* TIGR and SEQCORE leaders observed that scientists typically do not receive managerial and leadership training or team training as a part of their formal education. Therefore, organizations can benefit from preparing persons brought into an ongoing team. It is somewhat surprising that the teams within SEQCORE functioned so very well given the limited past investment in training on team concepts and processes, facilitation, conflict resolution, and team building and strengthening. Such limited investment might normally be expected to detract seriously from team performance. However, the strong positive aspects of recruitment for team fit, as well as for knowledge and skills, and the respect for diversity and use of divergent approaches engendered, helped to compensate for the limited training on team effectiveness. The open and sharing environment and the strong sense of mutual responsibility and trust also helped.

Lessons Learned[23]

This final section sets forth lessons provided by the experiences and performance of the three teams. It also addresses the organizational context within which the teams functioned, a context that facilitated their high performance.

❶ *The organizational context within which teams function is crucial in their advance toward high performance.* Particularly significant in the makeup of the positive organizational context for the three teams were four *organizational variables* cited as very important:

> TIGR's commitment to creativity and innovation across the organization;
> The organization's commitment to team approaches and team success;
> The organization's commitment to each team's success;
> The organization's commitment to each team's creativity and innovation.

Also important were commitment to an intellectual connection for persons working on the SEQCORE teams and the establishment of a qualification and promotion system that encouraged growth in knowledge, skills, and worth to the organization.

❷ *A number of team conditions were shown to be positively reinforcing for heightened team performance.* Eight *team variables* proved to be of high importance for the three case-study teams:

> Trust among team members and with the team leader;
> Mutual respect among team members and with the team leader;
> Commitment to team success by team members and the team leader;
> Team's commitment to stretching thinking and searching for new ideas and approaches;
> Team's commitment to creativity and innovation;
> Complementary nature of team members and leader;
> Willingness of the team members and team leader to take risks to achieve team success;
> Self-motivation of team members and team leader.

❸ *Integral to the organizational and team conditions that propelled higher performance was shared leadership and empowering leadership by the president of TIGR, the director of the DNA sequencing facility, and the team leader group.* The shared and empowering leadership was continuously present, providing technical and management assistance, resources and other support, encouragement, and recognition for team performance. Within this leadership context, many actual examples existed of organizational conditions and team conditions enhancing performance. Changes and enhancements in leadership were prominent in the events propelling higher performance.

❹ *A strong positive relationship existed among diversity of views and approaches, enhanced creativity, and increased productivity.* All teams strongly encouraged the valuing and expressing of diverse views. This approach contributed to expanded creativity in solving problems and in exploring and achieving new opportunities, which in turn contributed to increased efficiency, meeting and exceeding quality and quantity goals, and a happier SEQCORE staff, according to the president of TIGR. SEQCORE benefited greatly from the varied cultural backgrounds and experiences of staff, research associates, and team leaders. Training available to teams included a component on divergent views and divergent approaches. Both new and experienced employees learned to appreciate the dynamics that can result in a team whose members possess different experiences, cultural backgrounds, and motivations for action.

❺ *The environment has a direct bearing on the ease of securing the diversity of cultures, knowledge, experiences, and skills.* TIGR has never hesitated to host or sponsor persons from other cultures. As one team leader observed, "The people at TIGR are incredibly open minded and culturally aware. My name was never pronounced right in any of the jobs that I had before. Here, every single person says it exactly right. You see someone with a different culture, dressed differently, and all you have in mind is to talk to this person and see how he or she can fit with the team." The SEQCORE and TIGR environments reinforce the diversity that has been achieved.

❻ *The higher the interdependency of process and product, the higher the mutual trust and responsibility needed.* SEQCORE teams were highly interdependent, and their closed genomes constituted high joint work products—the highest of any cases analyzed. The teams evidenced an extremely complicated interdependence of process—highly integrated analytical, production, and closure processes. The crucial nature of the interdependence, likened to a lifeline, required that all team leaders and members understand that they are mutually responsible with others and that they cannot function without others. Team leaders understand and convey to others that there is no place for divisiveness or competition within and among teams, since these negatives diminish trust, responsibility, and performance.

❼ *Enhancement of organizational and team conditions for improved performance can have direct benefits in job satisfaction, staff loyalty, and diminished turnover.* As one example of organizational and team conditions enhancing performance, the R & D team increased the automation of laboratory tasks, diminishing repetitive manual tasks. Time saved by increased automation permitted members of SEQCORE's other teams to devote more time to creative and productive activities. The actions increased laboratory quality and enhanced job satisfaction. The actions also built additional SEQCORE staff loyalty and diminished job turnover, with positive influences on productivity.

❽ *Enhanced communication and interaction contributed substantially to conditions increasing team performance.* From the time the new SEQ-CORE director came to TIGR, both the ease and level of communication and the positive nature of communication and interaction increased—within and among the team leaders group, the teams, and the subgroups. Enhancement in communication and interaction has reinforced the willingness to advance ideas, to undertake innovative changes, and to take risks on behalf of the teams and SEQCORE. These developments in turn influenced success rates, efficiency, and productivity and increased the speed with which genomes were closed.

❾ *Teams' achievement of higher performance was aided by clear goals, a tracking system, and having those who must meet the goals participate in their creation.* The existence within SEQCORE of the clear goals for increased production, improved success rates, and reduced costs provided a reinforcing incentive for the teams. Team leaders were involved in the creation and support of these goals. Establishment and operation of an information tracking system, with readily available data on projects, sequences performed, success rates, per-unit costs, and related performance measures also served as an incentive for the teams. Team members knew and had easy access to the performance metrics. SEQCORE's experiences showed that those asked to meet the goals must see them as necessary and must help in determining what is possible. Together, the clear goals, participation in their creation, and tracking of performance fostered creative actions by teams to enhance performance.

❿ *Sustained high performance flourished in an atmosphere of shared and facilitative leadership.* When viewed from outside, the TIGR organization appeared to be performance driven. When viewed internally, one found that the performance was not driven by command and control but by a host of conditions and actions representing shared beliefs, contributions, and decisions in an atmosphere of shared leadership, trust, and responsibility. The teams' creativity and performance were not commanded, directed, or managed in the usual business sense of those terms but rather were encouraged, empowered, energized, and recognized.

❶ *Mutual trust and mutual responsibility powerfully influenced perform-ance.* Over and over in our interviews, growth in trust and growth in responsibility were reported as vital to performance. The nature of the joint products, requiring successive actions by the various teams, made high mutual responsibility an absolute necessity. In turn, mutual responsibility of a high order could not have been achieved without its companion, high mutual trust. A team leader indicated, "The trust that exists on my team and in SEQCORE is immense. So if you have a good idea, somebody here is going to listen. And if you put hard work into it, that idea can have an impact on the team and on SEQCORE's performance. The trust, the mutual responsibility, and the potential for impact—these energize my spirit."

❷ *Team members viewed growth in team and individual spirit as posi-tively affecting their performance.* Team leaders and team members experienced a fresh start, in 1998 and 1999, with many new things happening. The change in top leaders at both TIGR and SEQCORE, the change in leadership style—to shared leadership and leadership by example—plus people leaving and new people coming marked the kickoff in the growth of team spirit. As team leaders and team members learned to work together effectively and achieved successes, their trust grew, and their spirits grew as well. The sense of team spirit was evidenced also in the joy and inspiration that team members experienced from completed work. Those interviewed concurred that growing team spirit energized them and enhanced their performance.

NOTES

1. *TIGR—The Institute for Genomic Research* (Rockville, Md.: TIGR, 2000), and other infor-mation provided by officers and staff of TIGR.
2. Information about TIGR's projects can be found at its web site, www.tigr.org.
3. Information in this section is drawn from a personal interview with Claire Fraser, pres-ident of TIGR, Rockville, Maryland, May 24, 2001, as well as from documents provided by TIGR.
4. M. D. Adams, J. M. Kelley, J. D. Gocayne, M. Dubnick, M. H. Polymeropoulos, H. Xiao, C. R. Merril, A. Wu, B. Ide, R. Moreno, A. R. Kerlavage, W. R. McCombie, and J. C. Ven-ter, "Complementary DNA Sequencing: "Expressed Sequence Tags" and the Human Genome Project," *Science* 252L (1991): 1651–56.

5. *The Institute for Genomic Research, 1992–1999* (Rockville, Md.: TIGR), 1–5.

6. *Institute for Genomic Research*, 1–5.

7. *Institute for Genomic Research*, 11.

8. Information in this section is drawn from personal interviews with Claire Fraser, president; Tamara Feldblyum, DNA sequencing facility director; William Nierman, vice president for research; and team leaders and members, Rockville, Maryland, May 24–25, 2001.

9. Information in this section is drawn from personal interviews with the SEQCORE director and Team Leaders, Rockville, Maryland, May 24, 2001.

10. Information in this section is drawn from personal interviews with Claire Fraser, president; Tamara Feldblyum, DNA sequencing facility director; William Nierman, vice president for research; and team leaders and members, Rockville, Maryland, May 24–25, 2001.

11. *Guidelines and Criteria for Promotion* (Rockville, Md.: TIGR, 1998).

12. Arlen Leholm and Raymond Vlasin, *DACUM Approach—Developing a Curriculum* (East Lansing: Michigan State University, 2001); adapted from Robert Norton, *The DACUM Handbook*, Leadership Training Series no. 67 (Columbus: Center on Education and Training for Employment, Ohio State University, 1985).

13. *TIGR Sequence Facility Production* (Rockville, Md.: TIGR, 2001).

14. TIGR's genome sequencing as explained by William Nierman, vice president for research, in *Software Infrastructure for Managing Genomic Sequencing Projects* (Rockville, Md.: TIGR, 2001).

15. Nierman in *Software Infrastructure*.

16. Information in this section is drawn from the team leader group's responses to questions at TIGR, Rockville, Maryland, May 24, 2001.

17. The goals of the team leader group are the basic goals of SEQCORE, which as of 2002 were (1) reach and maintain average success rates for the whole genome shotgun libraries at 85 percent, (2) increase sequence production rate to 280,000 reads/month and meet all established deadlines for sequencing projects, (3) achieve a 30 percent reduction in direct costs for labor and reagents, and (4) continue to improve closure process in collaboration with the Bioinformatics Department.

18. Information in this section is drawn from the Prokaryotic Closure Team members' responses to questions at TIGR, Rockville, Maryland, May 24–25, 2001.

19. Information in this section is drawn from written and oral communications from Hoda M. Khouri, team leader, Prokaryotic Closure Team, TIGR, Rockville Maryland, May–September, 2001.

20. In the sequencing process, difficulties in closing a gap can result from any of several technical reasons dealing with DNA structure or the genes coded by the DNA.

21. Information in this section is drawn from R & D team members' responses to questions at TIGR, Rockville, Maryland, May 24–25, 2001.

22. Information in this section is drawn from written and oral comments by John Gill, R & D team leader, TIGR, Rockville, Maryland, May–September, 2001.
23. The text in this section is solely the responsibility of Arlen Leholm and Ray Vlasin.

5

Bosch Teams
Two Creative
Arrangements

► Ken Brochu, Kevin O'Keefe, Arlen Leholm, and Ray Vlasin

Why the Two Team Cases

This case begins with the Bosch Modulation Applications Team that conducted tests on the use of select Bosch equipment on prototype vehicles for one of the Big Three automakers. The team tested applications on vehicles equipped with Bosch antilock braking systems (ABS), traction control systems (TCS), or electronic stability control (ESC). Among the distinctive features of this creative and innovative team were its cold-weather and hot-weather testing of these applications and the team's quality performance under adverse climates and distant locations.

Also included is the Technical Platform Team, which represents an advance in teaming arrangements from those focusing on components (e.g., ABS) to those focusing on systems (e.g., Bosch braking systems) designed for the customer's various platforms (vehicle types). The Technical Platform Team was the core of a larger technical platform group for a large Bosch braking system project.

Both teams featured an intense dedication to meeting customer requirements and achieved goals through creative selection and use of skills and knowledge. The teams achieved high trust within the teams, with team leaders, and with supervisors that was fundamental to success. They demonstrated the crucial nature of communication among teams providing joint work products across different functional teams.

The teaming arrangements demonstrated that midlevel management can enable teams to be truly self-directed. Relying on their self-direction, the teams showed unusual creativity and high performance, benefiting from the team-customer environment they created. Team members with an array of team skills and technical knowledge melded into very complementary high-performing teams. Camaraderie, personal trust, responsibility and caring, divergent thinking, and creative problem solving enhanced team creativity and outstanding performance.

The Snapshot

The Robert Bosch Corporation is a familiar name in automotive equipment and its application and testing. It is the North American Subsidiary of Robert Bosch GmbH, based in Stuttgart, Germany—the Bosch Group. The organization has a long-standing, high commitment to and pursuit of quality in its products and services that goes back to the company's founding by Robert Bosch in 1886. The Bosch Group also is committed to excellence in innovation and technology and to teamwork throughout the organization, bringing together expertise and specialties to create the best products and services.

This case focuses on teaming—more specifically, on two particular teams that functioned within Bosch Braking Systems, headquartered in Michigan. One team was a Bosch *Modulation Applications Team,* which conducted modulation applications on prototype vehicles equipped with Bosch ABS, TCS, or ESC for one of the Big Three automakers. This longer standing applications team was responsible for the complete performance tuning of prototype vehicles used for testing ABS, TCS, and ESC.

The other team was newer and was the core group of the Technical Platform XYZ Project (XYZ refers to types of vehicles). We call it the *Technical Platform Team.* XYZ's technical platform manager explained, "It is the general day-to-day team, a core team that serves as the direct interface with the customer. It guides all the other support groups in the technical platform as to what's needed, what needs to be done, and where we have to go. For the most part, this core group or team deals directly with the customer and sets the course for the whole platform."

THE MODULATION APPLICATIONS TEAM

The Modulation Applications Team operated within helpful administrative guidelines. It had a clear sense of its mission and the jobs it would perform. The team was permitted to be self-directed and to operate with substantial flexibility. It reported to a director who was experienced, accessible, and knowledgeable about applications work and who treated the team in a hands-off manner.

The Modulation Applications Team conducted its work through strong cooperative relationships with other groups within Bosch and with the prime customer, a Big Three automaker. Within Bosch, the group cooperated most closely with a systems group for algorithm problem solving and with a software group for software systems applications and modification. The applications team also interacted closely with a number of other Bosch units and cooperated with several of the customer's units, including its garage that modified the prototype vehicles used in the testing.

The Modulation Applications Team included about a dozen professionals—mechanical engineers and electrical engineers, with more of the former because of the nature of the work demands. Led by an experienced engineering manager, Ken Brochu, the applications team divided its time among its three major functions: (1) working on the prototype cars, testing systems, and tuning the algorithm parameters (procedures for solving problems or accomplishing some specific ends) for optimal vehicle performance, (2) contacting and interacting with the prime customer and its units, and (3) related administrative support, including necessary documentation, technical report writing, and related contacts and interactions.

The first of these required 60 percent of the Modulation Applications Team's time. It encompassed the cold-weather and hot-weather applications testing by the team for Bosch's ABS, TCS, and ESC on prototype vehicles. Both cold-weather and hot-weather sites were at distant locations and necessitated on-site work by the team and its cooperators—Bosch's systems group for problem solving, its software group for software system modification, plus representatives from the customer's units. Much creativity was evidenced in these cold-weather and hot-weather tests and at other times. In addition, a unique camaraderie prevailed among the professionals during these testing periods and back at their headquarters. The camaraderie increased the team's ability to brainstorm and problem solve, even when divergent views were fiercely presented and defended, thus significantly increasing the team's productivity.

The Modulation Applications Team reported that its views, ideas, and recommendations for improvement were very well received. If the team detected a problem or a possible improvement on a prototype vehicle, both its cooperators within the organization and those representing the customer listened and attempted to use the team's ideas and suggestions. As is discussed later in the chapter, team members saw a number of team variables and organizational variables as being of major importance in the application team's performance achievements.

THE TECHNICAL PLATFORM TEAM

The Technical Platform Team for the XYZ Project operated within the administrative guidelines set for all teams and their members. The team also operated with the leadership, guidance, and coordination of its technical platform manager, Kevin O'Keefe. And it worked closely with the Commercial Platform for the XYZ project and its commercial platform manager, Brandon Berlinger.

> The Technical Platform Team, in operation for about three years at the time of the interviews, had clear central responsibilities: (1) to serve as the direct interface with the customer, (2) to coordinate closely with the commercial platform group, (3) to guide the other support groups in the technical platform regarding what is needed and where to go based on direct dealings with the customer, and (4) to set the course for the whole technical platform—its subgroups for foundation, actuation, modulation, and systems and engineering.

Some nineteen core members of the XYZ platform group comprised the Technical Platform Team at the time of the interviews. The team members represented a breadth of knowledge and an array of team skills and technical skills and experiences. Their technical skills encompassed foundation elements of the braking systems, actuation of those elements, modulation, computer and other electronics systems, and related engineering. Some these team members were professionals with a direct reporting line to the technical platform manager. Others served on the Technical Platform Team but had a direct reporting line elsewhere and an indirect reporting line to the technical platform manager. However, all team members were committed to the team's success. All understood the need to serve as a point of customer interface for questions, problems, and issues.

Customer interface roles were vital to the success of the technical platform for the XYZ project. Customer support ran the full gamut, from all manner of applications questions and modulation questions surrounding components and software of the braking system to utilization of parts on the assembly line. Team members were responsible for receiving and understanding the questions, for problems or issues involved, and for determining what support was needed to address them and what was necessary to resolve them.

The work of the Technical Platform Team as well as the broader XYZ project's technical platform and commercial platform groups was highly regarded. Managers and team members viewed the Technical Platform Team as one of the best, most innovative, and most successful of the automotive team operations. Team members observed that theirs was "the most successful team" with which they had worked or with which they had interacted.

Those interviewed cited a number of team and organizational variables that were of major importance to their successful operation. Team commitment to success for the customer was paramount. Team trust, self-motivation, mutual respect, caring, appropriate and complementary skills, new approaches, common vision, and willingness to take risks as a team were cited as being of major importance. The organization's commitment to dollar and nondollar support of the team also was viewed as being very important. These and other variables of importance to team success are reported later in this chapter.

The Industry Context

The Bosch Modulation Applications Team and the Technical Platform Team, operating from their location in Farmington Hills, Michigan, are a part of the Bosch Corporation, which is the American subsidiary of the much larger Bosch GmbH (the Bosch Group). The Bosch Group employed some 218,000 people worldwide in 2001, just over half of them outside of Germany. Its combined sales passed thirty-four billion euros, with foreign sales accounting for approximately 72 percent of that amount.[1]

This long-established, worldwide organization had a presence in 130 countries, where its associates developed, refined, sold, and serviced Bosch products. It had a strong presence in the United States, particularly in the Midwest, where the automotive industry is strong. Four key business sectors drove the organization, led by its Automotive Equipment sector, which accounted for about two-thirds of total sales and of the total workforce at the time of the interview. The three other business sectors were Consumer Goods, Capital Goods, and Communications Technology.[2]

The name Bosch has been closely associated with the automobile since Robert Bosch founded his Workshop for Precision and Electrical Engineering in 1886 in Stuttgart, Germany. Since then, Bosch's automotive equipment sector has become one of the largest manufacturers in the field, exceeding twenty-three billion euros in sales in 2001.[3] In addition to ABS, TCS, and ESC, its products included lighting technology, safety systems, engine management systems, bodywork electrics and body electronics, fuel injection systems, mobile communication, starting motors and alternators, and sparkplugs and wiper blades.

The Bosch organization has maintained many distinguishing traits, including an enduring commitment to quality—"an endless pursuit of . . . the highest quality products and services for our customers." As Robert Bosch expressed his vision,

> The best that can be produced by applying good will, mature considera-tion, and comprehensive testing, and by using the most sophisticated technical aids available, together with the best possible materials, only just qualifies to bear the name Bosch.[4]

A second distinguishing and enduring trait is the Bosch organiza-tion's commitment to continuing to deliver the levels of excellence in innovation and technology that its customers have grown to expect. A third key trait is the Bosch organization's belief in teamwork.

> At Bosch . . . every opportunity is completely unique. But one thing you'll find consistent throughout the organization is how important it is—for our people and our products—to work as part of a team. It's crucial to everything we do. Bosch people depend on their colleagues to bring their expertise and specialties to the table to create the best products in the industry. And to help ensure the best possible products for our customers, we believe in a high level of trust and commitment among associates.[5]

The organization's strong commitment to providing the highest-quality products and services, to delivering excellence in innovation and technology, and to fostering teamwork to ensure the most effective use of expertise and specialties would bode well for the organization and its teams. Together, these commitments provided a strong and reinforcing organizational context in which high-performing teams such as the Modulation Applications Team and the Technical Platform Team, plus their leadership, and their supportive administrative supervision could flourish.

The automotive group of the Robert Bosch Corporation and, more specifically, the Bosch Braking Systems component located in Michigan, has continued its founder's commitment to excellence in innovation and technology. One example of this has been Bosch Braking Systems' com-mitment to both high-quality components and their application and high-quality systems designed and applied to the customer's specifications. The modulation assistance initially provided to the customer focused primarily on antilock brakes, a core Bosch business. Bosch strengthened its ability to serve the customer by acquiring added capabilities in foundation and actuation supplies and services, merging them with the company's existing applications and engineering capabilities. Furthermore, the company developed a systems engineering capability to help coordinate these merged capabilities in service to the customer. Within the dynamics of the technology innovations are found the two teams identified here, the earlier Modulation Applications Team, and the later Technical Platform Team.

The Modulation Applications Team

ADMINISTRATIVE CONTEXT

Both the director, to whom the team leader reported, and the vice president, over that director, maintained an open-door policy. They spent time on the floor and were easy to approach and relate to, according to team leader Ken Brochu. One reason the team got along so well with them is that both the director and the vice president knew what it took to perform and achieve the applications job. They knew the work and they knew what had to be done to achieve the quality outcomes sought for the customer.[6]

The administration also provided guidelines within which the team functioned. For example, the team had QS 9000 (quality standards) and other engineering procedures to follow. These step-by-step procedures had greater application to production than to modulation applications, where very substantial innovation and application adjustments were required. As the team leader observed, "In modulation applications you don't have clearly defined A, B, C, and D. Thus, it is a bit more challenging. However, the guidelines are helpful. They are especially helpful to new professionals joining the team."

CLEAR SENSE OF TEAM MISSION AND JOBS

The team leader indicated that the Modulation Applications Team had a clear sense of mission and of the job to be accomplished. The team's number one job was to "make sure the vehicle is safe for customers." In addition, the team knew what specifications had to be achieved and the conditions under which the specifications had to be met. The team also knew the deadlines for conducting its applications work. Within deadlines, the team set its own timelines and test schedules, building in the development time that team members thought would be needed. The team leader observed, "Unfortunately, in the competitive economy, the time permitted by our chief customer for achieving applications goals is shrinking and shrinking."

SELF-DIRECTED TEAM WITH SOME CONSTRAINTS

The Modulation Applications Team's clear sense of mission and clarity of jobs to be performed, plus the administration guidelines within which the team could function, set the stage, allowing the team to exercise substantial judgment, self-direction, and flexibility in achieving its mission and performing its jobs. The team knew what to do to meet its assigned mission and objectives and had great discretion about how it organized for and achieved its mission and objectives. The team leader concluded, "We never are constrained unduly" by organizational guidelines or administrative actions.[7]

However, the team confronted two constraints beyond either administrative or team control. Brochu explained, "Time is one important constraint with which we must work. The customer sets the time [when the applications testing and modifications must be completed]. We try to plan around the time constraints imposed by the customer. Shrinking timelines introduce stress into the team's efforts. This stress would be much worse if it were not for the camaraderie and humor in the group. Sometimes we have to laugh about the tough challenges as a way of dealing with the stress."

"Weather is another key constraint. Scheduling is done to accommodate the availability of cold-weather and hot-weather conditions to permit proper testing. In addition, the impacts of weather can result in very tough conditions. For example, bad weather may result in a loss of power at the test site. If we don't have power at the winter site, we can't pump water to make ice. If we don't get snow, our tests are delayed. It turns out that weather is a chief constraint."[8]

TEAM COMPOSITION

The Modulation Applications Team comprised mainly mechanical engineers, with a smaller number of electrical engineers and one MBA.

Despite substantial and growing demand for testing/applications work, the team stayed fairly constant in size—between twelve and fifteen members.

The team leader, Ken Brochu, was the engineering manager for the Modulation Applications Team. A mechanical engineer by training, Brochu had twenty years of experience in the automotive field—the first eight years in automotive manufacturing followed by twelve years in automotive applications and testing. Brochu indicated that the team's mix of team skills and technical skills and talents was dictated by the complex work demands for which the team bore responsibility.

STRONG COOPERATIVE WORKING RELATIONSHIPS

The Modulation Applications Team worked closely with two main groups: a *systems group* (involved in algorithm parameters for systematic problem solving) and a *software group* (involved in software applications and modification). The team worked with these professionals on every system put into production. The working relationship with these professionals was both close and continuous, and the groups worked easily together. The Modulation Applications Team worked with several other groups (teams) within Bosch. For example, for the Bosch Braking Systems, the Modulation Applications Team worked with groups for (1) *actuation* (involving master cylinders and boosters), (2) *foundation parts* (calipers and pads), (3) *modulation* (hydraulics and electronic brains plus braking, traction, and electronic stability—the active braking on ice and other surfaces), and (4) *overall brake systems* (composition depending on the vehicle—might contain some but not all components).

The Modulation Applications Team also worked very closely with its customer, the automaker, on vehicles during their development in the prototype stage. The team leader emphasized the close working relationship with the prime customer, which accounted for about 20 percent of the team's effort. Several customer representatives cooperated closely with the Modulation Application Team, at times functioning as part of the team. Furthermore, to perform functions well, members of the team spent time at the customer's facilities. Team members needed close contacts with several groups at the customer's facilities. In particular, the team members interacted with chassis, suspension, and vehicle dynamics personnel. These interactions were especially valuable because the customer was continuously changing its prototype vehicles in ways that affected activation, performance, safety, and customer comfort. Each of these conditions was vital to the Applications Team's performance in testing and tuning the algorithm parameters.

FUNCTIONS PERFORMED

The team's work effort involved three broad functions that demanded roughly 60, 20, and 20 percent of the team's total effort, respectively. The Modulation Applications Team spent more than half of its time on the prototype cars, testing systems and tuning the algorithm parameters (procedures for solving problems or accomplishing some specific ends) for optimal vehicle performance. Roughly 20 percent of the team's time was spent with customers in contacts and interactions—consultations, problem solving, and a range of application issues and related matters. Another 20 percent was spent on related administrative support activities and necessary paperwork, such as documentation, technical report writing, and related contacts and interactions.

COLD-WEATHER AND HOT-WEATHER TESTING

The team's time spent testing and tuning the algorithm parameters included cold- and hot-weather testing of prototype vehicles equipped with Bosch components. The cold-weather testing involved a minimum of eight weeks a year and was conducted in Minnesota and Sweden. The hot-weather testing involved a minimum of between one and two weeks a year and was conducted in Death Valley, California. The same professionals were involved in both cold-weather and hot-weather testing, cooperating closely with the systems and software groups.

The team leader reported that the nature of the Modulation Application Team's work involved software and therefore could be very creative and inventive. By contrast, other teams that were more related to previously developed components lacked an equivalent opportunity for additional creativity and inventiveness. He pointed out that much creativity went into the design of Bosch's high-quality components prior to the team's applications testing on prototype vehicles. The early development of ABS, for example, was performed by Bosch in Germany. In addition, Bosch had spent more than ten years developing the stability systems just coming to the market at the time of the interview.

STRONG CAMARADERIE AND PROBLEM SOLVING

> Team leader Brochu observed, "There is a unique kind of camaraderie that goes on when we are conducting the tests and at other times—involving the Modulation Applications Team, the algorithm/systems people, and the software people. We go to the winter tests together. It is like going to camp together—people get along really well. We work very hard together. We play hockey together. We cook and have dinner meals together. It is a very different atmosphere and working environment than one might normally expect."

Camaraderie and team harmony provide major benefits, including a heightened capacity to brainstorm and solve problems very productively. Team members felt comfortable suggesting the full range of alternative approaches and arguing for their suggestions. Brochu explained, "Because we have such an easy working relationship within the team and with the other groups to which we relate, we can brainstorm and problem solve effectively and with ease." On reflection, he added, "That really is an accurate statement about our team and team relationships."

The Modulation Applications Team was receptive to and respectful of added or alternative perspectives from whatever source. For example, the garage technicians who worked on the prototype cars had excellent ideas, and engineers on the Modulation Applications Team used those ideas. "Our openness and receptivity to ideas happens at the engineering levels and right on through to those working on prototype cars in the garage," Brochu shared.

TEAM VIEWS WELL RECEIVED

Others at Bosch respected and listened to the Modulation Applications Team's views. Said the team leader, "The neat thing is if we see a problem on a prototype vehicle that needs to be fixed or changed, we give our ideas to the algorithm group and they try to correct the problem or change the situation. The same is true when we have information for other groups in Bosch or for groups in our customer's organization. Most of the time, the customer respects our opinions and suggestions and is willing to accept those we do make. The customer tries to use them but sometimes is constrained by its own engineering, cost, and/or scheduling considerations."

Managers and directors at Michigan's Bosch facilities ask for inputs on how to handle situations, according to Brochu. "Many of those in managerial and director jobs have the background needed. They have done similar jobs before to those now being performed. What is more, they know the prime customer. Everyone knows you have to come up with a solution, and those involved know they can use different ways to go about it. People do listen to one another."

Technical Platform Team[9]

CONTEXT FOR TECHNICAL PLATFORM

At the time of the interviews, the Technical Platform Team functioned within the larger Technical Platform Support Group of the XYZ Project. In turn, the Technical Platform Support Group plus a Commercial Platform Support Group constituted the XYZ Project. An explanation of the XYZ Project will provide a context or setting for the discussion of the Technical Platform Team to follow.

The overall XYZ Project was only a couple of years old at the time of the interviews. (The initials XYZ are symbols that refer to customer vehicle lines.) The project involved the entire braking systems—not just one component, such as ABS–on two vehicle lines. It was a large project in which members of the Modulation Applications Team participated along with quite a number of other professionals. Because of the project's size and span of responsibility, it was managed jointly by a "commercial platform manager" (CPM) and a "technical platform manager" (TPM). Furthermore, the range of responsibilities and the interrelated nature of the issues required close communication between the two managers and between the members of the Technical Platform Support Group and the Commercial Platform Support Group.

The Commercial Platform Support Group focused on the commercial use of the braking system and the related questions that would be relevant to the commercial production of the vehicles involved—that is, the business side of the platform. At the time of the interviews, the Commercial Platform Support Group comprised nine core members plus six additional persons serving the platform group. The core members performed such roles as exploring with the customer possible adjustments in components that might diminish their cost. The additional support persons performed such roles as tracking component costs.

The Technical Platform Support Group focused on the array of technical matters involved in a complete braking system and its effective operation in a vehicle line—that is, the technical side of the platform. The Technical Platform Support Group included nineteen core members plus seventeen additional support members. The core members tackled all technical matters in the design and interrelationships of foundation, actuation, modulation, software systems, and related engineering. The supporting members were involved in the technical design aspects or functioning of individual physical, hydraulic, electronic, or software elements of the braking system. The nineteen core members constituted the *Technical Platform Team*, the second team addressed in detail in this chapter.

CLOSE COOPERATION BETWEEN PLATFORM GROUPS

The Technical Platform Support Group and the Commercial Platform Support Group for the XYZ project worked very closely together. Each group was mindful of the possible implications of its work for the other group's success. The TPM explained, "The Commercial Platform Manager and I probably talk a couple times each day. Individual members of my team talk to their counterparts on the Commercial Platform Group a couple times a day. My team and I probably have well over fifteen contacts a day with the Commercial Platform Manager and his group. We are trying to keep them in the loop on the possible business implications of what we do. They—the Commercial Platform group members—are trying to keep us in the loop regarding possible technical implications of what they do on the business side."

SHARED PROFESSIONALS

The people interviewed referred to the professionals on the XYZ project as members of a "platform systems group." Such a group is designed to serve one or two "platform lines"—the different types of vehicles the customer plans to produce. Bosch has a number of such groups. O'Keefe pointed out that a professional might split between different platform systems groups but usually does so in "large chunks." Alternatively, a professional might spend 100 percent of his or her time with a specific platform systems group during one part of the year but less during another part of the year, with the remainder of his or her time devoted to other assignments. Such professional sharing occurred in addition to that between the Modulation Applications

Team and the Technical Platform Team, the core group of the technical platform for the XYZ Project.

COMPOSITION

Kevin O'Keefe explained that the XYZ project comprised four groups of professionals: (1) the foundation brake group, which was responsible for the physical equipment or hardware, such as front and rear calipers and rotors, (2) the actuation group, which was responsible for the power supply that connects the driver to the braking hardware, involving the booster and master cylinder, (3) the modulation group, which addressed the minisystems involved, including hydraulics, wheel speed sensors, stability sensors, software, and electronic brains plus braking, traction, and electronic stability, and (4) the engineering support group, which provided mechanical engineering, electrical engineering, systems engineering, and related support. All four groups were committed to the project's success.

Some Technical Support Group professionals were "direct reports"—that is, they directly served the TPM. Others were "indirect reports"—persons assigned to support the technical side of the project but reporting directly elsewhere. O'Keefe indicated that all members of the Technical Support Group for the XYZ project were dedicated to the project's success.

LEADERSHIP

Kevin O'Keefe served as the TPM for the Bosch Braking Systems XYZ Project. He also served as team leader for the *Technical Platform Team.* He held bachelor's and master's degrees in mechanical engineering and had served for more than ten years in the automotive industry, nearly eight of them with Bosch and a company that Bosch acquired. As one member of the Technical Platform Team explained, "O'Keefe was the person who held everything together on the applications, modulations, and engineering side of the project. He coordinated the overall effort from an engineering applications standpoint."

O'Keefe explained further that leadership for modulation applications within the XYZ project was provided by Eric Broman in cooperation with Brochu and that the project also involved cold-weather and hot-weather testing, in which Vicki Gouwens, Broman, and Brochu were central. In short, members of the Modulation Applications Team supported the

Technical Platform Team and the larger Technical Platform Support Group for the XYZ Project.

FROM COMPONENTS TO SYSTEMS

The concept of a "platform systems team" represented an innovation in the auto industry, a significant advance in assistance to the customer, both in products and application. What also occurred in the shift from components to systems was creation of a "new mental model" for teaming.

O'Keefe related how customer service for Bosch Braking Systems has changed. Modulation assistance had initially focused primarily on antilock brakes, a core Bosch business. To innovate and to strengthen Bosch's competitive position in the market as a brake supplier, Bosch purchased another company that provided foundation and actuation supplies and services. Foundation and actuation capabilities were brought from the company acquired and merged with Bosch's modulation applications and engineering capabilities. A systems engineering capability was developed to help coordinate these merged capabilities to serve the customer. As one team member observed, "Now Bosch can supply an entire system of brakes to the customer. So here you see Bosch's approach to selling a system, where before we just sold components and their application—for example, just antilock brakes."

ACQUISITION AND MERGER

To round out the background, team members indicated that the merger of Bosch professionals with those coming from the acquired company was not without its challenges. The transition did not go smoothly because professionals in both companies had their own ways of doing things. Substantial mistrust existed at the beginning. Those involved even questioned, "Who is taking over whom, and whose approaches and processes will prevail?" However, those involved worked at harmonizing approaches and processes for about three and a half years, resulting in a solid working relationship among those involved in bringing the diverse but complementary capabilities together. As a team member confirmed, "We worked to get to the point where we are now. You know, there's obviously a good team relationship now."

CROSS-FUNCTIONAL MODEL FOR XYZ PROJECT

At the time of the interviews, team members reported that this XYZ project was performing very well. Both the Technical Platform Team and the Modulation Applications Team were part of this solid and substantial performance. (It was the Modulation Applications Team's first total braking system modulation and applications effort with a larger group of professionals working together.) Team members reported, "This project is superior when compared to some of the other modulation systems projects" because it is dealing with the entire braking system for a customer's platform and bringing a broader array of team skills and technical skills and competencies to the process in a strong cross-functional team effort. He continued, "The project is one that is used as a benchmark or model for what other projects or programs could be."

Operation of the Technical Platform Team

EVOLVING PLATFORM APPROACH

A team started on a platform approach in 1998. It was the first full-system brake to which Bosch had made a commitment. Automotive manufacturers had been pushing for a full-system brake. They wanted companies that would supply everything—one-stop shopping. The platform approach for a full-system brake came after Bosch's merger with another company, which brought base brake and foundation capabilities to Bosch's ABS systems. It was the first model of a full-system brake platform approach. Some halting steps in the initial marriage of these capabilities resulted, in part because of insufficient understanding of the ABS systems side.

The Technical Platform Team was part of the second model of a full-system brake approach. It received new leadership, with O'Keefe serving as both the TPM and the leader of its core group, the Technical Platform Team. The new model dates from 1999, with those involved representing both a new approach and an expanded number of team members.

DEVELOPING CAPABILITIES

The Technical Platform Team has deliberately developed its capabilities over time to better support customer representatives and function internally with greater effectiveness. The TPM explained, "When some of us came on [merged with Bosch Automotive], we came from the foundation side [which was concerned with components such as front and rear calipers and front and rear rotors and their actuation through cylinders and boosters]. We were not experienced with the modulation side concerned with ABS and ESC hardware and applications, with wheel speed sensors, and ESC control sensors. Neither were those of us who came over to Bosch familiar with ABS, TCS, and ESC systems and related software. Consequently, we relied heavily upon Eric Broman and Ken Brochu to interface heavily inside Bosch as well as interact with customer representatives outside about such areas."

The TPM continued, "We would go along, but typically Eric and Ken had to be the lead persons because that was their role in the past." Broman added, "If there were customer questions about sensors or about the electronic control unit or the hydraulic unit, for example, I would go to those persons internal and talk to them. Then I would return to the customer." According to the TPM, however, the Technical Platform Team members "have transitioned and tried more and more to get away from that situation. Others developed specific capabilities to relate to modulation and systems concerns, and to the components involved. In turn, that freed Eric and Ken to serve greater roles in customer interface—to focus more on the customer's specific needs. It was key that Eric, Ken, and others on the modulation and systems side worked closely with the rest of us to help us through the transition."

A team member observed, "The transition turned out to be really important because now, these days, we get prototype vehicles for such a short time span, you are pressed to have the vehicles long enough to do the actual work. Without this increase in capabilities and the increase in the speed with which we perform those capabilities, the cars wouldn't go on the road."

MODULATION APPLICATIONS TEAM ASSISTANCE

The Modulation Applications Team assisted the Technical Platform Team through its capabilities for ABS, TCS, and ESC applications. Brochu explained, "The modulation group deals a lot with customer issues. The group handles anything performance related regarding ABS, TCS, and ESC. We have to make sure that the application and calibration performances match the specifications that the customer has set, so we do a lot of work in the customer's vehicles as well as a lot of summer and winter testing to perform this type of application."

SHOULDERING OF RESPONSIBILITIES

The TPM commented, "As one example of how we have advanced, now I can cover a meeting on an ABS item or issue. I'll either know enough or I'll know who to bring the information back to in order to make sure the right people are involved. And there'll be meetings when Eric [Broman] or some other team member will pick up on something that is going to affect us somewhere else, and they will get it to the right person. So issues are not just my issues or his issues. The team has really taken on new knowledge and new broader responsibility, so now issues are all team members' issues. Even if it is not your issue, you still take it on and get it into Bosch. Then you let the right person take it. That has really been a key."

UNDERSTANDING STRENGTHS AND LIMITS

Another reason the Technical Platform Team functioned so well was that individual team members understood the limits of their professional capabilities. As Broman explained, "This team works well because each person knows what they know and what they don't know. And if they are interacting with the customer, they avoid just speaking out and saying, 'Oh yeah, we can do that. No problem.' That has happened with other platform teams. Instead, our team members will say, 'Well, let me go ask the persons who specialize in this matter and I'll get back to you. I think I know the answer, but let me just make sure I know before I tell you.' Also, we don't want to make team members do something that our team can't do and then have to go back and explain to the customer. This understanding by team members of their own individual capabilities and limits and those of other team members has really made a difference in how well the team functions."

HIGH TRUST

The TMP shared, "The customer representatives now understand that they just can't get answers by pushing a team member on our front line to give an answer. They trust that we are going to get the right people involved and then get back to the customer with what is possible. The customer representatives trust that we will follow through. Knowing what each team member is strong at and what they are not strong at is a key to this approach for building the customer's trust."

High trust has developed within the team and with its leader, the TPM. He explained, "The trust factor is important. Since we know each other pretty well, we trust each other. If a team member says, 'I'll look into it. I'll get that quote, and I'll get back to you,' you can trust it will be done. We don't have to look over one another's shoulder to see that things get accomplished. Team members are going to get it done." Another team member exclaimed, "Yeah, it's trust!"

HIGH MUTUAL RESPONSIBILITY

The system orientation, the technical platform approach, and the array of talented professionals resulted in a mixture of reporting responsibilities for the various team members. Despite the potential for serious competing interests and diversionary time demands, such problems did not arise. A team member observed, "The technical platform systems approach is a big cross-functional effort. While we may not be directly accountable to the TPM, we are certainly responsible. And I think it is pretty neat how it has worked."

Again, the trust factor came into play as team members sorted out the matters for which they are mutually responsible. The TPM pointed out, "Because of the trust factor, if I call a person and say, 'I really need this. It must be done now. We've got to push this,' the person responds. You don't get the million and one conflicts for time or excuses. Instead, the person will say, 'Ok, it must be important. I'll respond.' And the same thing is true in reverse. There's a belief we're all trying to work for the same Bosch team, trying to make the customer as happy as possible. We are all responsible."

STRONG CUSTOMER RELATIONSHIPS

Team leader O'Keefe, explained the crucial relationship maintained with the customer. "To our customer, I am known as technical platform manager. The title serves as a name to go to if representatives of the customer have technical questions or concerns about anything relating to the braking system. Members of the team and I deal with the customer on many day-to-day matters. We have structured ourselves to give customer representatives one key contact for any technical issue or question concerning the braking system. And if the customer representatives have a question or issue on the business side about the braking system or its components, they have as a key contact the Commercial Platform Manager—Brandon Berlinger and his group."

O'Keefe continued, "My Technical Platform Group is in charge of all vehicles testing for the customer for brakes except for the ABS modulation performance. For all other performance characteristics the customer wants, including requirements the customer specifies, we run all the testing. Further, we are responsible for cascading those requirements down to the rest of the groups for action." He added, "If during or after running the tests we find issues, we work with the other groups to solve the issues and bring the results back to the customer. So my core group [the Technical Platform Team] is considered the front line with the customer and deals with the customer on a weekly and daily basis."

LISTENING TO AND UNDERSTANDING CUSTOMERS

Members of both the Technical Platform and the Commercial Platform Teams listened carefully to the customer and tried to fully understand the question, issue, or matter being raised before reacting. As the CPM shared, "I don't think any one of us, if questioned by the customer, would simply refer the person to the TPM or a Technical Platform Team member. Instead, we listen carefully to the customer and listen to what the question or issue is. If we can answer it and feel comfortable answering, then we do. If we don't feel comfortable answering, we make the phone call to the capable person as opposed to getting ourselves into a bind. And if we do answer the question, we notify the other person on the team concerning what was said, what took place, what we heard, and what comment we made. So if the other capable team member knew what you did and what you said to the customer, you would still have time to react in case you made a mistake. You could circle back and correct it and not put someone in a bind two weeks later."

BROAD CUSTOMER SUPPORT

The customer interface issues and questions for the Technical Platform Team ranged broadly across braking components and systems. They also ranged broadly across the platform responsibilities, covering all manner of technical matters—design and operations issues, questions, problems, possibilities, and opportunities. For example, at the time of the interviews, two members of the Technical Platform Team were working at two of the customer's assembly plants. Their customer interface role at the plants was to understand any issues or problems that might arise and to efficiently get the proper support required to resolve the issues or solve the problems.

Some assistances provided by the Technical Platform Team were triggered by the CPM and his core group. The Commercial Group also confronted a wide array of customer questions and issues. The CPM explained, "When launching a program cooperatively with the customer, there are a lot of things happening. Sometimes you're spread pretty thin. And in addition to our interactions with the customer about questions, issues, or problems, my team and I do a lot of interacting internally [with the Technical Platform Team and elsewhere in Bosch] to make sure that we're doing what we are supposed to be doing for the customer." If these customer matters and the possible responses to them had implications for the Technical Platform Team, the TPM or appropriate members of that team would be contacted and brought into the deliberations.

SOLID RELATIONSHIPS WITH SALES AND MANUFACTURING

The team also developed solid positive relationships with sales and with manufacturing. As a team member explained, "I think we have unique relationships between our engineering and sales and actually with manufacturing too on the modulation side. For this program, if you come up with something, I can call down to the plant and say, 'If I can get this to you on this date, can you do it? Can you implement?' And within a day, I can have cost and timing information. We just gel."

In addition, relations between the TPM and CPM were viewed as very good and very functional, as was the relationship between the two teams. The CPM observed, "I've been here the shortest amount of time, and I feel very comfortable in even dealing with the stuff the Technical Platform Group is responsible for. We know how to listen to the customer and understand the customer. We share and refer matters. We make sure that each considers the interests of the other and keeps the other in the communication loop. Our relationships are very good, and they work."

The CPM added, "Once you know your teams, your company, and your business, you don't offer things that you don't know you could deliver. You can work the job so that you stay involved. Where I sit and the way we work, I can see both the business side and the technical side well. That way you don't hide and then promise things to the customer from the business side that engineering may or may not be able to deliver."

A team member added, "Probably one of the major keys to our team's success is that we all understand our roles, no matter what they are supposed to be on paper. I know what he is doing. I know what you are doing." Another commented, "Also, we don't draw the line between commercial platform and the technical platform or between team members. Elsewhere, people may draw the line as to what their responsibilities are, and then they're hands off. That is not the case within the Technical Platform Group or between it and the Commercial Platform Group."

LIMITED ADMINISTRATIVE BOUNDARY CONDITIONS

The TPM reported, "One core boundary condition for the team is our annual budget and the profit or loss we make on an individual product. As long as you are not stepping out of bounds with the budget, you're ok. Even if you are going to exceed the bounds, if you can justify it and get more money, that is a separate matter. As another boundary condition, if you are planning a change and that change could cost Bosch some money, that gets reviewed. It has to go through a separate, different process. It is a boundary condition you must honor whether or not you are going to implement the change."

SELF-DIRECTED TEAM PERFORMANCE

The Bosch organization provided good support to the Technical Platform Team and the larger group. According to the TPM, this support took the form of both "dollar support" and "hands-off support." The TPM would establish a budget for the project and would receive funds at the beginning of the year. The TPM and team could determine how to spend it and shift funds among the necessary purposes and functions as long as they stayed within their budget.

Team members viewed this arrangement as highly desirable because they and their TPM knew what they were doing and performed so effectively. Likewise, they believed the hands-off support would have been modified if their TPM had gone off on his own and the team had not been performing well. As one team member observed, "Since our TPM receives hands-off support, it means the team is doing a good job. Yeah, or Kevin [O'Keefe] would have heard about it." The TPM concluded, "We are very much self-directed, very much." The Technical Platform Team and the Modulation Applications Team had earned and preserved their self-directed status and their hands-off support.

EMPOWERED TO ADD SKILLS AND KNOWLEDGE

The team leaders and the managers to whom team members reported bore the responsibility for deciding what training or educational updates team members needed. The TPM explained that these matters were taken up for the Technical Platform Team and larger group in his "direct reports" to supervisory levels. The team leader for the Modulation Applications Team also bore responsibility for deciding with his team members what training or educational updates a team member needed. The TPM indicated, "I don't think anyone is more self-empowered than our group of team members. If you [a team member] think you need it [added training or educational updates], you, with your team leader or manager's support, simply go out and get it. The same is true for those reporting to the manager of the software group and the manager of the sales group."

PERFORMANCE MEASURES FROM CUSTOMER

The Technical Platform Team's performance targets or measures were set by the customer. The team members explained that two targets or measures existed. First came those that required completion or delivery of an output by a certain date. One team member stated, "For example, we may have to have the logic done on a certain date, design freezes for calipers on a certain date, or meet other dates set by the customer." Second came targets or measures pertaining to costs. A team member added, "We may have to meet cost targets set for certain components or for certain systems." According to another team member, "A lot of things are tracked—topics, open issues, and a history of what is going to happen on each issue. It is a general form of evaluation of how well the technical platform or team is doing."

The TPM added, "If a customer is not satisfied with the response being received from Bosch personnel, the customer's main feedback goes to the vice presidents and directors of our groups. The feedback will come down to us. There're really no metrics for evaluating our team performance other than if we're missing customer dates, not supplying parts when they are needed, or not getting things done when the customer needs them. So much of our performance is customer driven."

ROUTINE TEAM MEMBER EVALUATIONS

As the TPM explained, "Underlying the evaluation process used for individual team members is the concept that each team member is responsible for his or her function and each is expected to perform and complete those responsibilities in a timely manner. If I or another team member must start doing someone else's role or responsibility for them, we do that to help customer satisfaction. But we try to correct the situation and not take on those roles and responsibilities permanently as a team or organization. We try to make that change where appropriate."

Individual evaluations may involve team judgments. These evaluations are about performance but do not involve a performance metric. A team member explained, "It is involved if a person really isn't pulling his or her weight on the project. Team members may observe the person is not meeting the performance expected or not meeting what's required. If the team members conclude they are not getting the support from a person that they need, it becomes a legitimate complaint for action." These team-level evaluations of an individual apparently have only occurred rarely.

The TPM continued, "In Bosch, the manager meets with the employee twice a year. It is a two-way street. You basically lay out what the goals are for the next six months or next year as well as what kind of training is needed. There's always a feedback from it."

ROUTINE TEAM-LEVEL EVALUATION

A similar evaluation process exists at the team level. For example, the Modulation Applications Team meets at least twice a year with its supervisory level. Brochu pointed out, "In Bosch, the manager meets with the employee twice a year for job evaluation. We share our goals for the next year. And maybe six months from then we sit down again and say, 'All right, maybe these goals have changed a little bit. Let's update them and make sure we are on track.' And we also get the employees' feedback. They may say, 'Hey, this is the training I want this year,' and if the team agrees, we'll make sure we put that on as a goal for the team, too."

BREADTH OF SKILLS AND UNDERSTANDING

The TPM tied together the crucial role of responding to the customer's needs, the difficulty of evaluation, and the need for breadth of skills and understanding, explaining, "Another reason why having specific metrics for performance evaluation would be difficult is because so much of what the team does is responding to the immediate needs of the customer. The job is a bit like firefighting. The team has functioned very well because our breadth of skills and technical knowledge and our flexibility make us able to respond quickly to the customer."

As the TPM explained further, "You may have a day with an open schedule and suddenly there's a meeting, then there's a car we've got to look at, and so on." Another team member added, "You have to be flexible and ready to jump from one thing to the next effectively. You've got to be able to go at a new issue, understand it, write it down, and analyze how we are going to attack it. Then you have to be able to put the people in place and make a whole plan. Incidentally, to track that process for evaluation could take more time than it takes to fix the issue."

INFORMAL OPERATING PROCEDURES

The Technical Platform Team and the Modulation Application Team followed an array of informal procedures that worked very well. The teams did not create for themselves a formal written operating procedure, which might have reduced some ambiguity, could have been shared with new hires, and could be reviewed and improved by all team members over time. However, the informal understandings about such matters as interacting with the customer, proper handling of questions and issues, involving those most capable, keeping others affected in the loop, never making customer commitments without being sure, shouldering responsibility, trusting others to respond promptly and accurately, placing customer interests first, cooperating with those who had the needed skills and capabilities, and hiring for team as well as increasing technical skills were equivalent to a simplified formal set of operating procedures.

COACHING

An established formal coaching function for enhanced teaming did not exist for the Technical Platform Team or the larger Technical Platform Group. Team members indicated that the broader systems framework or plan was provided and that it was up to the TPM and team members to make it work for this team. "Fortunately, we were able to make it work." said one team member. Another observed, "There were other teams created that were not working nearly as well as" the Technical Platform Group and its core team, the Technical Platform Team.

The coaching that did occur was termed coaching by example by the TPM and team members. New team members were encouraged to obtain views and ideas from across the team, determining how to treat issues as a team decision, not as individual decisions.

Team Standards for Hiring and Performance[10]

The Applications Team and the larger Technical Platform Team are well served by having three sets of standards: (1) core competencies sought, (2) skills and behaviors valued, and (3) quality principles required plus the goals they defined. These standards are used in pursing their mission and performing their jobs. The standards are both expected of team members and utilized in hiring decisions.

CORE COMPETENCIES

The Applications Team and Technical Platform Team sought the following core competencies when hiring new members and expected existing team members to demonstrate these skills:

> Understand business and industry;
> Solve problems and make decisions;
> Engage in strategic thinking;
> Build and use internal networks and teams;
> Communicate with others;
> Build partnership with external customers;
> Encourage risk taking, innovation, and organizational development;
> Demonstrate socially responsive and ethical behavior;
> Promote personal and associate development and empowerment.

SKILLS AND BEHAVIORS

The core competencies were related to valued skills and behaviors, including a careful look at personality for fit with the team and service to the customer. The list of valued skills and behaviors includes eighteen items, although some have been combined here for brevity:

> Professional/job knowledge and comprehension of company and business;
> Organization of work and total systems thinking;
> Teamwork/networking;
> Communication (oral, written, listening);
> Customer service/partnership;
> Dependability/accountability and adaptability;
> Self-motivation and initiative plus creativity/innovation;
> Continuous improvement orientation and practice;
> Ethical/social behavior;
> Safety/environmental accountability;
> Self-development/continuous learning and development of others;
> Encouragement/motivation/empowerment of others.

QUALITY PRINCIPLES

Both teams embraced the broader Bosch organization's quality principles, which the Board of Management established to show the company's uncompromising commitment to quality:

> We want satisfied customers. That is why the highest quality of our products and services is one of our major corporate objectives.
> The customer is the judge of our quality. The customer's opinion of our products and services is decisive.
> Our quality goal is always "zero defects" or "100% right."
> Not only do our customers assess the quality of our products but also the quality of our services. Deliveries must be on time.
> Inquiries, offers, samples, and complaints must all be dealt with promptly and thoroughly. It is imperative that deadlines be met.
> Each and every Associate in the Company contributes toward achieving our quality goals. It is thus the responsibility of all Associates, from Apprentice to Member of the Board, to ensure that their work is of the highest standard . . .

> All work must be done without defect from the very beginning. This not only improves quality but also reduces our costs. Quality increases cost-effectiveness.
> Not only defects themselves must be eliminated but also there causes. Prevention of defects has priority over their elimination.
> The quality of our products also depends on the quality of our sourced parts. Demand the highest quality from our suppliers, and support them in adhering to our mutual quality goals.
> Even when painstaking care has been taken, defects can occasionally happen. This is why we have introduced numerous and proven methods to identify defects at an early stage. These methods must be rigorously and consistently applied.
> Ensuring that our quality goals are achieved is an important management duty. When appraising the performance of our Associates, particular emphasis is placed on the quality of their work.
> Our quality directives are compulsory. Further, customer requirements must be fulfilled.

Every Bosch associate receives these quality principles in the Employee Handbook, which also explains and elaborates the principles. The principles reinforce the idea that everyone must work at quality every day. The quality principles also include the directive that anyone who identifies a problem that may jeopardize quality but lacks the authority to remedy it must report the matter immediately to superiors. The combination of these quality principles and the goals they define, the core competencies sought, and the skills and behaviors valued provides added focus and added clarity for enhanced team performance. The enhanced performance accrues to the teams, to the many others with whom the teams cooperate, to Bosch, and most important, to the customer.

What Made the Two Teams Special?

Those interviewed were asked to describe what was special or unusual about their team and to explain what they thought made their team high performing. Because the older and smaller Modulation Applications Team formed an integral part of the larger, newer Technical Platform Team for the XYZ Project, comments made encompassed both teams.

❶ One key reason that the teams were so special was *the trust that developed among team members and with the team leaders.* A team member who was with Bosch at the time of the Technical Platform Team's creation explained, "From my perspective, it is trust that makes us special. We know what each of us can do. We know and trust that if something needs to be done, it'll get done. You don't have to follow up on somebody else. Following up could be one of the most time-consuming things in our jobs if you don't know that the responsible person is going to do it and you've got to constantly check back and ask, 'Did you do this, did you do that?'" Also, there is the trust in team members' ability to know what they know and to know what they don't know. The team member continued, "Since we know the limitations of our knowledge, we avoid the problem of persons telling the customer things we don't know or making a commitment when one should not be made. We trust that a team member will take an issue from the customer, get information about it and write it down, and then bring it back to the right person for follow up. And it gets taken care of. That is something that I don't see in some of the other teams like ours."

Another team member shared, "You may not trust people that you have not worked with before. Since 1998 [when the Technical Platform Team was created], our trust level has gone way up as the team has worked together. . . . It's maybe a part of the evolution of a team. It just gets greater as it goes on." Still another added, "Without trust, it would all fall apart."

❷ A second reason for the team being special and performing so well was the *level and quality of communication among team members, with team leaders across teams, and with the customer.* It was expressed in various ways. According to one team member, "Good communication is part of the core skill set that a team member must have. Communication involves both knowing and sharing what your roles are and asking questions. If you don't know, you ask. Communication and trust have made this team work." Another team member added, "Good communication throughout the team has been possible since there has been a consistent core group here. Some members of the core group have been working together on this for several years. That plus a really good knowledge of our customer requirements have helped us in communicating. Even though we have had people leave the team and new persons join, the new people have worked in well."

Another team member stated, "Team communication with the customer is excellent. It has emphasized learning about the customer's questions or issues and getting as much information as possible about them. It is then possible to bring issues back to the Bosch person who has the skills to deal with them well. Communicating accurately with the customer is very important since meeting the customer's needs is the primary reason the teams exist." Still another team member commented on the level achieved: "Communication on this team is really good. I'm on another team also. The communication level for it is not as good as it is in this team. It is one of the things that I consider lacking there, but we're working on it."

Another team member added, "We have levels of urgency and approaches for them. If you really need someone, you page them or call them on their cell phone. For the next level down on urgency, you call them at their desk even if you know they are not there. You leave them a voice-mail message because they will always check their voice mail before they go home, even if they are driving back from a customer. At the lowest level of urgency, there is the use of e-mail. While this procedure is not a formal thing, we developed it to be helpful in our performance."

❸ Third, closely aligned with strong communication is *high responsiveness by team members to one another and to the customer.* A team member stated, "Very special about this team is its responsiveness. When I first came onto the Technical Platform Team, we had to increase communication quite a bit. I can't think of anybody on this team that didn't call back to me in a real quick way, even when they were at the cold-testing site or at one of the customer's plants. I pretty much talked to the team leader nonstop, but it was all the team members that I contacted. I think the communication, including responsiveness, on this team is the best I've ever seen. I've been on other teams and in other companies. If you need something and you are on a team member's voice mail, they are not going to skip over you. They continually return calls. I get a lot of questions from customers about a lot of things, some technical and some for other reasons. And it is important for me to get back to the customer quickly. These guys [team members] do a great job of that—helping me respond quickly."

❹ Fourth, imbedded in the high level of trust and in the very good communication and responsiveness is a *strong sense of mutual responsibility among team members to do the work and take care of the work* that is expected of them. As the technical platform leader shared, "Our group is the direct interface with the customer, the people we are talking to. We guide all the other functional groups behind us as to what's needed and what needs to be done. For the most part, we set the course for the whole platform. We see the issues that arise as team issues, not just an issue for the person who receives it. If a team member picks up on an issue or question that will affect us somewhere else, he or she gets it to the right person. Team members are responsible to one another for getting the information to the right person, and that person is responsible for following up on what is needed and getting back so we can respond to the customer quickly. Since team members are responsible, we don't have to check up on them to see if they are going to follow through."

The strong mutual sense of responsibility showed in team members' high level of caring for one another and willingness to fill in for one another and see that work was completed. As the TPM pointed out, "I think the level of caring among team members is very high. If anyone had a personal issue that required them to be away, the whole rest of the team I know would jump in and just cover. It wouldn't even be a question. You wouldn't have to establish who's going to cover. I mean, people would just start absorbing the workload until that person could come back and take it over." For example, after the World Trade Center tragedy, one employee's spouse was stranded on the West Coast and couldn't return home, leaving the team member with full responsibility for their three children. The rest of the team covered as much as they could. Everyone else just tried to pick up the slack. The TPM added, "When I had a meeting that I had to go to but could not, someone else went on my behalf. There was no concern with that arrangement. There was not the feeling of burden; rather, there was the feeling of trying to help."

❺ A fifth reason for the team being special is the *composite of skill sets that the team possessed.* The TPM explained, "We pretty much replaced all the team members in one area over the last two and a half years, and we didn't hire people with brake experience. We hired them for the skill sets that we needed. The first couple of persons were hired because of their skills in networking and their skills in teamwork. The questions we posed related to how well their skill sets would meld into the team and the larger organization and how well they could work as a member of a large team. That is really how we have been hiring. We get the right persons based on their skill sets."

He continued, "For example, one of the persons that I hired at the senior level had no brake experience. He came in from turbochargers. But he had the right set of skills to get in and manage a part of the team effort. Another person came in from a make-to-print manufacturer. His organization made some brake parts, but he had no knowledge of how they worked. [These two new hires] brought valuable skills we needed in teamwork, networking, communicating, and the like. We were allowed to go after these persons based on their skill sets, not based on their expertise. Now that is not always the case. For instance, you couldn't hire somebody to perform software design, application, and modification of software if they didn't know software. But hiring persons with the teamwork, networking, and other skills they have is critical, very critical."

❻ A sixth reason is the *strong commitment to product on the part of team members and their desire to perform as a team at a high level* for their customer and for Bosch. The TPM explained, "One of the most important reasons the team is special is that everyone cares about the product, not their own process or their own group. They care about a successful product and a successful end. They don't look for excuses. They don't look for reasons they don't have to do something. It is because they care about the product and the ending. There's nothing that gives us more satisfaction than that we get through the whole launch successfully, with little or no loss of time and with a good warranty. These are metrics that affect our customer. They and we take pride in that achievement. Even though the strong commitment to product doesn't show up specifically in our performance reviews, the achievement means a lot to us. It is important to recognize that team members care about the end product and not just their job and their specific function."

A team member further explained the high team commitment, a mutual commitment: "I think that with this team especially, everyone on the team has a personal level of commitment to this project to make sure that the things that they need to do, from their specific area of skill, get done." Another team member added, "The people on this team aren't out for themselves or for their own group. They are not trying to put forward their own agendas. Everybody's goal, a focused goal, here is to get the product out correctly and on time."

❼ A seventh reason given why the team is special is that *members of the team carried the ability to represent the team well, even when the issues are beyond their technical areas of expertise.* According to the TPM, "A unique thing about this team is that if we had a customer meeting or an internal Bosch meeting, regardless of the subject, you could send anyone from the team to it and know that no major mistakes would be made and that key information would be gathered. It doesn't mean that the person could answer on the spot the questions or issues raised, nor does it mean that the meeting would be as efficient as possible. However, there wouldn't be a concern by the team about the team representative. There would be total faith that the representative would know what questions need to be asked, what has to be done, and what information needs to be provided. So anyone from the team could replace anyone else on the team and the team process would still function effectively. It might be a little less efficient than the ideal, but it would function."

❽ An eighth reason why the team was special was *a combination of right and necessary skills, team self-sufficiency, plus accountability on the part of individual team members and the team.* Having the necessary core skills plus the full range of technical competencies required for the platform made the team quite self-sufficient for the challenges it confronted. This self sufficiency was further enabled by the hands-off support that the team received to perform its functions. Furthermore, team members were accountable to one another and to the team leader. As one explained, "When people are not accountable, you don't trust them. And when you have accountability, as on this team, you have trust." As two team members explained, "We do have a really good knowledge of our customer's requirements. And everyone here has a good knowledge of what we really need to do. We have the right core set of team skills and the technical competencies. We have worked together long enough that we know each other's strengths and weaknesses. And we have managed to find ways to work well together as a team. We are accountable to each other for our contributions to the whole team effort."

❾ Final reasons given for the team being special are ***team flexibility and team pride and respect.*** The leader of the Modulation Applications Team explained, "In addition to the other things mentioned, I'd say that pride, flexibility, and respect make us special, and they go together. We are a very, very hardworking group that wants to get the job done. We put in a lot of extra hours to get it done. Our customers have many demands. Many times they can't make up their minds on things. They can and do change things at the last minute. And because we are flexible, we get things done. Also, we have team members who are not afraid to stand up for what they think is right. We think that is real important. And we tell the customers that, too. We don't just lie down and take it. At times, we'll challenge the customer on their side. We receive respect from their side when it happens. And, we are proud of what we do."

A team member added, "I think all of us understand the importance of respect from individuals on the team. That respect creates an expectation—I don't ever want people on the team to think I'm not pulling my weight. And I don't want people to think that I don't respect them or that they can't respect me. I think that we all want to be respected for doing what we do. I think that's a big part of why we all want to do the right thing and why we all want to make sure that the customer's happy. And it is why we all feel like we have something invested in this team effort. I don't ever want people to think, 'I can't go to her because she is not going to do it.' I want people to respect me for what I do and know that it is going to get done. That creates a certain level of greater performance and expectations within the team."

The TPM added, "Respect also works the other way, in the opposite direction. If somebody on the team doesn't get something done that you expected, your first assumption is never that they let you down. It's typically something else got in the way. In other areas or places, when somebody doesn't do something, the first assumption may be that the person is lazy, they didn't get to it, or they care about something else more. Here in this team, it would be, 'Something else got in the way. What can we do next?' 'What's our next date?' 'Let's renegotiate with the customers.' Here, there is not an assumed problem that someone let you down. You assume that they made the decision for the right reasons at the right time. And you just respect that and assume that you've got to move on. You may disagree, and you may wish they didn't, but you respect it and just try to move on. At the team level, you don't see bickering or complaining because a date was missed. The very few persons who have fallen into that realm have left the team."

These perspectives on respect, flexibility, and team pride demonstrate a responsibility-based environment in action.

Key Variables Influencing Performance

Personal interviews with members of the Modulation Applications Team and the Technical Platform Team were used to identify the key variables influencing performance. Viewed as of highest importance to success of the teams were the following three variables: (1) *commitment to team success* by the team members and the team leader, reinforced by *substantial team zeal*, (2) *trust among team members and team leader(s)*, (3) the *self-motivation of the entire team*—team members and leader(s). Team members interviewed were unanimous about the very high importance of these three variables. Also seen as very important by nearly all team members interviewed was (4) *mutual respect among team members and with the team leader(s)*, reinforced by substantial *caring about the team by the team members and leader(s)*.

Team members cited several other variables as being of major importance, including (5) the *complementary nature (complementary skills) of the entire team*—members and the leaders(s), (6) the *team's commitment to stretching thinking, searching for new ideas and approaches, doing things in different ways, sharing different ideas, and respecting different views*, (7) the *existence of a common team vision and commitment to get into production*, and (8) the team members' and leader(s)' *willingness to take risks to achieve team success*. Viewed as quite important were (9) the *organization's commitment to dollar and nondollar support of this team*, (10) the *team's commitment to team creativity and innovation*, and (11) *team "optimism"* and *"team spirit"* among team members and leader(s).

Other supportive organizational conditions helped to provide an enhanced team environment. The organization was committed to team creativity and innovation and to team approaches and team success. The organization also was committed to growth in employees' in skills, knowledge, and education. The organization exercised shared leadership with the team and two-way communication between the organization and the team. As one team member commented, "The team is able to make 95 percent of the decisions that are necessary by the team." Another team member observed, "The organization pretty much stays out of the road of the team and its performance."

The team also contributed to its supportive environment, recognizing its members' contributions. The clarity of the team's mission and goals also enhanced the team environment. Several team members viewed the team as benefiting from an entrepreneurial nature. Also viewed as important was team members' confidence in one another's skills. Complementing these was the sense of caring that team members and team leaders had for individuals and their families.

COMPLEMENTARY SKILLS AND KNOWLEDGE, DYNAMIC VARIABLE IMPACTING OTHERS

During the interview process, team members shared information about the high importance of the range of complementary skills, knowledge, and experiences brought to the teaming efforts. They viewed it as a major cause of the high performance achieved. In this chapter, we use the variable complementary skills and knowledge as an example of the influence of a key variable as it works dynamically in the Technical Platform Team. As the intensity of this variable grows, it influences both the level of performance and the level of the environmental context in which that performance occurs.

As we worked with the two Bosch teams, we were impressed by the special roles served by growing team skills and technical knowledge and experience. As they became broader, deeper, and more complementary, skills, knowledge, and experience enhanced performance for the customer in various ways, which in turn increased the customer's trust. These gains plus the enhanced performance they helped create also stimulated a growth in effective communication, within the team, with the team leaders, with supervisors and upper management, between and across the two platforms for the XYZ Project, and especially between the two platforms and the customer and their many representatives. The growth was multidimensional and strongly cross-functional, a particularly vital asset because of the complexity of the work of both the Technical and Commercial Platforms and their need to serve the customer in a complementary, coordinated, and mutually reinforcing way.

We observed that as the Technical Platform Team's team skills, technical knowledge, and experience grew, they influenced many other conditions as well. For example, they increased trust among team members, with leaders, with supervisors, and among the two platform managers and their teams. They increased team members' and leaders' flexibility in performing team roles and responsibilities. They enhanced team members' ability to substitute for one another and fill in as needed, regardless of reasons. They gave reality to the notion that issues belong to everyone on the team, not just its leaders or the person on whom the issue falls. They helped team members understand their own strengths and limitations and those of fellow team members and leaders. They informed and empowered team members to further enhance their abilities through added training. They gave added insights for the hiring process, ensuring that the right persons that fit the team were hired. And the growth in team skills, technical knowledge, and experience increased team leaders' and members' ability to perform effectively in a self-directed manner.

DYNAMICS OF COMPLEMENTARY SKILLS AND KNOWLEDGE

As in the previous cases reported in chapters 3 and 4, instead of attempting to show the dynamics of the many influences, we display in simplified form the influences of this growth on two conditions—performance levels and environmental levels. The latter is the environment that the team helped to create for itself and within which it operated.

Simplified diagrams 1, 2, and 3 in figure 5.1 represent three positive connected dynamic loops. They depict the changing status and influence of complementary skills and knowledge on performance and on two environmental conditions, level of communication and level of customer trust. Complementary skills and knowledge are progressively greater in diagrams 2 and 3, as are the performance levels that result. Moreover, in diagrams 2 and 3, as skills and knowledge become progressively greater, the environmental levels, comprised of communication and customer trust, also increase.

Diagram 1 illustrates the starting level of skills and knowledge in 1999 on the Technical Platform Team (level 1) and the related initial level of performance that resulted. The initial level of communication was workable, and a level of trust existed with the customer that was based on the prior work of the leaders and core members who had worked together in the past.

FIGURE 5.1. COMPLEMENTARY SKILLS AND KNOWLEDGE: DIAGRAMS 1, 2, AND 3

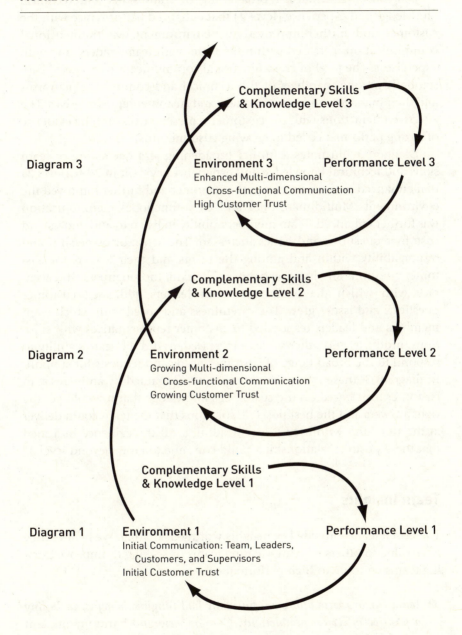

Diagram 2 illustrates a broadening of team skills and technical knowledge and experience (level 2) that enhanced performance with the customer and further improved the environment. Multidimensional communication increased within the team, with team leaders, and with supervisors. The level of cross-functional communication increased substantially among members of the technical and commercial platforms and their managers and between them and customer representatives. The effective interactions with the customer representatives and the evidence of strong performance led to growing customer trust.

Diagram 3 illustrates a further broadening and deepening of team skills and technical knowledge and experiences evident in 2001 (level 3) that enhanced performance with the customer and further improved the environment. Multidimensional and cross-functional communication was further enhanced. Team members' ability to listen to and understand customer questions and issues increased. The sense of ownership and responsibility within and among the teams and their leaders for customer questions and issues expanded. The skill, thoroughness, and accuracy with which the teams and their leaders addressed customer questions and issues grew. The carefulness and speed with which team members and leaders responded to customer representatives with solutions, products, and other services increased, as did the team's ability to respond to the broad range of customer needs and requests for support. In diagram 3, these improvements were accompanied by an increase in customer trust based on the customer's knowledge that it would get the right answers and the best possible solutions that the team could deliver at the time and within customer deadlines. All the evidence indicated that these positive relationships could continue to grow beyond level 3.

Team Insights

The Bosch teams provide key insights worthy of sharing. We believe they have value to others who are creating teams or seeking to improve existing teams en route to high performance.

❶ *Team camaraderie and team harmony had tangible benefits, including a positive effect on productivity.* Camaraderie and harmony made it easy for the team members to work effectively. This camaraderie and harmony increased the team members' ability to brainstorm and problem solve. As a result, the teams could consider a wider range of possibilities and solutions and converge on the best ones, thereby increasing the timeliness and quality of the team's performance and its productivity.

❷ *Achieved high performance does not imply that the team functioned within the best possible organizational context.* Some of the team members within the XYZ Platform Group reported to a program manager who previously focused on products or components. Team members and team leaders involved in the XYZ Platform observed that the ideal is to have all team members as well as the team leaders reporting to program managers who are platform and customer based rather than product or individual-component based. Team members and leaders indicated that their earlier efforts would have been less stressful, discord over priorities would have been diminished, and productivity would have been enhanced with centralized reporting to management fully oriented to the platform's success on behalf of the customer. The two teams apparently reported to managers and directors who were focused on the teams. The Technical Platform Team was innovative and performed well, overcoming the earlier program management shortcomings for the commercial side.

❸ *Training of team members in team processes likely would have been beneficial for the team.* The TPM received training from Bosch that was personality based and was focused on understanding, accepting, and learning to work with other people's personalities. Team members judged it to be useful in "understanding how people differ, how they think differently, and how they are motivated differently." The training also helped in hiring. As the TPM shared, "We do a lot in assessing technical capability, but we also hit the personality aspects. We explore initiative, self-starting, energy level, and their passion for the work." The fact that a number of team members had worked together previously proved helpful to the team's effective functioning. Neither the TPM nor the team members received training in team processes.

❹ *Another insight, according to the TPM, was "the importance of management support when we needed it while staying out of the road at other times."* The TPM continued, "There have been times when I knew we were going to ruffle some feathers with some things that were going on. But I had the comfort to just drop an e-mail or voice mail to my boss. I would share, 'This is what's taking place, this is what's going to happen, and there will be some fallout.' Once he was informed, I had a sense my support shield was in place. It was a guarantee that I would be supported." The combination of providing freedom to the team to be self-directed plus backup support from management when needed clearly helped the team's effective performance for the customer.

❺ *New hires coming to the team need mentoring, whether they are placed in technical (engineering) or commercial (sales) responsibilities.* The platform managers and team members have learned that new team members need assistance in learning what is expected in their job on the team. Both the technical (engineering) side and the commercial (sales) side of the project are visible to the customer and are crucial to successful outcomes for the customer. Coordination and cooperation of both sides of the project are vital. The team leader of the Modulation Applications Team pointed that out on the modulation side, new applications engineers have training checklists that they must complete. Also, they are assigned mentor engineers, who assist the new hires in becoming functioning parts of the team.

❻ *There is no substitute for personal responsibility and pride in what you do as a team and for the freedom to do your job well.* The TPM observed, "Both the commercial platform manager and I want the product to launch well. We are focused on the customer and take responsibility and pride in what we do. Team members are not afraid to stand up for what the team thinks is right. We talk to our boss about once a week. He allows us to be self-directed. He's the type of boss, on the engineering side, that keeps the next level of management off our backs. It is like a 'forever shield' so that we worker bees can get our job done. It gives strength to our backbone, our resolve to perform."

❼ *Coaching by example is viewed as important for the effective functioning of the team.* "Our coaching is a lot by example," said the leader of the Technical Platform Team. "When a new person comes on, many times he/she is dealing with an ABS issue. I'll give my opinion to the person, but I'll say, 'Call these other selected team members to get their views.' The new person learns by example not to run off with the first idea that is shared. We coach the new team member not to go to just one person and get all the answers. How we treat issues is a team decision, not an individual's decision. The whole team must be supportive of the actions taken. It is not forced coaching of the team but rather coaching by example."

❽ *Both the team and the company need to be flexible, particularly regarding new opportunities and their financial support.* The TPM explained, "Our team has been well supported. We've never had trouble getting the financial resources if we deemed it necessary and could justify the need. For example, a new possible program may not be in our business plan, but if we react now and proceed on the new program, we can avoid some negative impacts later. The organization's first position is to do what's right. The organization will spend the money if the justification is there to do what's right." Another team member added, "You have to do more work justifying it now, but they still do what's right."

❾ *Empowerment of the teams was vital to their high performance.* The two teams felt empowered by their supervision levels. As the TPM observed, "If we weren't self-empowered, the support situation would have been destructive. If we couldn't make the decision on a number of things we do, the team would crumble. We simply could not be running things up the organization for approval and continue to meet our tight timelines for the customer." Another team member observed "Our self-empowerment gives us greater ownership in our decisions and actions. It also contributed to our sense of pride in our achievements for the customer and for Bosch."

Lessons Learned[11]

A number of lessons can be learned from the Modulation Applications Team and the Technical Platform Team, their supervision, and their cooperators.

❶ *Important to the effective functioning of the team is the healthy respect that exists for divergent views and divergent thinking.* One team member observed, "I don't think any of us on this team are afraid to give their opinion or speak their mind. Further, they are not afraid of what their response is going to be. Team members are not judged on what they think." Another team member added, "Most teams don't give as much opportunity as we do for divergent views. Some come up with a decision to do something a certain way and don't worry how bad that solution is. Also, we don't have a few personalities that everyone will default to." The team leader added, "Everyone on the team is vocal. But when all the ideas get on the table, it tends to result in a final consensus that people back. They may not all agree, but if that's the way everyone is going, then they try to support it." Another team member added, "Because of our approach, everyone seems to have a bigger picture and bigger understanding. We take an issue, hash it and argue it, and then we come to an agreement. We focus on how we are going to make this work. And that is different from other teams."

❷ *Addressing team mission, vision, goals, and objectives, including the ground rules under which their team would function would have been useful at the time of the Technical Platform Team's formation.* The TPM observed, "addressing these would have served the useful purpose of getting the team together and spend time talking and understanding how the new team arrangement for the platform was supposed to work. Early on, we simply accepted the administrative vision of the platform approach without getting into these details about how the team would function. Later, we did address the role of persons on the team. We put them together and determined if there was anything we misunderstood. We aired out the assumptions that various team members had, and we addressed how we should function. But it would have helped at the beginning if we had determined how we would function and had set some key ground rules."

❸ *The two teams have developed team recognition arrangements because of their value.* The Technical Platform Team, with supervisor support, has created its own team recognition and rewards. "From my boss's standpoint, there has been a precedent of trying to provide these at our level. For example, we had an off-site meeting and seven of the eight hours were on structure of the team and what improvements could be made. One hour of it was reserved for pure fun—we went go-cart racing. Also, every year we arrange a day to get together and we take time to water ski. Human Resources has given us the freedom to do these things for the good of the team. But it really comes down to whether the manager or director sees the value of it and supports it. For the teams, the recognition is valued and supported, and it gives us added pride in our team and the organization."

❹ *Active information flow from team leaders to administrative levels above the teams is vital in keeping the organization in tune with team conditions and performance.* Unless upper administrative levels understand the team's operations, its achievements, and customer responses, they will have difficulty in properly evaluating the team and its achievements. The TPM shared, "The information flow upward can provide vital recognition needed by the team. I send communication directly to the team members' boss and the boss's boss to make sure it hits a couple of levels. The value of this communication shows up in the team's work. It is especially evident when management is focusing on team support. You definitely see it then."

❺ *A team system is needed to prevent burnout.* The team maintains a self-monitoring system to identify excessive workload and to help prevent burnout and employee turnover. It also maintains a commitment to sharing work. The TPM explained, "For my direct team [the Technical Platform Team], we track hours worked by each team member beyond a nine-hour workday. These are totaled for the month. I have used these when I see someone working, say, thirty hours or more excess load, I will take some of their work and place it with someone else. And, anywhere we can, we just try to fill in for people. The best thing that helps with burnout is that no one feels totally responsible for it all. Our monitoring and work sharing makes that feeling real." However, the intensity of the work by team members and team leaders also requires them to develop personal means of ameliorating stress. As one team member explained, "When I leave work, the minute I step out the door, I try to shut off as far as work is concerned. If I don't, I'll never get any sleep, and I wouldn't have a good home life."

❻ *When it comes to creative solutions to problems and related risk taking, total team support is vital.* As one team member explained, "Sometimes we come up with some pretty cool [innovative] ideas to get through a problem. It's important that the whole team understand and support the ideas since it is possible the organization may not. The action may appear risky or appear inconsistent with some policy to someone up the line. In such a recent action with team support, it solved the issue and avoided a major problem later. It's important that the whole team take the risk and not just an individual or two." He continued, "If one or two persons ask for a change they believe to be necessary and team members support it, that will carry greater influence with the organization. But if one or two persons say we need the change and other team members say, 'No, that's not the right thing to do,' it would end immediately right there."

❼ *The team learned that in dealing with problems and issues, members should strive for the best solution now, not the ultimate solution.* As one explained, "When a solution with full team support is proposed, the team's questions are, 'Is it the best solution at the time? Is it the right thing to do for what we have at the time?'" The team member continued, "One of my four favorite sayings is that the enemy of better is best. Some people outside the team fall into that trap. They don't want to do anything until they have the ultimate solution. For us, that would lead to major problems for the customer."

❽ *Hiring the right people first. The teams emphasized the importance of who they hire—it is important to evaluate potential team members' personalities for working with the team and with the customer as well as their skills.* According to the team leader, "Hiring is key. One of the big things is to hire people for their personality more than their specific degree. Then make sure they have a level of intelligence to do the job, and be willing to train them into the job if they have the right skills. They have to be smart enough to do the job in the long run, but the skills of working with the customer and the team have to be highly regarded." He continued, "We've nixed many an interview because the person was too quiet, not proud of what they had done, did not fit, even if they have a Ph.D. They may be the smartest person who is going to work in the corner. You must hire the right people first. If you don't hire someone who cares, it doesn't matter what system you put them in. They will get chewed up, get moved elsewhere." The TPM leader confirmed, "I totally agree. Personality is a key. In interviewing a person to hire, we spend at least three hours on those aspects and then we have another portion of the interview where we get into the technical aspects. Personality and fit and self-initiative are keys. You've got to find the right fit personality-wise."

❾ *Team members and leaders view trust as something earned through performance.* As one team leader explained, "I think you earn it. You can't force it to happen either. A team leader can't go in with the focus that I'm going to force them to trust me. You've got to earn it by example. Further, once you have earned the trust, one slipup doesn't cause you to lose that trust. So you have to earn it, but once you earn it, you are going to carry it for a long time."

❿ *Stress would be greater if it were not for trust and a sense of security between team members and team leaders and between team leaders and their bosses.* The TPM summed up these relationships: "On occasion, we let something drop, missed a deadline, despite our best efforts. I would tell my boss that I had missed it. But I had the security of knowing that he doesn't believe it's because I don't consider it important. Having that trust and support helped with the stress and burnout." The TPM added, "We are not tracking daily what anyone on the team does. If the job is getting done, team members can take some free time when they can fit it in. It's never easy, and people cancel vacations because of their work demands. If you ask them to cancel a vacation, you must be ready to allow them the flexibility to take it later when they feel it's necessary. That's really supported, too. Taking time away when you can do so really helps with stress and burnout." Another team leader shared, "It's important to recognize when team members become frustrated and need to blow off steam. It's important to let them vent and speak their mind. That helps with stress and burnout."

⓫ *The team members provided key insights about the role of recognition in team performance.* They observed that in recent years there has been a reduction in the awards and recognition going to individual teams as the automotive group has become larger. Such awards and recognitions were not a direct, significant loss but indirectly were quite important for motivation and pride. As one team member explained, "In my mind, the important thing is not the recognition but the pride that surrounded the recognition. I really think there are many people who are proud to work for Bosch, and that pride should be supported. And recognition would help because a lot of what motivates this team is the pride of the product and the name." Another team member explained, "It's important to have the recognition from your direct managers that you're doing a good job. It generates motivation and pride." Recognition of team members within the team by team leaders was substantial, as was the resulting motivation and pride of the team in its performance.

NOTES

1. www.bosch.com/en/company/facts/index.htm.

2. *Bosch, Creating the Future . . . By Making History Together,* brochure #rbus/01 (Bosch, 1999), 3. The business sectors subsequently were recast into three: automotive technology, industrial technology, and consumer goods and building technology (www .bosch.com/en/company/facts/struktur.htm).

3. www.bosch.com/en/company/facts/kfz.htm.

4. *Bosch, Creating the Future . . . By Making History Together,* 5.

5. *Bosch, Creating the Future . . . By Making History Together,* 6.

6. Comments by team leader Ken Brochu, Farmington Hills, Michigan, May 12, 2000.

7. Comments by team leader Ken Brochu, Farmington Hills, Michigan, May 12, 2000.

8. Comments by team leader Ken Brochu, Farmington Hills, Michigan, May 12, 2000.

9. The authors are indebted to the members who served the Modulation Applications Team, the Modulation Systems Team, and the Technical Platform Support group for XYZ who contributed freely with their responses, insights and suggestions. They include Ken Brochu, engineering manager, ABS/TCS/ESC Applications; Eric Broman, senior ABS/TCS/ESC applications engineer XYZ; Brandon Berlinger, commercial platform manager XYZ; Victoria Gouwens, senior development engineer XYZ; Jennifer Heideman, sales account manager; and Kevin O'Keefe, engineering manager and technical platform manager XYZ, positions they held at the time of the case study in 2001.

10. Information in this section drawn from materials provided by team leader via correspondence, October 5, 2001.

11. The text in this section is solely the responsibility of Arlen Leholm and Ray Vlasin.

6

Michigan State University Extension and Ohio State University Extension Self-Directed Teams

▶ Margaret Bethel, James Kells, James Chatfield,
Arlen Leholm, and Ray Vlasin

Why the MSUE and OSUE Cases

The Michigan State University Extension (MSUE) and Ohio State University Extension (OSUE) cases offer examples of high-performing teams in the public university sector. Three short case studies are presented, one of an administrative support team and two of virtual educational teams. The importance of being analytical about the role of administrative support functions and organizational basics for effective teams, including their helpful administrative boundary conditions, is described in the MSUE cases. MSUE used a systems approach to high performance that included (1) shared leadership actions throughout the organization, (2) careful attention to team and organizational conditions in creating and sustaining more than thirty self-directed educational teams, and (3) direct connections to citizen-customers for program advice and political and financial support.

MSUE teams were permanent, self-directed in operation, and tightly linked to public leaders and groups. Their programs integrated educational outreach, research, and teaching missions; the teams were dedicated to enhancing their knowledge, skills, and capacity; and they were empowered with resources.

OSUE's self-directed landscape horticulture team is an example of a high-performing team with a heroic leader and shared leadership that creatively used divergent views and linked directly to an industry support structure for team empowerment and enhanced industry benefits.

The Snapshot

MSUE and OSUE constitute part of the land-grant university system established in the United States by the Morrill Act of 1862 and by the Smith-Lever Act of 1914, which created the Cooperative Extension Service. A land-grant university has three broad missions—teaching, research, and educational outreach. MSUE and OSUE are part of their respective universities' broad outreach mission. They are in the lifelong learning business with a mission of helping people help themselves. They directly engage their citizens in the lifelong learning process.

MSUE and OSUE each have more than a thousand faculty and staff members, some on the main university campuses in East Lansing, Michigan, and Columbus, Ohio, and others at county and regional offices located throughout the two states. Educational programming is conducted in the broad areas of agriculture and natural resources; children, youth, and families; community and economic development; and allied areas. These educational programs are conducted statewide in both rural and urban areas and supported by funding from federal, state, and county sources.

This chapter has two major components. The first discusses organizational support systems put in place by MSUE to accomplish its mission of lifelong learning. A regional administrative self-directed support team illustrates how an organization can proactively apply sound organizational basics to increase the function of its production teams—educational program teams in this case. The second part of this chapter describes two educational program teams that operate as virtual teams. One is from MSUE and the other is from OSUE. These high-performing teams are an application of virtual teams in an educational context.

One administrative support team and two educational teams that operated at very high levels provide key lessons that can be applied in a wide range of organizational environments. Members from the three teams contributed insights through a personal interview process.[1] The three teams were the MSUE Field Crops Team (an area of expertise [AOE] team), MSUE West Regional Administrative Team, and the Ohio State University Extension Nursery, Landscape, and Turf Team.

The self-directed team approach connected university faculty to stakeholders and tied research to outreach education with an interdisciplinary problem-solving focus that produced results for a wide range of priority issues. A trend of enhanced motivation among campus and off-campus team members and stronger credibility with stakeholders emerged as a result of the self-directed team approach. Improved credibility translated into renewed stakeholder pride in "their" land-grant university and helped ensure continued public support. The systemwide achievements covered here indicate that the self-directed team approach can be very beneficial for educational organizations.

Crucial Role of Organizational Support Systems for MSUE Teams

MSUE launched self-directed work teams in 1994. Because of this comprehensive action, in which it created a number of educational program development teams, it dramatically increased the quality, timeliness, and relevance of products and services to its stakeholders. This action was taken cooperatively by administrators, program leaders, on-campus specialists and off-campus educators, and regional directors for MSUE. It was taken in cooperation with the administrators and faculty colleagues from MSU's academic research units.

Described here are the broader support systems in which MSUE's self-directed teams were created, operated, and supported. Improvements made in MSUE's support systems played a major role in propelling the self-directed educational teams to higher performance levels. These changes emphasize the fact that teams were built within a supportive organizational structure, and not built in a vacuum.

SUPPORT SYSTEMS ADJUSTED

To enhance support systems for teams, MSUE made adjustments in five systems—personnel, communication and information technology, core competency, finance, and evaluation and recognition.

❶ *Personnel System:* Stakeholders were directly involved in personnel search committees for both off-campus and on-campus teams.

❷ *Communication and information technology system:* MSUE invested during the mid-1990s to make sure the geographically disperse "virtual" team members could be connected electronically to e-mail, listservs, two-way interactive computer video systems, satellite uplink and downlink capabilities, and backup technical support. Communication strategies and support systems are especially important for virtual teams.

❸ *Core competency system:* MSUE identified the core competencies required for effective educational outreach. This was done systematically using a self-assessment applied to measure the level of competence possessed by individual team members. A curriculum was built for each of the core competencies, which were provided centrally for all teams. The ten core competency areas include (1) professional development, (2) written and spoken communication, (3) program implementation, (4) organizational knowledge, leadership, and management, (5) marketing and public relations, (6) education and information technology, (7) program planning and development, (8) applied research and evaluation, (9) diversity and pluralism, and (10) audience identification and development. Technical competencies were designed and provided by each AOE team for its members.

❹ *Finance systems:* MSUE provided base-level operating dollars to each of the AOE teams and decentralized decision making regarding use of those support dollars. However, the accounting function for those funds remained centralized to keep that burden from the teams.

❺ *Evaluation and recognition system:* For off-campus team members, a portion of each individual's compensation was based on the overall performance of the team.

EARLY ORGANIZATIONAL SUPPORT FOR AOE TEAMS AT MSUE

In the early 1990s, MSUE went through a major strategic planning and reorganization process. One of the organization's concerns was growing dissatisfaction from the users, especially large agricultural interests, which did not feel that they were getting the quality of assistance that they needed to make timely decisions affecting profitability. At the time, MSUE was organized with educational program leaders and faculty specialists located at the central campus and generalist agricultural educators at the county level.

In 1992, Arlen Leholm arrived at MSUE as associate director and was greeted by complaints from the Extension's agricultural constituents, who were unhappy at the level of educational programs being delivered by educators at the county level. Some constituents also complained of a perceived disconnect on campus among colleges and among campus departments relevant to the constituents' needs. These stakeholders said that Extension was becoming a dinosaur, not worthy of the considerable support it receives from the state legislature. Leholm and colleagues knew it would take more than tinkering at the margins to meet the expectations of this constituent group. Needed was a new set of entities focused on specific areas of need with the requisite Extension and research expertise. These entities would be flexible, largely self-directed teams, linked to stakeholders and their needs.

Very few public organizations at the time had launched such self-directed teams. Leholm and his colleagues at MSUE were not aware of any

U.S. Extension organizations that had developed self-directed teams around areas of expertise. Many had committees that coordinated educational outreach and research functions, but they had not developed ongoing, integrated, self-directed, research-outreach education teams that served as the program creation and delivery unit. Certainly none had redesigned their educational delivery system around self-directed teams. They knew they would have to look primarily to the private sector for guidance.

As a first step in the development of AOE teams, Michigan agricultural interests were asked what they wanted from their land-grant institution. They responded that they wanted a quality, cutting-edge educational product from Extension and research that was timely and customer-focused with a multidisciplinary systems approach to problem solving. Stakeholders did not distinguish Extension programs from research programs. MSUE responded by involving its stakeholders in the design and implementation of customer-focused, self-directed AOE teams charged with responsibility for meeting the stakeholders' applied research and educational needs.

A new structure was created to generate greater contact between state-level researchers and the user community. Commodity-based AOE teams eventually were created to more systematically link research and technical staff with users. As an initial action, some boundary conditions were established for the organization and operation of AOE teams. These guidelines helped to reduce uncertainty in team-organizational relationships as teams progressed.

BOUNDARY CONDITIONS FOR MSUE AOE TEAMS

A committee representing the range of potential interests during the formation of the initial AOE teams created eight boundary conditions, which constituted some key "what-to-do" rather than "how-to-do" items. They served as supportive conditions for the creation and operation of teams and for their movement from solid performance to very high performance.

❶ *Mission, vision, and operating guidelines:* Each AOE team was asked to develop a microvision and micromission that would align the team and the organization. These would provide a basis on which the team could build its goals and objectives, its core values and operating principles.

❷ *Customer/problem-solving focus:* Each AOE team was asked to develop a customer-focused and/or problem-focused program directly beneficial to those served. It should be directly consistent with the knowledge-based educational and technical assistance orientation of MSUE. Furthermore, it would link research, Extension, and those served.

❸ *Active involvement of stakeholders:* Teams should develop a clear picture of the stakeholders being served and their geographic concentrations. Teams also should address ways to seek and obtain stakeholder input for their programs—as advisers to or members of specific projects and/or programs or through other means. Stakeholders could be involved in designing, performing, and assessing projects and programs, including possible local/community research applications.

❹ *Regional distribution of expertise:* The organization and the team would strive to achieve appropriate regional distribution of team expertise across the state consistent with stakeholders' needs. The distribution would enhance the availability of and access to such expertise and would open new creative possibilities for expertise trades among counties within regions, with each off-campus educator having a home-county base.

❺ *Curricula, staff development:* Each AOE team would address what knowledge and skills were needed to enable it best to perform its microvision and micromission and reach its goals and objectives. Teams would identify technical content knowledge/skills as well as process knowledge/skills that would benefit team performance. Based on those analyses, within-AOE and across-AOE staff development—knowledge and skill building—were undertaken. Leadership for technical knowledge/skills came from within the teams, while team process skills and other core competency skills (those common to all teams) would be provided centrally.

❻ *Mentoring:* Each AOE team would provide or otherwise arrange for mentoring opportunities for team members who sought and could benefit from such mentoring. Mentoring would be self-selected rather than assigned.

❼ *Entrepreneurship:* Each AOE team would be entrepreneurial about its resources and programs. Funds made available from MSUE would be used to leverage community and other funding opportunities to conduct necessary programs. Some operating money would be provided to each team. Entrepreneurial teams would be self-rewarded by a wider range of resources and cooperators.

❽ **On- and off-campus** *co-chairs:* To ensure MSUE personnel easy access to the teams and their capabilities, teams were required to select one person from off campus and one person from campus to serve as team co-chairs. This arrangement also would help ensure that each team gave full representation to on- and off-campus views and considerations.

These boundary conditions have served the MSU AOE teams well. The boundary conditions have continued to be helpful since their inception more than ten years ago. The initial 1994 teams were for Livestock, Dairy, and Field Crops, but by 2003 some twenty-eight AOE teams were operating over the full range of the MSUE mission.

DEVELOPING A CURRICULUM

Consistent with the boundary conditions for staff development, a process called developing a curriculum (DACUM) served as an initial step in creating teamwide general areas of competency in both technical and process skills. DACUM helped educators to be effective AOE team members.[2] Under DACUM, Extension educators and specialists who excelled at their jobs were asked to explain in their own language what they do and how they do it and to develop a profile of the skills team member need to effectively perform their jobs. These DACUM results were used to build curricula for staff development and to develop job descriptions for new AOE team members. The DACUM process helped the teams be analytical about technical and core competencies required for team members and the team to succeed.

Stakeholders in agriculture were involved in reviewing the DACUM results and providing input on the general areas of competency expected and required from an AOE educator. The DACUM process helped to develop internal and external ownership of the AOE teams and their educational functions. For several teams, the DACUM process had an added benefit of building communication and trust among members of the potential team where it may not have existed before.

EXTENSION, RESEARCH, AND CLIENTELE LINKAGES

Linking Extension and research functions has been a considerable challenge to land-grant institutions. A seamless interface between Extension and research is central to meeting the future needs of an information-based society. Self-directed teams have potential to help make the seamless interface possible and effective.

One of MSUE's most important goals was to achieve a seamless interface between Extension and research. The two areas were closely integrated to enhance the effectiveness and relevancy of these two key land-grant functions in serving the needs of Michigan's citizens. The close integration of Extension and research helped to keep educational outreach and research priorities consistent with Michigan citizens' priorities.

Figure 6.1 illustrates the AOE team approach, with campus and off-campus educators working together as an integrated team. This approach maximized the potential for improving both the research and

FIGURE 6.1. RESEARCH, EXTENSION, AND CITIZEN PARTNERSHIPS AND LINKAGES

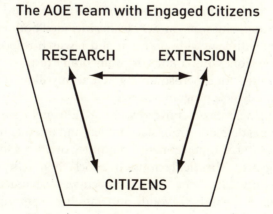

The AOE Team with Engaged Citizens

RESEARCH   EXTENSION

CITIZENS

educational outreach functions. The AOE teams also actively involved their citizen-customers, resulting in a dramatic increase in timeliness, effectiveness, and impact.

Along with creating strong linkages among campus researchers, Extension faculty, and off-campus educators, it was essential to continuously develop, nurture, and use partnership relationships with industry and customer-citizen groups. A key to effectively meeting their needs was to involve them directly in identifying those needs and to engage them actively in the research and educational outreach. This involvement included problem identification and clarification, research and analyses, applications of results, and delivery of Extension education with and for clientele. In addition, citizen stakeholders were involved in the hiring decisions for new AOE team employments.

Crucial Context for MSUE Teams

At MSUE, AOE teams constituted a highly trained group of Extension and research faculty and staffers who directly involved citizens in educational outreach functions. The AOE teams were fully responsible for planning, implementing, and evaluating educational programs in a self-directed manner. Most teams contained between ten and twenty members, with every member of the team sharing responsibility for performance. Team members developed specialties through a series of in-depth training and educational opportunities and integrated knowledge from several disciplines. Recognition and some compensation were linked to team performance. A portion of team members' compensation was linked to their performance through merit team awards.

The Extension educators on AOE teams included both university faculty members with statewide outreach and research responsibility and Extension educators with county or multicounty responsibility. Trades across county lines for expertise among AOE teams allowed for both specialization and diverse program coverage.

Within Michigan State University, the AOE teams were formed as a result of external demands from stakeholders and internal recommendations from the 1992 Empowerment Committee of Michigan's Council of Extension Agents.[3] The field crops, livestock, and dairy teams were launched in early 1994. The AOE approach was expanded in 1995 to include teams for children, youth and families, community, natural resources, and economic development, tourism, state and local government, and leadership development. The AOE teams addressed issues in rural, urban, and metropolitan environments.

Development of MSUE's AOE Model

FOCUSED EXPERTISE

An AOE team planned, implemented, and evaluated educational programs that met the needs of Michigan citizens in some targeted problem or opportunity area (figure 6.2). Each team included off-campus educators, specialists (those having both Extension and research appointments), and selected others (such as customers and cooperators) with interest and expertise in the area of focus—a particular farming system, food industry, or educational specialty. Within an area of expertise, the team may have defined one or more specializations. For example, the livestock AOE team created beef cattle, swine, sheep, and equine subgroups.

WORKABLE ARRANGEMENTS

Teams did not have specific size requirements except that they could not be so large as to render them ineffective. Each AOE team included some campus-based members with expertise that linked to one or more university academic units as well as county educators willing and able to partner with them. Each team developed its microvision, mission, and operating procedures in a way that was consistent with those of MSUE.

The AOE team had co-chairs that provided leadership on a rotating basis (usually one to two years, depending on the team's operating procedures). Co-chairs were selected by the team and served as program/team facilitators. They did not have administrative or supervisory roles. Campus department chairs conducted performance appraisals for the campus-based faculty AOE specialists, while county Extension directors or regional directors conducted performance appraisals for the AOE off-campus educators. A particular strength was the exchange among chairs and Extension supervisors of input from county educators about campus specialists' contributions to teams and from campus specialists about county educators' contributions to teams.

GIFURE 6.2. MSUE'S AREA OF EXPERTISE MODEL

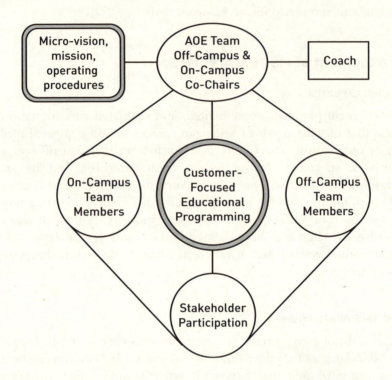

A coach served each team, helping to reduce barriers, fostering team development training, serving as "wise counsel," and communicating within, among, and beyond the teams. The coach also provided an important coordinating function across AOE teams for the development of complementary programs and effective resource and budget strategies. Each coach served approximately six teams in complementary program areas. Over time, the coaches became less involved in the internal aspects of teams and more involved in relationships among teams. The coach's role was essential for team performance even with mature teams.

SELF-DIRECTED WITH SUPPORT

The teams were expected to be self-directed in all aspects of their educational programming throughout the state. Each team developed plans for program delivery and team capacity enhancement. The teams assessed and prioritized customer needs, planned and implemented educational responses to meet stakeholder needs, mentored new team members, and developed team expertise. Teams also evaluated program impacts and documented team progress.

Technical support was available for program evaluation. Interpersonal or "soft" skills training required for effective team performance were provided centrally for all the AOE teams. Technical skills required for each AOE team's operation were designed by the AOE team, starting with the DACUM process. Many teams developed and implemented a curriculum for their AOE team members.

The Extension director's office allocated funds for starting up teams. The funds were used to assess stakeholder needs through focus-group interviews, to enable participation in out-of-state training programs, to procure reference materials, to acquire computer software, and to cover team travel and logistical needs. Beginning in 1996, teams received operating budgets for their priority programming. Teams were encouraged to look for external funding, and a number sought and secured significant additional outside resources.

GROWTH IN TEAM APPROACHES

The number of MSUE teams has grown almost tenfold since 1994. Some approaches to team formation were the same for all the teams, such as the boundary conditions, the use of DACUM or similar means for identifying the competency required in technical skills and process capabilities, and the development of a team's microvision, mission, and operating procedures. However, human resources available for the individual teams, particularly on-campus faculty, varied substantially, requiring a range of approaches to team formation, operation, and support.

PROJECT TEAMS VITAL

An interdependent "project team" can provide the functional linkage needed among Extension, research, stakeholders, and other resource persons. Created by one or more AOE teams, a project team represents one excellent way in which a university truly can engage society.

The development of the concept of a project team had a very positive influence on the success of the AOE teams. The project team was a short-term team connected to AOE teams that provided an applied research product or service for issues identified by MSUE's stakeholders or citizen groups. Project teams created and used by the AOE teams included both AOE members and non-AOE members (as depicted in figure 6.3). Project teams also were created between or among several teams to solve interdisciplinary issues beyond the boundaries of an individual AOE team. Often, faculty members who lacked Extension or research appointments were willing to contribute to the applied research efforts because funding for the project teams was provided. The project team approach was more familiar to them and did not involve a long-term commitment. The coaches facilitated formation of these cross-disciplinary project teams.

These project teams developed competitive proposals for funding their applied community action research projects. They received some support and could compete for added internal MSUE and other funds. Project teams also were encouraged to use their limited funds to pursue and leverage external funds. Project teams have succeeded in all educational programming areas and have tapped talent that otherwise would not have been available to the AOE teams. At the same time, the AOE teams provided continuity to the stakeholders for long-term educational programming.

MSUE demonstrated that project teams can operate within or with a larger self-directed team. MSUE's Field Crops AOE Team, with fifty-two

FIGURE 6.3. PROJECT TEAMS AS CRUCIAL COMPONENTS OF AOE TEAMS

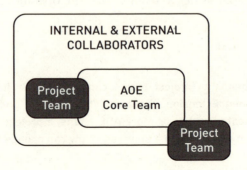

members at the time, used a number of individual project teams to link with stakeholders and to bring research results and Extension education programs to clientele. The project teams were small, efficient, and workable. They readily involved stakeholders and determined stakeholder needs. They created specific performance goals and objectives, involved the most appropriate research and Extension professionals, recruited and involved other professionals, established performance criteria and timelines, and achieved intended outcomes.

COMPREHENSIVE STAKEHOLDER INVOLVEMENT

A comprehensive stakeholder involvement system was developed by MSUE and is illustrated in Figure 6.4. The stakeholder system proved invaluable and connected to stakeholders in three ways.

❶ *Advisory committees for the AOE teams* were comprised of stakeholders who had an interest in a particular issue; they gave advice to specific AOE teams and sometimes influenced MSU's research agenda.

❷ *County Extension committees* were developed in 1996 and initiated in 1997. The committees represent all the voices in a county and performed three functions: (1) educational program needs assessment and direction, (2) advocacy of Extension efforts with policy makers, and (3) leadership development within the county's communities. Some of the AOE advisory committee members were members of the county Extension committees.

❸ *The State Extension and Research Council* was made up of eighteen members from the county Extension councils and six members at large. This council provided invaluable advice to MSUE on a wide range of issues and served as a key political advocate for Extension at state and federal levels.

All the AOE teams involved their stakeholder or citizen groups. Stakeholder participation ranged from active and continuous involvement through all stages of a team's development to more selective and occasional involvement. Several of the teams formalized stakeholder involvement with advisory/partnership committees whose members served a

FIGURE 6.4. STAKEHOLDER INVOLVEMENT

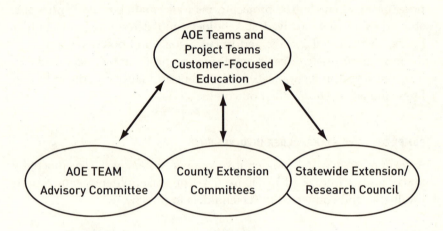

two-year term. These advisory committees explored needs and possible programs and evaluated the team's impact on critical issues. AOE teams actively involved stakeholders in project teams and specific projects and programs.

MSUE also involved citizens formally through the county Extension committees. Committees in all eighty-three Michigan counties provided strong collective voices. Complementing these county committees was a State Extension and Research Council. Both the county committees and the state council understood MSUE's role and could explain to key policy makers the value of the entire MSUE system and its programs. Having citizen involvement at these two levels significantly strengthened MSUE's AOE team programs. Furthermore, rural and urban interests began to understand diverse needs and possibilities and the common ground that linked them.

OTHER SUPPORTIVE ADMINISTRATIVE ACTIONS

Creation of the self-directed teams was undertaken in an environment of shared leadership across MSUE. It resulted in shared budgets that were decentralized to the regions of Michigan and shared responsibility between campus and off-campus personnel for decisions and actions pertaining to educational program coverage across the state. One key innovation was to move from position replacement to the concept of program coverage, which proved immensely more flexible in its application and more effective in providing needed programs to stakeholders. It would change the way MSUE did business for the foreseeable future.

The creation of the self-directed teams, along with the creation of County Advisory Committees and a State Advisory Council involving a broad range of stakeholders in Extension programs, changed MSUE's program, political, and financial support. During the past decade, MSUE has undergone both operational and structural changes. Today, state and regional educational programs are planned and delivered largely through twenty-nine self-directed teams of Extension educators and researchers popularly known as AOE teams. These AOE teams are based on common issues, connected by technology, and empowered by their own leadership and by support systems from the organization.

RESULTING TEAM PERFORMANCE

MSUE's experience with the development and operation of AOE teams ranged broadly. Several of the teams were judged to be very high performing. The majority of teams were solid high-level performers, with a few not meeting expectations. Almost all of the AOE teams performed their mission levels far higher than was the case before the AOE teams were created.

Detailed evaluations of six of the AOE teams in 1996 and again in 1999 revealed very satisfied customers.[4] Moreover, the AOE teams that faltered did so because they failed to adhere to team basics or because they reported to a team leader who was unable or unwilling to empower the team members. A few teams failed to truly establish a mission, vision, or shared work plan. They were reconstituted or closed out.

MSUE's ten-year experience with self-directed teams has resulted in enhanced staff motivation and retention, increased credibility with stakeholders, and a larger statewide pool of skills from which to draw as a means of meeting its citizens' educational outreach needs. The resulting organizational self-esteem has been high.

The West Regional Administrative Team, described below, represents another form of organizational support put in place by MSUE to increase the effectiveness of its educational programming. A shared leadership approach by this *administrative support team* plus a series of innovations proved to be a major success factor in maintaining educational program team effectiveness. Also it resulted in new entrepreneurship and enhanced ownership for problem solving and for taking advantage of new opportunities by the local county staff.

MSUE West Regional Administrative Team

"We are committed to our staff, our most important asset. We will continue to build and empower county staff teams that are well trained and recognized as specialists in their fields. As a learning organization, we are committed to on-going professional development of all our employees. We support the commitment, creativity, entrepreneurial spirit, and multidisciplinary approach demonstrated in our work. We are committed to open organizational communication that promotes a healthy working environment. We believe in rewarding effective, scholarly work and recognize that it evolves from the complementary strengths of our off-campus and campus based staff. We celebrate the joy, passion, satisfaction and fun our staff derives from bringing knowledge to life."[5]

ADMINISTRATIVE CONTEXT

In 1996, newly appointed MSUE Extension Director Leholm rallied his top administrative team and reflected on the early successes of the AOE teams. Nearly twenty AOE teams had been launched by that date, and many were exceeding expectations. Collectively, the administrative team made the judgment that while the self-directed (AOE) teams represented a great way to improve the educational delivery network, other improvements would be needed to achieve long-term organizational success.

Federal and state budget shortfalls were extremely challenging. Without additional innovative approaches to Extension education, the AOE teams' good work would be threatened. The MSUE administrative team had been modeling shared leadership practices since 1992 under Director Gail Imig (who departed in early 1996), Associate Director Leholm, state educational program leaders, and a regional team of district directors, including Maggie Bethel, who became the West Region director in 1992. The top administrative team, bolstered by the major success of the AOE teams, made a leap of faith, committing to more extensive shared leadership.

Starting in July 1996, Leholm started sharing salary savings from all off-campus staff vacancies with the counties. All salary savings previously had been held centrally, with the director making decisions on position reinvestment. After one year of closely monitoring the regions' capacity to handle this new level of responsibility and accountability, the regions were fully empowered to create new approaches to staff vacancies. The regional directors and MSUE's director crafted the approach for making regional staffing decisions. These guidelines delineated the ground rules so that everyone knew what to expect.

The new guidelines stated that all salary savings accrued within a region would stay in that region. The regions would return to the director's office one-sixth of the total vacancy dollar savings to handle structural deficits resulting from state and federal budget shortfalls. The regions could make the decisions but were jointly accountable with the director to be fiscally responsible—the budget had to balance. The regional directors, in turn, formed a committee of county Extension directors that would bear responsibility for developing a regional staffing plan and making hiring decisions regarding which positions would be filled at the county level.

TRIGGERING EVENT

Events sometimes trigger a change in the way a group or team performs. Such a triggering event occurred for the West Regional Administrative Team. Maggie Bethel stated, "Once the management team trusted their empowered status, not only their mind-set changed, but the change in team member behavior was equally dramatic. During times of tight financial resources, where there once would have been complaints about what 'they' [central administration] were not filling in positions, shifted to how 'we' can leverage our resources to achieve educational program coverage. Also, dramatically diminished was the competition among team members for resources for their particular unit, which shifted to working together as a team to apply resources across geographic boundaries and units."

In the process of developing the staffing planning guidelines, Bethel experienced a triggering thought that stimulated a change in mental models: "What if we switched our thinking from replacing a specific job position to one where we would think about our most pressing educational program needs and how we could provide program coverage geographically across county boundaries? In essence, don't tell me what position you don't have; tell me what you need in program delivery." Bethel's revelation freed the organization from a "concept prison" of simply replacing vacated positions, permitting innovative program coverage through creative program staffing arrangements. This process included asking staffers to develop interdisciplinary skill sets, increase leveraging of partner resources, and expand networking.

The MSUE West Regional Administrative Team practiced an open-books budgeting policy, allowing anyone to review its financial records. The team established operating guidelines agreed to by all team members. They sought to move the team from a mind-set of competition for internal resources to one of leveraging external resources. As trust increased among team members, subteams became empowered to make decisions between meetings of the entire team. All staff members within the region were asked to provide creative input to the regional team, resulting in the implementation of many innovative ideas.

Expanding and sharing authority for staffing decisions and moving those decisions closer to the ultimate citizen-customer was augmented by the decision to empower regional staffers to find new funding partnerships. The only caveat was that the new funding partnership had to be central to MSUE's mission. In one case, a thirty-five thousand dollar salary savings that previously would have stayed at the state central office was leveraged fivefold, all within MSUE's mission.

MEMBERSHIP OF REGIONAL TEAM

MSUE was divided into six Michigan districts. The West Regional Team comprised fourteen counties. Each Extension office was led by a county Extension director, with educators covering programs in agriculture, family living, youth, community and economic development, and natural resources. With additional empowerment of local county Extension educators, Bethel and her team of county Extension directors built operating procedures and a microvision and mission as a regional administrative team. They formed subteams to design and carry out various management roles. One subteam received responsibility for rewarding both teams and individual members who performed at very high levels.

JOINT WORK PRODUCT

The MSUE West Regional Team needed to operate as a real team. They had to work together to develop staffing plans, and the resulting hiring decisions required joint action by the entire team because all counties would be affected by all decisions. Instead of sitting back and giving in to budget shortfalls, team members became very strategic and proactive. They used some of the salary savings now in their control to hire a part-time grants person, resulting in substantial increases in short-term project money plus money to leverage new staff positions, thereby increasing further the positive impacts of the AOE program teams.

KEY VARIABLES FOR REGIONAL TEAM

Both organizational variables and team variables played important roles in the West Regional Administrative Team's high performance:

> Shared leadership actions throughout the team;
> Entrepreneurial approaches to financial and human resources;
> Citizen and stakeholder involvement in establishing educational priorities;
> Clarity of vision and mission for the team;
> Commitment of the team to performance goals;
> High professional respect among team members and administrators;
> High levels of trust among the team members and between the team and regional director.

STATEWIDE IMPACT

Across the state, the combination of having salary savings accrue to the regions and empowering regional directors and regional staffing teams proved pathbreaking. County and other local recurring dollar support grew between 1997 and 2000 from twelve to twenty-one million dollars.

TRANSFORMATIONAL EDUCATION INFUSED

Under Bethel's leadership, the West Regional Team initiated the concept of transformational education. At the end of 2000, Bethel succeeded the departing Leholm as MSUE's director. Bethel continued the organization's shared leadership and AOE team opportunity and extended the concept of transformational education to the entire MSUE organization. She sought to meld the concepts of shared leadership, the system of AOE teams, and empowerment of county staff into the highest possible enduring benefits for local citizens.

Extension organizations traditionally have focused on information delivery, technology transfer, and facilitation. In transformational education, locally based educators who work with a community of interest over a significant period of time build on the social capital and leadership in communities to make sustainable advancements. The currency of social capital is trust. MSUE's AOE teams build ongoing trust relationships with clientele groups on a wide range of issues. Combining locally based educators who have earned social capital with university-based faculty who have specific expertise can result in powerful impacts. Together, in direct partnership with a local community of interest, they can produce even more significant benefits through their trust relationships. These impacts can transform a community of interest, result in significantly new community capabilities, and make huge differences in individual lives.

Dynamics of Shared Leadership for Regional Team

The most influential variable identified by team members that propelled the MSUE West Regional Administrative Team to its very high performance levels was *shared leadership*. Figure 6.5 illustrates the influence of the shared leadership variable at three levels of intensity.

In diagram 1, during 1994–96, shared leadership level 1 is accomplished by creation of self-directed teams. Together they influenced the level of performance, performance level 1. In 1996, the MSUE administrative team decided to decentralize budget and hiring decisions to the regional level (environment 1), causing a higher intensity in the shared leadership variable as shown in diagram 2. With decentralized decision making in the hands of the regional director and her county Extension directors, performance elevated to performance level 2 and resulted in a new environment, environment 2, in which the regional team felt so empowered that it leveraged human and financial resources. This in turn caused the shared leadership variable to intensify further to level 3,

FIGURE 6.5. SHARED LEADERSHIP: DIAGRAMS 1, 2, AND 3

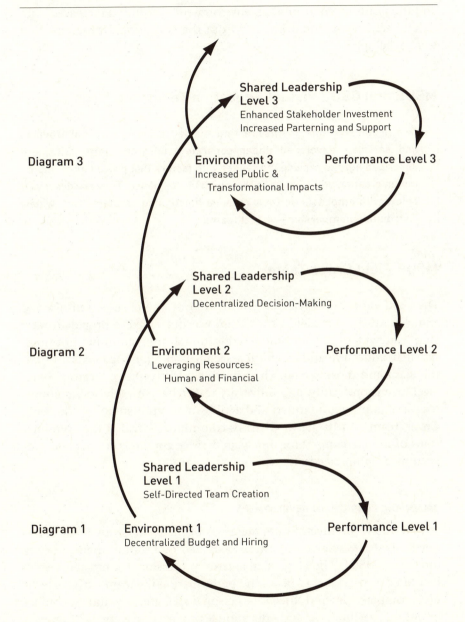

Diagram 3

**Shared Leadership
Level 3**
Enhanced Stakeholder Investment
Increased Parterning and Support

Environment 3
Increased Public &
Transformational Impacts

Performance Level 3

Diagram 2

**Shared Leadership
Level 2**
Decentralized Decision-Making

Environment 2
Leveraging Resources:
Human and Financial

Performance Level 2

Diagram 1

**Shared Leadership
Level 1**
Self-Directed Team Creation

Environment 1
Decentralized Budget and Hiring

Performance Level 1

as shown in diagram 3. Performance then rose to performance level 3, and the resulting environment, environment 3, featured increased public and transformational impacts from the educational programs that were developed.

MSUE and OSUE Virtual Education Teams

Two virtual education teams creating and delivering educational products and services, developed under separate land-grant universities, are described here to provide the reader with factors that proved most important in creating and sustaining their high performance. They are described below with emphasis on their creative functioning as teams with widely distributed membership—virtual teams.

MSUE Field Crops Team

The Field Crops AOE Team began in 1994 as one of three self-directed teams at MSUE. The Field Crops Team was organized to provide leadership statewide in determining educational programming priorities, research, education and technical assistance, and training needs for both the team and those served. The team included county educators, state-level Extension faculty, and university researchers. An advisory committee was comprised of farmers and agribusiness representatives. The Field Crops Team and its active advisory committee provided the combinations of inputs required for timely analysis of current concerns and projections of future needs.

DACUM AND CURRICULUM DEVELOPMENT

In May 1994, seventeen future members of the Field Crops Team developed a DACUM analysis that was facilitated by Leholm, then associate director of MSUE. Fifteen general areas of professional competency were identified as necessary to be a solid performer on the team—twelve technical competencies and three interpersonal skill areas, including conflict resolution, facilitation, and educational program delivery. Within each general area of competency, the tasks that would have to be performed ranged from that required for a new team member to tasks that the most veteran team members would have to master to meet the performance levels expected by the team.

Using the DACUM analysis, the team then developed a core curriculum for mastering technical skills. The curriculum for mastering competency in the "soft skills" identified by the team would be provided centrally by MSUE. The technical curriculum designed and delivered by the team included foundation training through four short courses: (1) pest management, (2) soil management, (3) crop management, and (4) farm financial management. Two of these courses were taught per year, with the entire curriculum repeated in a two-year cycle.

The DACUM process provided the team with a helpful starting point, even though many of the members would have preferred to begin by developing a mission statement and a common working approach. Focusing first on the DACUM analysis created a readiness to move on to other components of the Field Crops Team. The team members had a history of working well together on committees and on special projects. Still, the experience of being analytical about the competencies was new to them, and it energized the entire group's thinking.

FIELD CROPS MISSION

Having addressed both technical competencies and team process competencies that likely would be needed, the Field Crops Team clarified its mission:

> The Field Crops Team is a group of county and state Extension staff working together to help crop producers improve themselves, their businesses, and their environment through an educational process that applies knowledge, demonstration, and research to critical issues, needs, and opportunities.

The team then addressed the ways in which it would carry out this mission and created operating procedures.

LAUNCH OF AOE TEAM

The Field Crops AOE Team started operating in June 1994 along with the Livestock and Dairy AOE Teams. Three teams had to be launched at the same time because MSUE lacked adequate resources to have a skilled county educator in each of these areas in every county. Each county educator on the three teams had a home county base even though the educator would serve more than one county. Further, the elected Michigan county commissioners would be made aware of the reasons for making this change in operations to meet citizens' needs.

Trades for professional Extension services then occurred across geographic county boundaries with only a minor internal resistance and virtually no external resistance. MSUE took a very analytical approach to this step, seeking to avoid problems that had arisen elsewhere; several other states had tried a multicounty approach that placed people in regional offices disconnecting them from the counties. Some experienced great harm to performance outcomes and to their Extension organization. In summary, necessary specialization through the initial three AOE teams was accomplished through multicounty trades in program coverage while preserving the strong political capital relationships and program support that existed at the local county Extension offices.

TEAM MEMBERSHIP

Eventually, the Field Crops Team grew to fifty-two members–thirty-six off-campus county educators and sixteen campus faculty specialists from five academic departments (agricultural economics, agricultural engineering, botany and plant pathology, crop and soil sciences, and entomology) located in two colleges on the MSU campus. The Field Crops Team knew that such a large real team would be too cumbersome to be effective for many of the performance challenges it would face. However, the members recognized that having a comprehensive team to coordinate priorities with an advisory committee could be a big advantage. They chose to keep the fifty-two-person team for coordinating program priorities but to break into subteams around key priority educational programming areas, with co-chairs for each key priority area.

The overall team chose co-leaders—one from on campus and one from off campus—who would rotate on a two-year basis. James Kells served as the first on-campus co-chair, and Dan Rossman served as the first off-campus co-chair. The team asked Kells to continue as on-campus co-chair for the first six years, while the off-campus co-chair rotated every year. According to Kells, "In the early stages, the Field Crops Team had some difficulty in getting support from line department administrators. They also had trouble in convincing their own peers that such teams would have the authority to determine programming strategies and actually direct funding allocations. However, over time those doubts were removed."

FIELD CROPS ADVISORY COMMITTEE

The external advisory committee consisted of twenty-five members: twelve farmers (two from each of Michigan's six Extension regions) selected by AOE Team members, twelve commodity representatives selected by their respective commodity groups, and one industry representative selected by the Michigan Agribusiness Association. The advisory committee members served two-year terms, reviewing the team's progress and helping to identify future priorities.

TEAM OPERATING GOALS

The Field Crops Team identified its key roles and responsibilities and established a series of operating goals:

> Fitting team vision and mission with state vision and mission;
> Active and continuous involvement of citizens/stakeholders;
> Issues identification and program planning;
> Identifying the general areas of competency required to meet the team's vision, mission, and program impacts;
> Active and continuous entrepreneurial approaches to resources;
> Utilizing project teams/subgroups for enhanced engagement;
> Team member support—recruitment, mentoring, technical training, process, and other core competency training and team recognition;
> Program support—program coordination, budget management, external funding, impact assessment and evaluation, reporting, and marketing;
> Communication—within teams, across teams, and with program area, citizens/stakeholders, collaborators, and regional and national counterparts.

The Field Crops Team met many previously unsatisfied needs and tackled problems of larger size and scope than individual researchers or research teams would have been able to manage. The research and Extension interests were melded in new and more functional ways because of the mutual research, Extension, and client participation. The team began to develop and deliver more cutting-edge knowledge and to meet needs in a more timely manner. Local clientele developed a greater sense of ownership of the team's output and how it was achieved. Clientele became eager to receive the team's output, implement its recommendations, and encourage others to use those recommendations.

MANY PROGRAM IMPACTS

The Field Crops Team interacted with the broad base of research and Extension personnel at Michigan State University, as well as counterparts in the Michigan Department of Agriculture, the farmer and agribusiness community, and other key stakeholders. Team members monitored changes in the agricultural industry and predicted technical and economic concerns. The team became responsible for designing and overseeing new educational programs, information delivery, on-farm research and demonstration activities, and related agribusiness industry involvement. The AOE team's organizational structure helped farmers become more familiar with the people working to solve problems and have a greater voice in shaping the research and Extension agenda.

One interesting outcome that illustrates the impact of the Field Crops Team's performance was the development of a memorandum of understanding (MOU) with the sugar beet industry. Before creation of the Field Crops Team some sugar beet industry members had strongly criticized Extension educators, viewing MSUE programs as having limited value for the industry. However, after the Field Crops Team had been in operation for several years, the sugar beet processors and producers became very pleased with its performance and offered to make a significant direct investment in the educational programs and to supplement the salary of one county educator for a three-year period. At the end of that initial MOU, the sugar beet industry was so pleased with educational assistance received that it made the MOU permanent, providing an excellent example of a public- and private-good partnership, and greatly increasing the MSUE Field Crops Team's capacity to deliver quality educational programs. Subsequently, the team received some seed money from the director's office and leveraged it five to seven times.

KEY ORGANIZATIONAL VARIABLES

The organizational variables that were significant to this team were discussed in more detail earlier in this chapter. The most important organizational variables included a high commitment to the team, shared leadership, empowerment, development of support systems, creation of helpful boundary conditions, assistance in curriculum development for technical and soft skills, and support for professional development. Also important to successful implementation of the Field Crops AOE Team were four main factors: (1) adherence to team basics as described by Katzenbach, (2) recognition of organizational basics, including a supportive environment for the teams, (3) an Extension administration that understood and practiced a shared-leadership and empowerment philosophy, and (4) an Extension and research administration that supported the teams created.

KEY TEAM VARIABLES FOSTERING HIGH PERFORMANCE

The Field Crops Team was clearly a very high performing team. Its key constituents both state- and nationwide recognized its achievements. Although much could be written about the team and its close fit with the organization, some team variables played a particularly important role in its high performance:

> Clear focus on performance;
> Clarity of goals and objectives;
> Engaging citizen-customers at high levels;
> High professional respect among team members and of administration;
> Increasing levels of trust over time;
> High emphasis on subteams taking leadership actions;
> Members comfortable in leadership roles and as followers;
> Strong on evaluation of their impacts in metrics important to their clientele;
> Attention to both team curriculum and professional development;
> Emergence of team spirit.

The very high performing Field Crops AOE Team had an intensity not found in most of the other MSUE AOE teams. The level of caring and respect among team members was very high, enthusiasm approached zeal at times, and creativity and performance were extremely high. Mutual respect was high, as was mutual accountability. Levels of burnout and staff turnover were very low. Members of this team described their team's spirit as a major factor in its performance and members stated that their personal spirits had been energized through their active involvement on the team.

Ohio State University Extension Nursery, Landscape, and Turf Team

The Ohio State University Extension Nursery, Landscape, and Turf Team (OSUE Team), distributed across the state, was comprised of fifteen active core members and some twenty additional members. Together they contributed to a mission of delivering accurate, practical, and timely educational resources to the Ohio nursery, landscape, and turf industries. The OSUE team members represent a wide range of interdisciplinary backgrounds with faculty located on campus and with county and regional educators throughout the state. The team actively engaged industry partnerships to achieve their performance objectives.

TRIGGERING EVENT

The OSUE Team is an example of a team born out of crisis. Jim Chatfield, one of the team's key leaders, recalled the triggering event: "Crisis was the motherhood of invention, at least for this team. The Horticulture Department at Ohio State University was reduced from thirty to twenty-one faculty in the early 1990s as a result of a statewide budget crisis. Luther Waters, chairperson of the Horticulture Department, called a special meeting with faculty and industry representatives present where he laid it on the line. Waters exclaimed, 'Look, we are in a crisis here, budgetwise, and it isn't going to get better! I don't think this is just a temporary thing. Are we going to give up and stop delivering educational programs to our constituents, or can we change the way we do our work and somehow get the job done?'"

Two responses came from the people at the meeting. One group retorted, "We've had it. We don't have anything left. We don't have the resources anymore. We simply can't serve [the landscape, nursery, and turf industry] anymore." Others in the room said, "Now, wait a minute.

The Extension Landscape Nursery program is not dead. Look at the assets in this room. We have people in entomology, we have people in plant pathology, in horticulture and agronomy, and we have people with a research focus who may not have Extension appointments but may be able to help. Just look at all the county educators in this room. What if we got our act together and did a better job of coordinating all the assets that are left?"

At that point in the meeting, the president of the Ohio Nursery Association announced, "I like where this discussion is going. If you come to us in sixty days with a proposal of how you will be organized, what you will do for this industry, you will not be able to get to the bank fast enough to cash the check we will write you. We will partner with you to get the job done." Chatfield recalled, "The gauntlet had been laid down. Now we had to respond. It was fantastic as defining moments go."

INDUSTRY PARTNERSHIP

Chatfield and his colleagues spent several months in 1992 developing the specifics of a proposal for their industry partner. The developing team members discussed with the Ohio Nursery Association the concept they had in mind. It was financial support from the industry beyond the current financial crises. Both partners agreed "that the money that the industry would provide would be for team development and not faculty salaries. It could be used by the team for specific uses for the partnership. The money was to make us a team, at that time, of about twenty people that they could call instead of the one person that had been their main contact and whose position was lost due to the budget crises." Ken Cochran, an original team member, recalled, "Chatfield flew into my office and said, 'I've got a good idea. We are going to lose key positions that will really hurt us. Why don't we just get together and do this team thing? Do you want to be part of this team with me?' I said I was interested, and I still am, ten years later. What I remember most was how enthusiastic Chatfield was and that I felt I could be part of his team."

Hannah Mathers, a recent addition to the team, added, "I've heard different accounts of what happened at that special meeting over a decade ago. But there clearly was a group who were just totally defeated by the loss of positions. Some individuals never recovered. Others took up the challenge. I believe with Jim Chatfield's leadership, our team has more than met the initial challenge and is operating at very high levels today."

HEROIC LEADER AND SHARED LEADERSHIP

The most distinguishing characteristic of this team was its key leader, Chatfield, and the development of a core group of team members who shared leadership actions. The OSUE Team practiced shared leadership, but it is doubtful that the team would have been formed or would have operated at high performance levels without Chatfield's presence and influence. Key leaders have the ability to create a vision and achieve wide ownership and acceptance for that vision among team members and cooperators.

ORGANIZATIONAL SUPPORT

OSUE's organizational support for the team was more enabling than strategic. Key organizational leaders supported the experiment without stepping in and saying, "Well, wait a minute. Now, you can't do that." The organization had a visionary district director, Barbara Ludwig, who had provided leadership for early experimentation with county-based educator specialization, achieving excellent results. Ludwig's efforts, along with top organizational leadership from Keith Smith, Bobby Moser, Don Pritchard, and Steve Baertsche in the early days, set the stage for the OSUE Team to form and try new approaches to delivering educational programs to a key industry constituency. Chatfield recalled, "The top leadership of the organization wanted to be informed and was very open to us creating something new that would build on the early county educator specialization."

KEY TEAM VARIABLES FOSTERING HIGH PERFORMANCE

Team leaders deliberately sought *divergent thinking* to get the best input from all team members and industry partners. The OSUE Team was particularly impressive in the way the members actively sought all ideas, regardless of source, before seeking convergence on a strategy or on specific actions. Erick Draper, a county educator on the team, claimed, "We trusted one another to know that even if we're challenged in an idea, that's fine because what we're all doing is challenging one another to become better."

Trust levels, particularly among core team members, were very high, with team members describing being a member of the team as the best part of their job. Several members described membership on the OSUE Team as not feeling like work and as a great deal of fun.

The team practiced *mentoring of new members.* This specific strategy addressed the need of new on-campus faculty members to achieve tenure within academic departments.

Caring among team members was especially high. Members readily stepped in to help members needing family time, assistance with particular problems, or assistance with professional needs.

The OSUE Team exemplified *communication strategies.* Sixteen team members initiated publication of *Buckeye Yard and Garden Line,* a weekly newsletter. A great deal of coordination was required to ensure the accuracy of horticulture reports. In the first two years of the team's operation, Chatfield and then one other colleague wrote all the newsletters. As trust and confidence built on the team, the number of contributors grew to ten, and the newsletter came to reflect a joint work product with an increasing amount of shared leadership actions over time, demonstrating the growth in team maturity and performance.

Lessons Learned[6]

FROM MSUE TEAMS

❶ *Shared leadership plus team basics and organizational basics are necessary conditions for high team performance.* The unleashing of creativity and entrepreneurship associated with the practice of shared leadership at MSU added a new level of performance not previously achieved. Most of the AOE teams in this shared leadership environment have performed very well, and a few have achieved unusually high performance. They have surpassed the expectations of their citizen stakeholders and Extension leaders.

❷ *Central to this shared leadership was a belief system of trust.* The MSUE administrative team held that the teams and their members should be trusted to do excellent work. The MSUE administrative team collectively believed that the organization bore the responsibility to provide teams with the support and resources necessary for success.

❸ *Self-directed work teams are not created in a vacuum.* The teams are created in an administrative support structure that can be positive, neutral, or negative. For MSUE, that structure complemented performance by the AOE teams through revised systems for personnel, communication and information technology, core competency, finance, and evaluation and recognition.

❹ *Helpful boundary conditions aid team effectiveness.* MSUE established boundary conditions that would be honored by all self-directed teams. These boundary conditions applied to all teams and added clarity to their mission.

❺ *During the early stages of AOE development, the rest of the parent organization—deans, department chairs, faculty, and county directors—must be brought along by directly involving a subset of them.* Not everyone will appreciate or support AOE teams in the early formation stages. In later stages of team development, a few very high performing teams may cause organizational anxiety and possible resentment. Careful attention to these matters and open communication can help to create a supportive organizational environment for high-performing teams.

❻ *Empowerment is crucial but not sufficient for very high performing teams.* An organization must both profess and practice empowering the teams through information, resources, shared authority, responsibility, and accountability. Disempowerment is possible and highly disruptive to team performance, and the organization must guard against this phenomenon.

❼ *Mentoring and coaching are functions crucial for team success.* The MSUE and OSUE teams developed a procedure for mentoring new members. Coaches assisted MSUE's teams, and without such assistance high team performance would have been difficult to achieve, particularly given the number of teams with multidisciplinary responsibilities. Without a coach to communicate within the teams, particularly during startup, and among and beyond the teams on an ongoing basis, self-directed teams would likely have looked inward and failed to see how their contributions fit into the broader organization. MSUE coaches provided wise counsel when asked and helped mentor the team co-chairs. The coaches also avoided doing things for the teams that the teams could do for themselves.

❽ *The power of new mental models can propel team performance.* MSUE's West Regional Administrative Team transformed its operation and greatly enhanced its effectiveness by changing its mind-set about fund use and position replacement. Under a shared administrative arrangement, the team received decision authority for providing needed educational content rather than for replacing vacated positions. The result was enhanced educational program coverage in which team members and their cooperators and stakeholders had high ownership. The increased ownership stimulated local partners to greatly increase their financial support.

❾ *Political effectiveness strategies proved valuable.* Any organization relying on public support must be attentive to political support to carry out its mission. MSUE's self-directed teams both benefited from and contributed to the organization's political effectiveness strategies. As part of these strategies, it was important that stakeholders knew about and owned the educational programs and the purposes they served. That closeness helped keep the teams targeted on stakeholder needs, informed the political process, and generated financial support.

FROM OSUE'S NURSERY, LANDSCAPE AND TURF TEAM

❿ *OSUE's Team illustrates how an organization can look to self-directed work teams as a possible way to reorganize when faced with a major challenge.* However, sound team and organizational basics must be applied to make the use of self-directed teams the logical and effective choice.

⓫ *Strong partnerships with those served can result in empowerment for the team far beyond what its parent organization can provide.* High trust levels within the team and with industry partners enhanced the OSUE Team's performance, resulting in timely impacts. Strong mentoring within the team and members' caring about each other's professional well-being further reinforced the team's trust and effectiveness.

⓬ The *OSUE Team actively practiced divergent thinking before seeking convergence on either strategy or action.* The team demonstrated that divergent thinking can be a powerful tool in deciding what to do, when to do it, and how to do it to benefit those served. For the OSUE Team, it yielded high technical accuracy in its products and high competency in its human resources.

NOTES

1. The authors are indebted to the members of the three teams who contributed their insights to this case study: Steve Poindexter, Natalie Rector, and Dan Rossman from the MSU Field Crops Team; Dave Guikema, Norm Meyers, Sandra Draheim, and Betty Blase of the MSU West Regional Administrative Team; Ken Cochran, Erik Draper, Dan Herms, and Hannah Mathers of the OSUE Nursery, Landscape, and Turf Team.

2. Robert Norton, *The DACUM Handbook,* Leadership Training Series no. 67 (Columbus: Center on Education and Training for Employment, Ohio State University, 1985).

3. D. Guikema, "Areas of Expertise: Editorial," *Michigan Association of Extension Agents Newsletter,* 1994, 1.

4. M. Suvedi, *Farmers' Perspectives on Michigan State University Extension: Summary Reports* (East Lansing: Michigan State University Extension Program Support Systems, 1996, 1999).

5. From MSUE's West Regional Administrative Team mission.

6. The text in this section is solely the responsibility of Arlen Leholm and Ray Vlasin.

The Women's Interest Group
The Hill Women

▶ Mary Andrews, Ashok Kumar Seth,
Arlen Leholm, and Ray Vlasin

Why This Case

The women's interest group is an example of a high performing team. The group achieved its high performance from a start with meager resources, limited knowledge and skills, and low technology. By teaming together, the group members overcame daunting obstacles, increased their family income and well-being, and improved their small hillside community. Their team spirit was among the variables that helped to propel them into high performance.

This women's interest group was one of many groups assisted by the India government as a means of reducing poverty. The group of twenty-five women lived in a small farm village (panchyat) in northern India's Himalayan foothill country. Located an hour by bus from Shimla on a winding road cut into the hillsides, the local village families lived on meager incomes. The women were the farmers, tending crops and livestock on small plots of land tucked into the hills.

This chapter describes how the women's interest group formed, operated, and excelled. It explains how members used meager resources, educated themselves, and used that learning to increase their farm production and incomes. They explored, studied, and improved existing agricultural enterprises and created new ones. They undertook new roles as group members and planned and took individual and group actions for their mutual benefit.

The chapter describes how intense caring and sharing, dedication and zeal to improve, enthusiasm, and energized human spirits within a group led to unusual achievements despite resource constraints. Group members increased household income and addressed community challenges in safety, education, and substance abuse. They developed a new positive outlook for themselves and their families, including the desire that all of their children graduate from college. These women dared to undertake and achieve things they never dreamed possible.

The Snapshot

The case that follows contrasts sharply with the cases described in chapters 3–6 and the team settings involved. This case describes a team formed by northern Indian village women who were farmers.[1] Starting on their own, they benefited from some government organizational and production assistance. Their women's interest group was a real team—they worked on enterprise projects that were planned, implemented, and funded together. They achieved their joint projects through mutual trust and mutual responsibility and shared in the necessary leadership actions.

The hill women in this group started with few monetary resources, low technology, and limited education. Some were illiterate at the time of the group's formation. Most were responsible for the production from their family's small farm plots because most of their husbands sought work off the farm. The men left in the morning for work in Shimla or adjacent areas and returned at day's end. While the spouses might decide what was to be done on the farm plots, the women made day-to-day decisions about operating the field plots and about tending the livestock. They also shouldered the work.[2]

The women's group started on its own initiative. Taking advantage of some modest governmental help, group members educated themselves in farm production, improving existing farm enterprises and creating new ones. They saved and contributed rupees to the group's revolving loan fund, enabling members to advance their crop, livestock, vegetable, and fruit enterprises. As a result of their combined creative efforts, they substantially increased the income from their small farm plots and increased their total family incomes. Their tenacity for enterprise education, their inventiveness in individual and group enterprise improvements, and their income generation gave them new standing in their families and in the village community.

The members of the women's interest group used their team skills, including intense caring for one another, to move beyond farm enterprises to community problems and opportunities. They tested their soils and improved their use, reduced the risk of fire, established protection from marauding monkey packs, resolved difficulties with their local school, and attacked substance abuse. They developed new hopes for themselves and their children. Their goals included complete schooling for their girls as well as their boys and a collegiate education for all their children. The achievements of this team of twenty-five hill women ranked with those of the best of the high-performing teams we have observed.

Context

ECONOMIC AND SOCIAL CONDITIONS

Rural areas of India, including the northern region around Shimla, contain much poverty. Millions of India's rural families exist on less than ninety rupees (two U.S. dollars) a day. India has for years attempted to help rural families better their lot, improve their production and income, increase their available food, and improve their health and housing. The Indian government also has attempted to help villages with forestry management, natural resource conservation, and improvement of village water supplies, roads, and schools. But the needs in rural India are enormous, and the available government resources are stretched thin.

The women in the farm households are the primary farm production workers. They prepare the land for crops, plant them, cultivate them, and protect them. They harvest the crops and preserve them for family use or sale. Likewise, they tend the family's dairy cows or other livestock. They obtain and provide feed for the livestock. They are responsible for the production of milk and other products, again for family use or for sale.

To say that the life of typical farm women is hard is likely a gross understatement. When one sees them walking along rural roads, working in the fields, or tending the livestock, one can nearly feel the personal burdens they seem to be carrying. Some, in fact, are carrying heavy physical loads—sticks they have collected, livestock feed they have cut or otherwise obtained, or farm produce they are taking to a nearby market. Their countenance seems to reflect their burdens—eyes downcast, faces without smiles, a dispirited, weary pace.

GEOGRAPHIC CONDITIONS

The urban center of Shimla, in the state of Himachal Pradesh, is a large northern Indian trade center built into the sides of several adjacent mountains. In some areas, the city appears taller than it is wide, a truly picturesque mountain place. It is also a historic city, formerly the summer capital of the British government. A number of old government structures, government yards, and a church from that era have been preserved and serve as points of interest for visiting tourists. Shimla serves as the major trade center for the *panchyat* Anandpur that is home to the hill women's interest group. It is the marketplace for the products produced in the *panchyat*—milk, vegetables, root crops, fruit, and berries.

Anandpur is located about forty kilometers from Shimla. Narrow winding roads cut into the hillsides lead from Shimla to Anandpur. At first, the trip by bus or car is slow going because of trucks, bicycles, carts, and pedestrians, but traffic quickly diminishes. Where the hillsides are steep, the downhill edges of the roads are marked by white-painted stones positioned along the shoulders, a low-cost safety practice that serves as one of many reminders of how India's people can be creative and make do with the limited resources available to them.

THE HILL VILLAGE

The ride takes just over an hour but seems much longer. Anandpur's commercial center is located at a curve in the road with a place to pull off. A few small shops serving travelers and villagers sit at the back of the flat pull-off area—Anandpur's commercial center. At the time of the interviews, forty-five families comprised the Anandpur *panchyat*. (Anandpur is located within the Shoghi circle, in the Mashobra block, in the Shimla district of Himachal Pradesh.)

Homes dot the hillsides both above and below the road. Flat small fields for crops and vegetables are nestled into the hillsides. Sloping areas, some covered largely with grass and others covered with pine trees and grass, surround the small fields and extend up the hillsides. A few narrow dirt roads lead back to homes, while a few narrow dirt paths snake up and down the hillsides.

Meeting with the Women's Interest Group[3]

VISIT BY WORKSHOP TEAM

We arrived at the hill village for our initial visit and parked at the turnoff area. A state government representative and an agricultural agent led the way. We walked off the road and up a steep, narrow, curved, rocky path. We met, greeted, and passed two school-aged boys in matching shirts and trousers walking to the local elementary school on an adjacent hill. We came to a modest one-story home and were greeted warmly by our host, Satya Thakur, whom the government representative described as the "link worker" for the women's interest group. Thakur served as the liaison between the women's interest group and the state agency and district personnel who provided assistance to the group. She shared her group leader roles and responsibilities with two other women.

Thakur and the group had assembled in her home, its regular meeting place, awaiting our arrival. Thakur was considered to be courageous, hardworking and confident, popular with the group, and a capable group leader. She was a widow with four young daughters whom she was educating and supporting on her own. At the time of the last interview, one daughter was studying for a bachelor's degree. Thakur aspired to have all her daughters complete college, as did other group members.[4]

GRACIOUSLY RECEIVED BY THE GROUP

Thakur invited us into her modest but very clean home. The two main rooms were connected and open. Together they were large enough to permit the group's twenty-five members, most of whom were present, to meet and conduct their meetings.

Few group members spoke English, so an Indian-born female colleague and male agricultural agent served as interpreters.[5] In every instance, the responses appeared frank, considered, and thoughtful. The group members appeared eager to participate in the discussion, and clearly were full participants in the group venture, were proud of what they had achieved, and were self-assured. Despite their enthusiasm for participating, the women also demonstrated that they knew how to function as an orderly group, acting in a respectful and considerate manner toward other group members. Their actions were consistent with the strong sense of caring for one another that they demonstrated throughout the day.

MUCH INFORMATION SHARED

The discussions were very informative. We learned that the average age of the women's group members was about forty and that the group was fairly homogeneous, cohesive, and highly motivated. Each member owned an average of less than one hectare of land. One of their main economic activities was production of vegetables, including root crops, with efforts at off-season vegetable cultivation and production. Dairying was another main economic activity—most of the women had dairy cows. With a ready market for their milk, they were eager to further increase their production. They also produced fruits, berries, and corn.

They did not store any of their crops for use as seeds. Rather, they sold the crops they did not use for their family and then bought fresh, higher-yielding hybrid seed varieties commercially if they could not obtain them from the state Department of Agriculture.

Group members shared with us copies of some of the farm enterprise bulletins that they had obtained and were using. The subjects included production of tomatoes, beans, peas, onions, mushrooms, and cauliflower plus household water systems. Bulletins existed on other topics as well. The members shared all the bulletins they possessed.

The group met about every two weeks to address an ordered set of topics designed to improve farm enterprises, increase production and family income, and to enable the members to help each other and care for family members and the broader community. The group contended with a number of constraints—lack of irrigation, transportation difficulties, and crop damage by monkeys and rabbits.

Group members demonstrated substantial trust of one another, a sense of mutual responsibility, and a willingness to share both information and assistance. Information shared also showed they cared intensely for one another, deliberately addressing members' problems and needs and planned actions to help.

SUBSEQUENT VISITS[6]

Rajvir Singh conducted follow-up interviews in January 2001 as a part of a larger set of discussions involving leaders and facilitators of ten interest groups in the Shimla district, and Ashok Seth led a third visiting delegation in March 2003.

Operation of the Women's Interest Group

GOVERNMENT ASSISTANCE[7]

The government's "women's group" program (Mahila Mandal) had started some years earlier. The program initially focused on household activities and their improvement. The state government, with financial assistance and guidance from the Indian government, formulated a program to give village women a general awareness of family issues, including the importance and necessity of small families; of clean houses and a clean village for good health, particularly for children; and of formal education for all children. The program also addressed the elimination of prevailing social evils such as dowry and alcoholism. Women were encouraged to organize into groups known as *mahila mandal* to obtain financial assistance to meet and obtain information.

In 1995–96, the Ministry of Agriculture introduced the pilot Women in Agriculture Program to improve agricultural enterprises. in seven states, including Himachal Pradesh. The program subsequently expanded into five additional states.

The Women in Agriculture Program provided support, through the state government, to enable groups of women farmers to develop into viable units. The groups would concentrate their activities on agricultural enterprises. The program would provide various types of support (financial, production supplies, information, and education) so that the women might orchestrate their own activities, resources, and group interactions. The hill women's interest group in Anandpur was one of ten groups in the Mashobra block.

ORIGINS OF THE HILL WOMEN'S GROUP

The hill women began working together as a smaller group in 1993–94, undertaking several agricultural activities. One member related, "At first, it took a lot of work to get the women to become a group. They had operated as individuals for so long. When they began to see the benefits from working together, the women came together as a working group—a whole group." The group grew to about twenty members at the time it became affiliated with the Women in Agriculture Program. They had taken advantage of information available under the earlier Mahila Mandal program.

Under the Women in Agriculture Program the state Department of Agriculture provided group members with improved seed varieties as well as information and some extension education on crop production for those who could take advantage of the offerings. State support provided funds for a liaison position and for the training of someone for that position as well as for two assistant contact women. The program linker served as the chief contact between the women's interest group and the government offices that provided assistance. Also, the women could request and obtain support for education concerning particular enterprises. Though the support was modest, it represented a new opportunity for increased skill and knowledge and helped cover bus fare for members to take advantage of education offered.

The group leader and members were ready to find and use assistance to advance their agricultural objectives. Said a group member, "When the NATP [National Agricultural Technology Program] became available, we were invited to a meeting where information on project ideas was provided. We were encouraged to join as a group and select one activity for support under the project. We did join and selected dairy. We have a history of working together and trust each other. We chose dairy because we each had one or two animals in the family and we were responsible for looking after them. Our animals were local breeds with low productivity. We knew if we could get better breeds, better heifers, we could produce more milk. We had a good market with families in Shimla and could sell additional milk easily."

INITIAL SPOUSAL OBJECTIONS

The hill women needed to convince their husbands that spending time with the women's interest group and traveling for training would be beneficial. As one agency member explained, "Traditionally, Indian rural society has been man dominated. Hence, men discouraged the house women from frequent visits to outside places or institutions. Men, particularly with illiterate or semi-illiterate backgrounds criticized involvement of women in village affairs and for their frequent movement outside the village. The women, because of their home responsibility, were hesitant to go on vocational training and study tours outside of the district for more than one day." Thus, particularly in early stages of the group's formation and operation, some men saw women spending time away from their households as improper, unnecessary, or unproductive. This spousal commentary stressed group members and the group process. The situation had to be overcome, largely by the individual women involved.

As the group progressed, enterprise improvements and production increases became visible. Female farmers began to bring added income to their households, a development that more than anything else changed husbands' opinions about wives' involvement. One team member related, "Many men opposed our spending time away from our homes. We could only change this by bringing new income into the family. Once we brought the new income the men would say, 'Go, go to your meeting,' instead of saying, 'Why don't you stay here and take care of the kids, the cooking, and the washing?'"

GROUP SIZE LIMITATIONS

The women's interest group began with twenty members from among the village's forty-five families. As the group progressed, other women from the village asked to join. The group had been meeting at the leader's home and determined that the maximum number of women that could meet there was about twenty-five. In addition, the state agricultural agency had recommended that women's interest groups not exceed twenty-five. The group capped its membership at twenty-five. When other village women asked to join the group, they were refused membership but were offered help in other ways: the women's interest group offered to answer any questions and to demonstrate the group's improved practices as well as to help create a second women's interest group. At the time of the initial interviews, assistance was being provided to nonmembers, although a second group had not yet been formed.

MAIN PERFORMANCE OBJECTIVE

The women's interest group clearly expressed its main performance objective: to increase farm production and consequently family incomes. They sought to improve and expand their existing agricultural enterprises and undertake added enterprises. But they needed a number of things, including more farm enterprise education and information, improved seeds and plant varieties, improved dairy breeds, and funds to invest in and operate the enterprises.

However, at the time of the workshop team's visit, the women's interest group had already developed strong community objectives. Some had direct bearing on the agricultural conditions, such as soil testing of all farm plots, collecting pine needles to enhance mulching and preserve moisture for vegetables, preventing destruction of farm produce by the marauding monkey packs, and reducing damage from rabbits. However, other objectives focused on the community conditions that affected families, such as improving schooling and reducing the abuse of alcohol. The agendas for the regular meetings routinely included both farm production and broader community aspects.

PERFORMANCE GOALS

With the district agency's help, the liaison/leader and group members established performance goals to better meet their agricultural production and income objectives:[8]

> Participate in meetings of the group and in training events;
> Maintain harmonious relationships and coordination within the group by participating in members' good and bad family occasions;
> Participate in training necessary to adopt new technologies to increase production and income;
> Create demonstration plots;
> Emphasize milk production and marketing;
> Provide members with credit for investments and expenses from the group's savings;
> Maintain linkages with departments to obtain production supplies, technical knowledge, and other information.

REGULAR OPERATING MEETINGS

The women's interest group met regularly to plan and transact operations. The meetings appeared to play a central role in the team's effective operations and its coordinated actions and achievements. At the regular meetings, a variety of activities occurred:

> Discussion of activities in progress;
> Discussion of constraints and problems faced;
> Sharing of experiences, including training and study tours;
> Collection of contributions for the revolving loan fund;
> Assessment of group and member needs, including training and production;
> Discussion of immediate future action plans;
> Sharing of literature, inputs, and skills;
> Sharing of members' problems and joint exploration of solutions;
> Planning for members' major activities;
> Discussion of community-wide problems and actions.

Caring for one another constituted a deliberate, natural part of the group's operating plan and process. All parts of their agenda reflected a concern for sharing and working as a group. In addition, the last three items on their agenda addressed directly the needs of others and assistance to be provided by the group for those needs.

INFORMAL OPERATING PROCEDURES

The regular meetings of the women's interest group formed the centerpiece of the group's informal but understood operating procedures. The meetings and other elements of the group's effective operating procedure were gleaned from the discussions conducted:

> Regular biweekly operating meetings with an agenda of action items;
> Keeping of a journal by the group indicating those attendees at the meetings and progress made since the previous meeting;
> Requirement that everyone make entries in the journal—members who could not write were expected to learn so that they could make entries in the journal, take advantage of educational programs, and participate fully in the group;
> Contributions to the revolving loan fund;
> Sharing of activities in process and progress made;
> Attendance at and active participation in group operating meetings as well as in the group's plans and activities;
> Helping group members with major farm activities and other significant life events (births, weddings, illnesses, and deaths of family members).

Keeping a journal was a greater achievement for the women's interest group than it might appear. A number of the women were illiterate before the group formed, but all members have subsequently learned to read and write. Writing in the journal enabled all members to share a summary of their progress. Literacy further permitted all members to participate fully in the regular meeting as well as in training programs and to read and use all bulletins. Women who had been illiterate when they joined were among those requesting more intensive training for various production enterprises.

ACTIVITIES IN PROCESS AND PROGRESS REPORTED

A major part of each meeting was the sharing of activities in process and the progress made since the last meeting. Information shared might include results of recent soil tests, some new tillage approach, a technique for preserving moisture for a root crop, a new way to stake and tie tomato vines, the production obtained from varieties of French beans or corn, the yield from a specific blueberry variety, and so on. Or it might cover some new approach to sorting and selling tomatoes, an attempt to store a vegetable for off-season marketing, the purchase of an improved breed dairy heifer, the milk production for a particular breed of cows, or the success from direct marketing of additional milk to a select family or two elsewhere. Group members might share information about new seed and horticultural varieties and where they might be obtained—from government or increasingly from commercial sources.

Included were reports of progress made by subgroups. If a subgroup had been working on some idea or some needed action, the subgroup would be expected to describe its actions. It would share what it learned and the source, possible actions to be taken, and possible benefits. If the subgroup believed that the entire group should act, it would share its recommendations. This sharing, by individuals, subgroups, the liaison/ leader, and assistants informed, educated, and motivated the group.

REVOLVING LOAN FUND

The women's interest group created a revolving loan fund to provide members with money for new enterprises or for improving existing enterprises. Loans were made only to group members and were repaid with interest. Members could also use the fund to cover emergency expenses if they had no other means of meeting such expenses. Each member was expected to save and contribute ten rupees to the fund at each meeting. (When the revolving loan fund started, the contribution was five rupees each meeting, with the amount increased to ten rupees when regular meetings began to be held monthly rather than biweekly.)

At the time of the initial interview in 2000, all members contributed 5 rupees per meeting to the revolving loan fund. Funds were held in two bank accounts totaling some 26,400 rupees. Two families held membership in another women's interest group as well and made deposits into its revolving loan fund, thereby obtaining even greater access to capital and credit. Thus, self-help among the members was clearly on the increase, as was the potential for self-generated loan funds and members' access to them.

The revolving loan fund succeeded. All group members who received loans paid them back with interest (last reported at about 2 percent per month). None of the members took a commercial bank loan. These women would not have had access to funds for farm investments and expenses without the women's interest group.

SHARED LEADERSHIP

Satya Thakur, the group leader and agency liaison, was a longtime village resident. She obtained and shared information from government agencies and other sources, arranged for assistance, and brought the group together regularly in her home. She was the only member of the group to receive some (modest) outside compensation for her service. Members viewed her as a courageous, hardworking, and confident leader. Agency personnel viewed her as an excellent liaison, dynamic and self-assured. She shared leadership of the group with two alternates who served as assistant contact farm women. The three received annual training for their roles under the Agricultural Technology Management Agency (ATMA) program.

The group also vested leadership in their subgroups. If a particular situation needed exploration, a subgroup of two, three, or four members would do so. Each member could take leadership actions on behalf of the subgroup—that is, lead in exploring and analyzing the matter, identifying possible actions, and forming recommendations.

Likewise, each member of the women's interest group could undertake leadership actions. Individual members could advance problems or constraints for consideration and possible action or could secure training and share the information and skills obtained. Any member could be a part of a subgroup and exercise leadership in that manner. Furthermore, any member could plan and provide assistance on some major activity for another member or for the village. The women's group nurtured its members' leadership capabilities while advancing agricultural enterprises and community betterment. Future strong shared leadership for the women's interest group from within its membership seemed assured.

AGRICULTURAL EXTENSION EDUCATION[9]

If support could be arranged (from the ATMA and/or from within the group), members could take advantage of a variety of agricultural extension education offerings as a way of improving or establishing a farm enterprise:

> *Sandwich (specialized vocation-oriented) training:* a ten-day program organized in three phases available to the group, not individual members. The topic would be identified by the group and focus on some agrobased vocational activity.
> *Reinforcement training:* a five-day program organized on a specific agrobased need identified by the group.
> *Mahila Goshti:* a one-day agricultural education exhibition with resource persons available for consultation; all group members were invited.
> *Study tour:* two study tours of agrobased activities were held each year (one inside and one outside the state) for twenty-five women members.
> *Training for the liaison and two assistant contact farm women:* three days per year, with ATMA support for travel expenses, literature, and seed and fertilizer samples.

As the members explained, the sandwich program consisted of three objectives or parts focusing on some specific farm enterprise or activity: (1) to learn as much about a particular enterprise as participants could from materials and teaching provided by the district and other available sources, (2) to go to a location where such an enterprise and its operation could be observed firsthand, (3) to explore what resources or improvements would be required to create or improve the enterprise on the farms of the group. Women in the group reported that they especially liked the sandwich programs, in which the three parts provided a focused approach to evaluating enterprises.

The district's ATMA project offered a variety of topics for technology training:

> Agriculture and crop related areas;
> Agro-forestry;
> Animal care and nutrition;
> Homestead agrobased production, such as mushroom cultivation, beekeeping, sericulture, or fisheries;
> Integrated nutrient management;
> Integrated pest management;

> Household water management for kitchen gardening;
> Marketing and technologies to help reduce drudgery;
> Development of appropriate agricultural skills through practical training.

However, the women's participation in the training depended on whether it could be arranged and whether the whole group or the appropriate group members could find the funds and tap family savings to cover the costs of attending that exceeded what the liaison could arrange from the ATMA project or other sources. Participation also depended on husbands' willingness to permit the women to leave the village for training programs, particularly programs requiring more than one day away. When all these conditions could be met, group members participated in technical training.

At the time of the initial interviews, members reported they had been involved in various training programs. They all had received and put into use training in preparing feed for dairy animals; however, they wanted more intensive training in dairying and in animal husbandry. They also indicated that they wanted additional training in vegetable production—particularly off-season vegetable production and storage and mushroom production—and in new enterprises such as rug making. Further, group members wanted the training to be of the sandwich type—education about the enterprise, observation of it in operation, and analysis of what it would take to implement it on their farms.

STRATEGIC MARKETING OF MILK AND PRODUCE

The women's interest group was interested in effectively marketing its produce as well as producing it efficiently and more abundantly. For example, the group decided it could easily sell additional milk by continuing its direct marketing to select families. As one member explained, "We sell our milk production individually. We see no advantage in marketing our milk as a group. It would be difficult to bulk our milk since we are so spread out." Another member shared, "We believe we can get a higher price and cover our travel costs by selling a fresh, good product directly to one or more families. We like the direct contact with the purchasers and their families. The families expect our quality product, and we have a place to sell our milk that we can depend on."

For vegetables, root crops, and fruit, marketing strategies depended on such factors as type of product, time of product availability for sale, range in quality, whether direct sale was possible for high-quality products, and available and dependable transportation. Attention was also given to whether marketing could be enhanced by advancing or extending the cultivation, production, and home storage of vegetables beyond their regular season.

When asked about collecting (bulking) and selling their produce cooperatively or to a jobber for resale, group members voiced reservations. They pointed out that mixing of high- and low-quality vegetables likely would not bring them the best return for their produce. While it might help in the disposition of lower-quality products, they did not see it as the most profitable way for the group to proceed with its marketing. Also, they were mindful of the logistical difficulty of bulking produce for sale because the farms were spread throughout the *panchyat*.

However, some group members had developed a system of tomato and ginger root collection in which a truck would come daily during the harvest season for those crops. The women would take their produce down to the road and would be paid by the trucker for the amount of produce contributed. The trucker would then resell the produce in the Shimla market.

Important in this case was the fact that the women's interest group analyzed the market possibilities. As a result, they viewed direct sale by individual members to families in the Shimla region and benefiting from the quality products they produced as consistent with the group's overall plan to advance farm enterprises and increase family incomes. They did not view these individual approaches as contrary to group action by the women's interest group.

Accomplishments

SELF-ASSESSMENT

We asked members of the women's group what they viewed as their successes. They were modest in their responses but indicated rather clearly that much had been achieved:

> Major increases in production of milk, vegetable crops, and other produce and increased family income from their sale;
> Better living standards in the family, including better nutrition;
> Improved literacy of women members and improved education of children;

> Thrift among the members, with saving habits increased;
> New investments in farm assets, particularly in improved dairy animal breeds—Holstein, Friesian, and Jersey—plus investment in soils;
> Awareness and effective use of development agencies;
> Enhanced communication among group members and beyond their group;
> Enhanced member and group status, esteem, and influence within their households, within the village, and beyond;
> Improved decision-making ability and acceptability;
> Increased access to capital and credit through the revolving loan fund, to which all members contributed;
> Increased desire by members for training in new enterprise areas and for more intensive training to improve existing enterprises;
> Sustainability of the women's interest group.

Although this listing is very impressive, it does not tell the entire story. During our three visits, members shared additional outcomes that indicated even greater achievements by this very special and highly productive group.

LIVES OF MEMBERS AND FAMILIES CHANGED

One member related that being a part of the group had changed her life and that of other members. "Since the start of this group, we feel stronger. We feel more able [self-assured] to do other things as a part of the group. Kantajee [a member] produced high-quality vegetables that were exhibited in a local show. This was reported in the local press. We have traveled to different places to learn things with help from the [ATMA] project, which we would not have done before. We are making more independent decisions than before. Our children are doing better. We have more money to look after them. They go to school. We can give them milk and still have enough for sale."

The woman continued, "Two of our group members have been elected to the *panchyat* [village government]. Satyajee [a group member] has become a member of the ATMA governing board. Others want to copy us—our women's group. Our lives have changed for the better." Another member explained, "I feel that I am not alone. If I need help, I can turn to my group. As an individual, I feel more confident." Still another member added, "My workload is bigger, but I now organize my time." Yet another related, "We are happy to be taking this additional [enterprise] responsibility as our success has made our family life stronger." One member pointed out, "It has made other differences in our group. We have a great sense of humor now. Since we are a group, we are very open with other members. If one of the group members has some large-scale work that needs to be done, she tells about it in the meeting, and we decide when group members will help. We even help the health worker and come together for the health worker."

FAMILY MOTIVATION AND PARTICIPATION

Not to be overlooked was the group's influence on husbands and children. One member shared, "Because of the group's work, we are getting good participation by our husbands and our girls and boys. Our work is not separating women from men. Neither is it keeping men from as much participation in farming as they wish. Our work increases household discussion of the farm activities and the whole farm system approach." Another group member observed, "Some women are getting good involvement from their husbands before they go to work off the farm and after they return from that work. Also, we are getting good participation by girls and boys in the farming. It contributes more income Another member shared her insights about motivation: "Because of our work and our education about farming, our children want to complete their schooling and go to college. Motivation in our girls is high because of what they see happening to our women." The members of the women's interest group thus constituted positive role models for the girls of the village community as well as a motivating force for husbands and children of both sexes.

INNOVATIVE GROUP ACTIONS

The group members were not content to limit their innovative efforts to their individual farms. The members jointly explored, studied, planned, and implemented a number of group actions that benefited all panchyat farms. For example, one member noted, "We started soil testing. We received training on how to remove soil samples for testing and how to get the samples tested. Now, every field belonging to the women's group families has been soil tested. We did it to manage the soil and fields better. We know how much manure to use on each field. Now all families [in the *panchyat*] test their soils and manage the amount of manure they use on fields."

Another woman observed, "I bought a Holstein heifer in Shimla some time ago. I kept the heifer, and after a while I got it artificially inseminated. It worked out well. Now all the women are using artificial insemination for their cattle, and their breeds are improving." Building on that statement, another member pointed out, "All the women who have milk cows have added or switched to Holsteins, Jerseys, or Fresians. We get more liters of milk than before. Now we get twenty to forty-five liters of milk daily per family that can be taken by bus to Shimla and sold to families there. We get about fifteen rupees per liter for cow's milk." Another woman said, "Because of the greater number of livestock, we now get so much cow dung that it is more than we need on our fields. We sell some of our extra dung to the university and state farms," generating more income.

The women in the group also observed that the heavy buildup of pine needles on the tree-covered hillsides constituted a fire hazard. At the same time, their experimentation had revealed that pine needles made an excellent soil cover around vegetables and root crops. The cover retained added moisture for their growth, a vital endeavor since the women lacked an irrigation system. The women also discovered that removing some pine needles from the hills would increase vegetative growth on which they could graze some of their dairy animals while still protecting the soils. The women's interest group organized and managed the pine needle collection process and then reaped the benefits of the changes.

The women's interest group also took actions to help nonmembers in the village with their farm practices and production. As one member pointed out, "The other women wanted to join us so they could get training and get new and better seeds. Our group is helping those women get the better varieties of seeds, and the women are accepting advice that we give them on crops and livestock." Thus, all of the *panchyat*'s farm families benefited from the women's interest group's actions.

MEMBERS' INFLUENCE IN FAMILY DECISIONS

Prior to their involvement in the women's interest group, the wives in the village had a limited, traditional role in family decisions pertaining to finances and household enterprises. Although the women were the farmers in most of the farm families—preparing plots, planting and caring for crops, tending livestock, and performing most other farm work—husbands and family elders made decisions about the enterprises and related finances.

Because of the knowledge and skills developed by the members of the women's interest group and because of the income they generated, these women became a new force in their family decisions. As one member explained, "Our husbands are asking us for our advice before deciding what agricultural crops to plant and where to plant them. We feel our status in the family has improved. We manage money jointly and consult with our family or husband before making major decisions to spend money. We are contributing more to make family life better, and our husbands can see this."

Another woman lived in a household with three generations of family. The "family minister for money" opened a bank account and deposited the woman's earnings. As the woman explained, "The family minister keeps the money for the family. If I want to use the money, I must discuss it with the family and then the family decides together if I can use it." She continued, "If I have an idea that I want to follow—say, spending it on a better dairy heifer—I bring the idea to the family. I tell what it will cost and what it will do for the farm and family. The family discusses it with me and then decides whether I can go ahead and use the money." At that point she broke into a broad smile because, she said, "I am the one that had the idea, and I brought the idea to the family and discussed it. It was because of my idea that the new investment happened." She was quite proud of her new role in the family.

In May 2000, we asked other women how much their standing had improved as a result of their participation in the women's interest group, and after chatting among themselves, a group of women replied, "At least 75 percent." Furthermore, they indicated, "Our standing in the community has grown about 75 percent, too." One woman explained, "Earlier we were cautious to talk about agriculture to the men. Now we do it freely. We ask questions of the men, and we give our ideas to the men."

SELF-EMPOWERMENT

The women's interest group benefited from government programs and state assistance. However, the group also became increasingly self-empowered, a process facilitated by some of the same conditions that empowered other teams analyzed in this volume: (1) access to needed information and technical knowledge, (2) access to financial and other resources, (3) decision authority for actions taken, and (4) accountability and responsibility for actions taken.

Over time, the women's interest group *obtained considerable information and technical knowledge* about enhancing existing farm enterprises and creating new ones. Such efforts were made possible by the excellent work of the liaison and her two assistants, the training programs on technical matters in which group members participated, the regular operating meetings at which all members shared information and knowledge, the production bulletins obtained and shared among the members, and such other sources as the demonstration plots managed by the women.

The members of the group *achieved access to financial, technical, and human resources*, particularly as they pertained to farm enterprise improvements. The revolving loan fund constituted a chief group resource. The new farm income they created and brought to their farm family provided an additional source of funds for enterprise investment and improvement. Their active and intense caring for one another, their deliberate sharing with others, and their assistance to one another constituted still additional resources for both individual members and the entire group.

The group members *achieved increasing decision authority for farm enterprise actions.* As the women members became more technically knowledgeable, more effective in managing the farm enterprises, and more adept at increasing income from their farm enterprises, they achieved new and higher standing in their families that resulted in their husbands' and larger families' vesting more decision authority in the members.

Members of the women's interest group *grew in accountability and responsibility for the actions taken and in mutual accountability and mutual responsibility within the group.* They were responsible and accountable, collectively and individually, for (1) sharing activities in process and their progress, (2) sharing knowledge from training, (3) sharing literature, inputs, and skills, (4) contributing to the revolving loan fund, (5) addressing group constraints and problems faced, and (6) assessing and helping to meet members' needs. They also were responsible for (7) sharing members' problems and jointly working out solutions, (8) contributing to group action plans, (9) helping with members' major activities, and (10) participating in solving community-wide problems.

WOMEN'S SPIRITS

> The group's growing sophistication for analyzing enterprise problems and opportunities allowed and empowered the women's interest group to address a wider range of possibilities. As members received more training and education, they became more valuable resources to the group for planning, analyzing, and implementing new actions. This success built the women's self-assurance and further empowered them to address other community-wide problems and opportunities. The women in the group became a new force both in the family decision process and in changing village conditions. In both family and community, their roles broadened and their voices were being heard.

Those conducting the interviews concluded that the women's achievements, their new roles, and the fact their voices were being heard in the *panchyat* as well as at home had energized their group spirit and their individual spirits. Their growing mutual trust and responsibility, their intense caring and sharing, and their dedication, commitment, and confidence further energized that spirit. In contrast to their women counterparts elsewhere in rural areas, their eyes shown brightly, their heads were held higher, their faces were alive, and their enthusiasm seemed undaunted. Clearly their spirits were energized.

To test the group members' attitude toward all they had achieved and the many changes that resulted, we asked, "How many of you would like to go back to the way things were before you became a women's interest group?" Every woman at the May 2000 meeting said, "No, No, No!" They said it loudly and repeatedly, some shouting it. They said it with strong negative facial expressions and vigorous hand movements to match. They could not and would not return to conditions of the past.

What Made the Team Special?

MUTUAL COMMITMENT AND CARING AND SHARING

Two distinguishing attributes that helped make the women's interest group special were its individual and group commitment to common objectives and its related intense caring for and sharing with members and others. Group members would do almost anything for one another to advance their group objectives. They worked together on farm enterprises, jointly advancing their incomes and savings. They helped one another with major projects, cared about one another's children and families, and helped address common community problems. The intense caring and deliberate sharing were empowering individually and collectively. These attributes increased group strength and compensated in part for the lack of other resources.

One member summarized the sense of commitment and caring: "We feel very close to each other. Many of us have been together in this group for a long time. Our faith in each other has slowly improved. We do a lot of things together. For example, as a group we recently decided to help a woman outside the group who was sick. We are happy to do things like that."

INDIVIDUAL AND GROUP SPIRITS

The high spirits of the group and of its individual members was a third distinguishing feature that made this group special. Their spirits were high because of their farm accomplishments and their increased standing and roles in their families and in their *panchyat*. Members also reported that their spirits were high because of their sense of security. As one member observed, "We know that if we run into a problem, the group will help us. We can take a loan from the group's fund for an emergency need, and that gives us a feeling of security. We feel more secure and happy now." Their spirits also were high because their voices were being heard within their families, throughout the village, and beyond.

ENHANCED PRODUCTION AND INCOME

The group's great success, given its initial resource constraints and spousal objections, was a fourth distinguishing feature that made this team special. The women's interest group achieved great success in terms of enhancing productivity of enterprises and in contributing to family income. As one member shared, "We are involved in different activities, like vegetable production and dairy. Both are paying very well. We like dairy because it is our responsibility totally. We received technical training from ATMA, but for it we got no grant or subsidy. This condition made us rely more on our own abilities. We also learned about health problems related to animals. Feed has not been a problem for us. Our income has tripled since the start of ATMA [its availability to this group]."

SUSTAINABILITY OF THE GROUP'S OPERATION

A fifth distinguishing feature that made the group special was its high potential for sustainability. Group members were very proud of their many accomplishments and wanted to continue them. The women showed determination that their women's interest group would sustain itself into the future. One member shared, "We are very confident that our group will continue, even if the project [help from ATMA] is over. But we do not want to ask our members to contribute more money [above regular contributions] to the loan fund, as some members could not afford to do so. Some of our group members now belong to another interest group and have to contribute some rupees in each group."

Members' hopes for the future also enhance the group's likely sustainability over time. As one member pointed out, "Our group is already diversified. But some of us would like to grow more vegetables. We can produce and sell more milk. We would like to learn new [enterprise] skills, such as rug making."

ALCOHOL REFORM

A sixth feature that made this group special was its willingness to take on the most difficult community issue, minimizing the use of alcohol. Group members pointed out that heavy consumption of liquor had been a serious problem. When the men returned to the *panchyat* after working away, they stopped at the two liquor stores by the village road. The liquor was not cheap, and its consumption took a sizable segment of the men's earnings away from their families. In some instances, heavy alcohol consumption led to abuse of family members.

Members of the women's interest group individually and jointly approached male members of their families and of other families in the village, asking them not to consume alcohol regularly in huge quantities. Government officials from the regional office reported, "The women were successful in diminishing the alcohol consumption and in creating a better social environment. They were successful because they adopted a group approach." The women reported that they also asked that the local liquor shops be closed, but the people who held the liquor contracts had the power to ensure that the liquor stores remained open. Nevertheless, the women's bold actions raised village awareness, reduced liquor consumption and income loss, and improved the village environment.

OTHER CONDITIONS

District government personnel who worked with the hill women's interest group reported that several additional factors helped make the group special.

> *A close sisterly relationship prevailed among the group's members.* Members participated actively in other members' significant family events, both good and bad.
> *A high sense of security existed among members of the group.* The members' willingness to help one another with farm enterprises and other needs advanced security.
> *A high level of trust existed among the group members and between them and the group leader.* Continuity of membership and leadership contributed to this high trust.
> *The level of communication and interaction within the team and with the team leader was high and aided productivity.* Both organization and meetings were vital.
> *Members developed a strong group approach to both farming and community matters.* Collectively, the women achieved things that no one of them could achieve alone.
> *The group was homogeneous regarding resources and felt needs.* Their small units and marginal resources permitted them to identify with one another's situations.
> *The leader gave full attention to every member and maintained full transparency in her actions.* She was an ideal shared leader and liaison.

Dynamic Influence of Team Spirit

As in the previous chapters, instead of attempting to show the dynamics of the many influences on performance, we display in simplified form the influence of team spirit on the women's interest group. Those conducting the interviews concluded that the high team spirit was central to the hill women's self esteem and performance. We indicate this factor's influence, including the growth in level of caring and sharing, assistance to others, and group zeal, on two conditions—performance levels and environmental levels. *Performance* refers to the various outputs of products and services achieved by the women's interest group. *Environment* refers to the set of circumstances that the women's interest group members helped create for themselves and within which they operated.

Simplified diagrams 1, 2, and 3 in figure 7.1 represent three positive and connected dynamic loops. They depict the changing status and influence of the increasing team spirit. As the interest group's caring intensified, the assistance provided within the group and beyond increased, the level of performance grew, and the environment within which the group worked improved. These conditions set the stage for more intense team spirit—caring, sharing, assistance, and zeal—for greater performance and for an enhanced environment.

Diagram 1 illustrates the starting level of team spirit for the women's interest group (level 1). It began with high caring for other members of the group and a commitment to mutual assistance regarding production enterprises. The performance that existed initially is reflected in performance level 1. As the group progressed, its members began to take actions that changed their environment. They focused more intelligently on improving existing enterprises as well as possible new ones. They increased their literacy, which in turn enhanced team members' effectiveness in receiving and sharing training and learning (level 1). These group enhancements led to an increased level of team spirit (level 2).

Diagram 2 illustrates the increased level of the women's interest group spirit, including effective assistance within and beyond the group (level 2). Increased team spirit in turn enhanced performance (level 2). The increased performance and the increased planning, analyses, and actions that made it possible influenced the environment. Loans from the revolving loan fund became more readily available because contributions to it continued and loans were repaid with interest. The group became more strategic about marketing, important because output by members increased. And the members not only enhanced their literacy and knowledge but aspired to have their children become better educated. These conditions constitute a new environment (level 2). Motivation from the enhanced environment plus the increased level of performance led to an even higher level of team spirit (level 3).

Diagram 3 illustrates the still higher level of team spirit with its increased zeal for achievement and its intense caring for group members and others in the community and sharing with them. Members' advanced knowledge and skills increased the assistance group members provided to one another and to nonmembers, factors that combined to yield higher performance (level 3). Increased investments, such as for new dairy breeds, permitted improved farm enterprises and new ones. Creative community-wide approaches became more prevalent, such as soil testing and improved field use. Community conditions were improved, such as strengthened schooling of children and cooperation in matters of family health. Husbands and children became more involved, and women's voices were truly heard. Together, these conditions represent a new environment (level 3). The information shared by those interviewed and by those who assisted in the interview process indicated that the positive relationships could continue to grow beyond level 3.

Insights from the Women's Interest Group

This unusually creative and productive women's group provides many insights worthy of sharing, most of which have already been discussed. Seven additional insights supplement the lessons learned presented near the end of the chapter.

❶ *Government assistance can serve as a catalyst for the organization and initial empowerment of those in poverty, helping them increase their knowledge, production, and income.* Government action provided the women's interest group with important support when it needed to move ahead. Money for seeds, funds to help support a liaison to the state agricultural agency, and funds to help defray initial farm enterprise education clearly helped to move the group ahead. The state agency's district offices and personnel provided advice. Furthermore, in later years, the ATMA model of assistance emphasized capacity building rather than financial support, a development that benefited the women's interest group's sustainability.

❷ *The hill women's desired outcomes truly represented joint products; therefore, a directive single-leader unit would have been less effective.* The exploration, analysis, planning, and implementation of farm enterprise improvements and creation of new enterprises constituted multiple joint products. They required mutual commitment and responsibility of members working in cooperation. No directive single leader could undertake what the group could undertake cooperatively. No single leader possessed all the skills that the group could

FIGURE 7.1. TEAM SPIRIT: DIAGRAMS 1, 2, AND 3

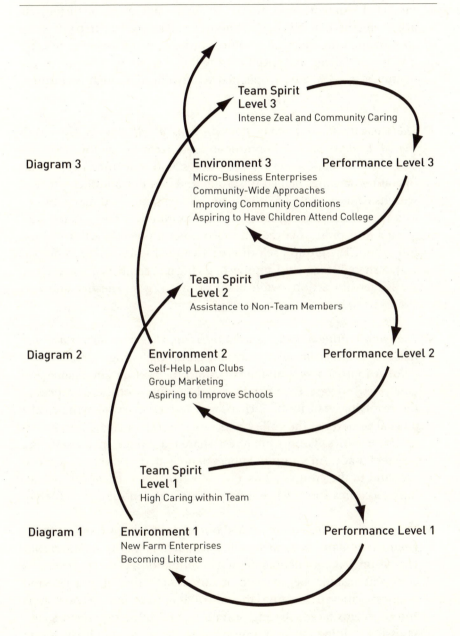

Diagram 3

Team Spirit Level 3
Intense Zeal and Community Caring

Environment 3
Micro-Business Enterprises
Community-Wide Approaches
Improving Community Conditions
Aspiring to Have Children Attend College

Performance Level 3

Diagram 2

Team Spirit Level 2
Assistance to Non-Team Members

Environment 2
Self-Help Loan Clubs
Group Marketing
Aspiring to Improve Schools

Performance Level 2

Diagram 1

Team Spirit Level 1
High Caring within Team

Environment 1
New Farm Enterprises
Becoming Literate

Performance Level 1

bring to bear on a problem or opportunity. No single leader could predict the outcomes from start to finish and direct or dictate the achievements that resulted. Moreover, no single leader could have commanded the financial resources or possessed the stature to carry out major village improvements with local support. Instead, the women's interest group operated as an effective, high-performing team.

❸ *The women's interest group functioned as a self-directed team with shared leadership.* A commitment to objectives, an informal but agreed-upon set of operating procedures, and well-structured regular operating meetings helped the group to determine and then proceed with its courses of action. While the women performed many actions as a group, for some problems and opportunities they created subgroups to explore, analyze, and recommend possible actions to the full group. The group's self-direction worked well. It was combined with a shared leadership approach, giving all members opportunities for leadership actions while maintaining a group leader and two assistants to coordinate the process.

❹ *Though operating procedures were informal, they were understood and followed by group members.* Regular group operating meetings were held. A journal was maintained to record meeting attendance and enterprise progress. Each member of the group contributed rupees to the revolving loan fund. Each person was expected to write in the journal or develop the ability to do so and to participate fully in the group activities. Group members shared activities in process and progress made. All group members participated in the regular meetings and in the group's plans and activities. The existence of operating procedures appeared vital for the unusual performance achieved.

❺ *The group meetings were action oriented and helped the women's group coordinate its farm production and community improvement.* The group was very deliberate in its agenda for regular meetings. Its ten-point agenda began with member activities in process and progress achieved. Meetings then moved on to reviewing constraints and problems faced, sharing of training and other experiences, and assessing training needs and production inputs required. The group developed immediate future action plans and shared literature, inputs, and skills beneficial to the plans. The agenda focused on members' problems and jointly developed solutions as well as on members' major activities and how the group could help. Finally, meetings addressed community-wide problems and opportunities and the actions that could be taken.

❻ *The farm women's group addressed and changed the village environment.* When the original performance objectives–increased farm enterprise production and increased family income—were being accomplished, the women's interest group formulated new family and village objectives. The group targeted village conditions that needed to be improved, including safety, schools, and substance abuse and related family income loss. Because of the group's caring for its team members and others; its self-developed analytical, planning, and implementation skills; its increased confidence and village standing; and its group approach, the members addressed and changed their village environment.

❼ *The standard of living changed the most.* When asked what had changed the most about the families of the women's interest group, the quick response from the women was the standard of living. One woman explained, "We have more family income because of the things we have done. In earlier times, we depended on local breeds of cattle. Now we use breeds of cows that produce much more milk. We have one person in the cornfields to warn us so we can protect the corn, fruit, and vegetables we grow from the monkeys." Another woman added, "We use better seeds and better plant varieties. We save more moisture in the soils. We have increased yields manyfold. We eat better and have more to sell. We can buy more of what we need. And we can educate our children better."

When asked how much their standard of living had improved, three of the women conferred before answering, "At least 75 percent." Based on what the visiting team saw and heard in May 2000, that number may well substantially understate the group's improvements.

Lessons Learned[10]

The women's interest group truly represented an unusually high performing team. Members achieved remarkable results despite serious resource constraints. They provide a powerful example to those who might believe that their restraints are insurmountable or that a group of individuals can do little because they lack resources. The women's interest group's experiences provide important lessons for those who seek to create teams under adverse circumstances and help them advance toward high performance.

❶ *Good ideas can come from anywhere, especially from team members, but the organizational context must exist or be created that permits those ideas to be translated into positive and effective group action.* Government programs provided very modest assistance to enable the hill women to organize effectively. The women's group received assistance through the district agency for a leader, for participating in agricultural extension education opportunities, and for limited production supplies. This assistance helped in the initial and subsequent growth of the organizational context. Once well under way, the women's interest group functioned as a productive team. It encouraged ideas from members and analyzed those ideas for possible use. Members provided a vital source of good ideas. With limited agency support, the group translated these ideas into productive actions.

❷ *Even in conditions of abject poverty, highly effective teams can emerge with clear performance objectives to which the team members are strongly dedicated.* From the beginning, the women focused on improving their family income through improvements in their farm enterprises. They committed themselves to learning, through extension education programs, the technical aspects of dairy production, animal husbandry, soil testing and management, vegetable and root crop production, fruit and berry production, and other types of crop production and management. They committed to improving their literacy skills to make themselves more effective in their farm enterprise pursuits. And they committed to creating, from their own meager savings, a revolving loan fund that would enable them to implement enterprise investments and improvements. These objectives were the group's central focus and were not ignored as the group undertook other community objectives.

❸ *The women's interest group did not receive training in team processes; however, it developed operating procedures and expectations about member participation that helped it become an effective team.* The group's operating procedures included a plan to meet regularly, reports by group members of their progress, active participation in meeting discussions, monetary contributions to the loan fund, and group consideration of ideas regarding farm enterprises. If the group judged an idea important to pursue, subgroups often were created to explore and report back. If an idea was pursued further, the women involved would analyze it, observe it in operation, and determine requirements for its implementation. The thorough procedure served the group well, minimizing enterprise failures and increasing the benefit from enterprise actions.

❹ *Shared leadership was effective in this group situation, in which initial literacy and initial technical capabilities were low and initial financial resources were nearly nonexistent.* Though the women's interest group was served by a capable leader, the group members shared in the leadership responsibilities. Members took leadership responsibility for identifying enterprise problems and opportunities and presenting them to the entire group for discussion. Members took responsibility for serving in subgroups that analyzed ideas and advanced them for group consideration and action. Members took responsibility in broader agricultural and community matters. Shared leadership, despite constraints, was fundamental to the achievements made.

❺ *Human development of team members proved vital to creative team performance.* The women's interest group members recognized that they needed to overcome the literacy barriers that held them back. Those who needed literacy skills worked hard to achieve them. The requirements of writing in the group's journal, serving as members of subgroups, and participating in technical educational programs about crop, livestock, and other enterprises provided added incentives to those needing to advance their literacy. The combined literacy improvement plus technical skills obtained through educational programs enhanced members' active participation and their usefulness. Development of members strengthened the group's performance.

❻ *Even in conditions of extreme poverty, high mutual commitment, high mutual responsibility, and high mutual caring can serve as team strengths and substitute in part for lack of other team resources.* For example, fruit and vegetable crops were threatened by packs of marauding monkeys from the river area down below the hills. Monkeys are protected because of religious beliefs and therefore are not exterminated or harmed. All hill women took turns at watching and mobilizing the village if the monkey packs approached. When alerted, village women came together in force and beat on pans and used other noisemakers to drive the monkeys back to the river area, protecting the agricultural enterprises. No expensive security system or noisemaking devices were required.

❼ *When a group is empowered, it can broaden its performance goals and objectives, further enhancing individual and family life and community conditions.* As group members worked together for enterprise production, their caring for one another increased. They became concerned about problems and conditions beyond their farms. Having established the ability to analyze farm problems and take action, they could apply these skills to other family and village problems. Thus, the group addressed educational inadequacies and worked to diminish the heavy consumption of liquor by the village men.

❽ *Major benefits can accrue to an organization or social group when members, previously without a voice in decisions, have their voices truly heard.* As the members of the women's interest group increased farm production and bolstered their family income, they received greater standing within the families. Husbands and other family members sought out the women's views and recommendations, earning them larger roles in farm decisions. Their voices became more fully heard at home. Their roles in community-wide actions also increased—for example, in soil testing, marketing approaches, and school improvement. Their voices became increasingly heard in community matters. Women from the group came to hold positions in local government. The many group achievements listed earlier provide strong evidence of the positive benefits of women's voices being heard.

Powerful Implications

Organization, implementation, and empowerment of women's interest groups may constitute one of the most powerful ways of harnessing the creativity of the rural poor in India as well as in other countries. We were fortunate also to observe women's interest groups in the state of Uttar Pradesh, in northeast India, that creatively restored saline soils and brought them back into production. We observed women's interest groups in the state of Kerala, in southern India, including one that was processing wood from rubber trees that were no longer productive and was making saleable wood products. These women's interest groups, plus the hill women's group near Shimla, provided convincing examples of what empowered teams of women can achieve in production, enhanced incomes, and improved family and community life.

NOTES

1. District government personnel referred to the team as the Women's Group Anandpur, Block-Mashobra. We refer to it here as the women's interest group and the hill women's group or simply as the group, generic terms used respectfully to refer to the team in Anandpur Panchyat.

2. We are indebted to Rajvir Singh and colleagues, who brought the women's interest group and its achievements to our attention.

3. The initial visit occurred on May 23–26, 2000, as a part of a workshop on participatory extension management hosted by the Agricultural Technology Management Agency, Shimla District, Himachal Pradesh, India, and conducted cooperatively by Michigan State University Extension and MANAGE, the Institute for Extension Management in Agriculture, Hyderabad, India. The workshop team members visiting the hill women included, Dr. B. Najeshwar Rao, Dr. H. S. Bhalti, Dr. Sutsh Dev, N. R. Hayagreeva, Virender Kumar, Snneh Wadhwa, and resource person Dr. Sashi Pal along with R. Vlasin.

4. Information drawn from interviews with the women's interest group by Ashok Kumar Seth and colleagues from the Agricultural Technology Management Agency, March 2003.

5. The translators likely polished responses, making them more complete in English and possibly eliminating some of the interviewees' word choices and local expressions.

6. Interviews by Rajvir Singh, Agricultural Technology Management Program, Shimla District, January 2001; interviews by Ashok Kumar Seth and Agricultural Technology Management Agency team members, Shimla District, March 2003.

7. Information in this section obtained via correspondence by Rajvir Singh, project director, ATMA-National Agriculture Technology Program, Shimla, Himachal Pradesh, India, January 11, 2001.

8. Goals drawn from interviews conducted by Rajvir Singh, January 2001.

9. Information in this section obtained via correspondence and attachments by Rajvir Singh, project director, ATMA-National Agriculture Technology Program, Shimla, Himachal Pradesh, India, January 11, 2001.

10. The text in this section is solely the responsibility of Arlen Leholm and Ray Vlasin.

Broader Lessons from the Cases Explored

▶ Arlen Leholm and Ray Vlasin

The Broader Lessons

A major goal for this book is to arm its readers with lessons that may be helpful as they enhance performance of their current teams or ones they hope to create. Each of the preceding five case-study chapters provides key lessons specific to that case and its unique organizational context.

This chapter covers the broader conclusions about organizational and team conditions that apply to the high-performing teams analyzed. We believe that these conclusions hold important insights for many other teams that provide joint products or joint services and seek to carry their performance to higher plateaus. We believe these lessons have value whether they are applied to co-located or geographically distributed virtual teams that seek to advance to high performance and sustain that performance over time.

In Chapter 1, we set forth the hypotheses that guided our research. They were: (1) interdependent work teams producing joint products or services could achieve high performance under an array of situations as long as the teams possessed the empowering conditions and operating relationships that allowed full expression of team creativity; and (2) while one cannot deliberately command or direct an interdependent team into unusually high performance, together the organization and its teams can take a series of actions that will materially increase the odds that the teams will become very high performing. Our analyses and the observations of team members and leaders associated with the teams in the five case study chapters provide confirming evidence for our guiding hypotheses.

In the course of conducting our exploration with high performing team members, plus team and organizational leaders, we asked if the important lessons they had learned from their experiences would have application to other teams—within their organization and beyond their organization. We benefited by their informed judgment and combined it with observations provided by the masters of team performance from Chapter 2, along with our own observations and experiences. From these combined observations, we have selected for presentation here 21 of the broader lessons. We have grouped them into four categories for ease of reference by the reader.

Starting Right

❶ *Being diagnostic is the place to begin in aiding one's team or its organization to enhance team performance.* It is imperative that one start with an assessment of where the team and the organization are, not where you want them to be. For example, the Quaker Oats leadership was very diagnostic and thereby avoided taking what might have been customary but fatal first steps. The leadership of the Institute for Genomic Research (TIGR) teams also was very diagnostic regarding the conditions needed to advance the teams toward higher performance. Michigan State University (MSU) Extension was diagnostic about the need for teams and the capabilities they would require before implementing a team-based system.

❷ *A strong focus on performance is central to the high-performing teams, and all teams evidenced both individual accountability by team members and mutual accountability with other members of their team for performance.* Team participation in determining performance goals was vital. But in no case did a strong focus on performance alone suffice to permit team success. Many other conditions or actions were involved in advancing the teams to high performance. The TIGR teams and the Bosch teams shared the many creative processes and approaches they found necessary for their unusual successes.

❸ *Organizations and teams need to strive together for clarity of purpose regarding performance goals and other team objectives.* Goals and objectives undertaken by the high-performing teams usually were both clear and specific. The means for carrying out the objectives were left largely to the teams and sometimes presented a substantial challenge. The performance to achieve team objectives received high priority. The TIGR teams and Quaker Oats's Labor Management Leadership Team achieved great clarity of purpose and enabled team members to take a wide range of leadership actions leading to the unusual performance achieved.

❹ *Hiring the right people first.* The Bosch teams emphasized the importance of who they hire—their personality for working in the team and with the customer as well as their skills. As one Bosch team member emphasized, "One of the big things is to hire people for their personality more than their specific degree. People have to be smart enough to do the job in the long run, but the skills working with the customer and the team have to be highly regarded." Moreover, "We've nixed many an interview because the person was too quiet, not proud of what they had done, or simply did not fit. . . . You must hire the right people first. If you don't hire someone who cares, it doesn't matter what system you put them in."

❺ *Deliberate attention to complementary skills needed for team performance is especially important when team products and services are complex and varied, need for innovation is high, and team processes are complicated.* In all cases, teams sought and engaged complementary knowledge and skills. Teams embodied the team skills required, added persons with needed skills, or obtained education in team skills through the parent organization or on their own. The Bosch teams, the teams of TIGR, and the women's interest group provide excellent examples of achieving needed complementary skills that led to greater performance.

Knowledge and Skills

❻ *Investment in the knowledge and skills, including process skills, of potential team members before team formation can facilitate orderly team introduction, maintain productivity, and be financially sound.* At Quaker Oats, which invested substantially in intensive and systematic education and skill development prior to team introduction, production continued without a loss and increased following team implementation. The MSU Extension education teams also gave attention to skill building prior to and during initial team operation, thereby enhancing early team performance.

❼ **Professional development of all team members appears vital to creative and innovative actions and enhanced performance.** While some of this training and development must be technical, it must also encompass team and other process skills, sometimes called the soft skills. Quaker Oats, for example, provided training in communication, consensus decision making, effective meetings, problem solving, and conflict resolution. MSU Extension was diagnostic about educational needs via use of the DACUM or related processes and provided follow-on education in technical and interpersonal skills. Through its "sandwich education program" and other means, the women's interest group developed members' capabilities for new and existing enterprises and for community actions.

❽ **One of the important elements fostering success in high-performing teams is the positive treatment of divergent views and approaches.** Team member training needs to include positive treatment and understanding of the importance of divergent views and approaches in creative decision making and action. The most creative teams analyzed actively sought divergent views and approaches for discussion before reaching convergence. They sought divergence within their teams, including from subgroups, from other teams, and from other sources beyond the team, including clients, cooperators, public agencies, and other stakeholders. The TIGR teams, those of Bosch, and the Ohio State University Extension team offer excellent examples of the search for and creative use of divergent views and approaches.

Cautions

❾ *Self-directed or self-managed teams can be highly effective for those joint objectives and joint purposes that require it, but not for all possible objectives and purposes. They also are not appropriate for all organizational settings.* In all cases, the self-directed teams analyzed were responsible for a range of products, services, and/or outcomes necessitating joint actions by team members. Furthermore, effective performance also required shared responsibility, shared accountability, mutual trust, and other forms of cooperative action. For all the high-performing teams, the objectives sought apparently could be achieved best by a self-directed team, not by a single-leader unit in which the leader decided who was to do what and how. However, such a single-leader unit may be the more functional work system model in a strong command-and-control environment where a team would not be reporting to a supportive shared leader.

⑩ *Size of a self-directed team is basic to its effective functioning and its achievement of strong performance. The lesson here for team formation is to stay small but make sure the team has the complementary knowledge and skills for the performance sought.* Each team's membership permitted it to be highly workable, from the largest at twenty-five members to the smallest at eight. One exception, an MSU team with fifty-two members, divided itself into complementary subteams around projects. With fewer than ten members each, these subteams performed as smaller self-directed teams, with close participation from Extension educators, researchers, and stakeholders. The teams of TIGR and the women's interest group very effectively used temporary subgroups. In all cases where subgroups or subteams were used, they communicated thoroughly and effectively with their whole team.

⑪ *Reducing ambiguity and uncertainty within teams and in their relationship with their parent organization is vital for effective teams— whether co-located or virtual. Ambiguity and uncertainty are the enemies of effective team formation and high team performance.* Any division of responsibilities or functions between administration and teams should be clearly defined and stated. Furthermore, a team's mission, vision, values, and goals must fit those of the organization— e.g., TIGR and Quaker Oats. A team's operating procedures must fit with the organization's operating guidelines—e.g., MSU Extension's administrative boundary conditions. A team should be clear about its code of conduct and stand ready to share it with team members, team recruits, and administrators—e.g., the Bosch teams. A team should be clear about the mentoring functions it provides and the coaching provided to it—e.g., MSU Extension. The virtual teams in the case studies paid special attention to communication strategies that linked the geographically distributed members together—e.g., Bosch, OSU Extension, and MSU Extension dispersed teams.

Concepts That Make a Difference

⑫ *Establishing and fostering a trust environment is fundamental, if not crucial, to the formation and successful operation of self-directed teams.* Trust among team members and trust between team members and those in leadership positions were vital to team success. Mutual trust between the team and organization was also important in influencing team performance. Trust levels within the high-performing teams analyzed were very high and had increased over time. Trust levels between the team and the broader parent organization were typically high but varied substantially. Quaker Oats, the women's interest group, and Bosch offer excellent examples of the role of high trust.

⑬ *Trust is something earned through your performance and has lasting influence.* As one Bosch team leader explained, "I think you must earn it. You can't force it to happen either. A team leader can't go in with the focus that 'I'm going to force someone to trust me.' You've got to earn it by example. Further, once you have earned the trust, one slipup doesn't cause you to lose that trust. So you have to earn it, but once you earn it, you are going to carry it for a long time."

⑭ *Also important in team formation and team operation are the concepts and practices to be employed concerning leadership actions.* The high-performing teams analyzed typically had a point person (a team coordinator, team chairperson, or team leader). However, that person plus the other team members viewed leadership actions as a shared responsibility. They did not treat leadership as associated only with a single position. In all the teams analyzed, team members performed various leadership actions for the good of the team. These actions were varied and ranged across the team's roles and responsibilities. It was not uncommon for a team member to serve a leadership function one day and then a support role the next. The teams of TIGR and the women's interest group provide examples of highly effective leadership actions by subgroups.

⑮ *Those working with teams should recognize that team zeal and spirited enthusiasm are real forms of team energy contributing to performance. They add to physical, mental, and emotional energy, as set forth and documented by Moxley.*[1] A well-functioning team can generate added zeal and enthusiasm among its members, enabling the team to operate as if it could achieve nearly anything. Zeal and spirited enthusiasm were evident in each high-performing team analyzed, though these traits were manifested in different ways and to different degrees. Team zeal and spirit emerged as teams progressed and experienced successes and increased over time. Several members of teams described having their "spirits energized" by their active involvement in their team. The women's interest group offers an excellent example of zeal and spirited enthusiasm and their influence on greater performance, moving the women to undertake and achieve things they never before dreamed possible.

⑯ *Stress can be reduced in various ways.* A team can be proactive in reducing stress by maintaining a self-monitoring system to identify excessive workloads to help prevent burnout and employee turnover. If high trust exists between team members and team leaders and between team leaders and their bosses, a sense of security can develop. If a team is operating with a great deal of zeal and a high level of caring among team members, their burnout will be lessened. Team members who cover for each other in work and family crises or otherwise share workloads will experience less stress and burnout. Finally, clarity of team purpose, values, a code of conduct, and operating procedures will reduce ambiguity and uncertainty, thereby diminishing stress. The teams of TIGR and Bosch best exemplified this lesson.

Administrative Context

⑰ *Shared leadership by administration and teams is a necessary condition for teams to be self-directed and advance toward high performance.* Shared leadership requires a belief system that team members can and will perform well in a self-directed or self-managed mode if given proper support. Shared leadership was a key organizational and team variable experienced by the high-performing teams analyzed. The women's interest group and the MSU Extension teams constitute very good examples. All teams analyzed experienced a shared leadership environment, most within a shared leadership organization. If a team operated either continuously or occasionally within a command-and-control structure, a team leader or supervisor provided insulation from that environment.

⑱ *If top leaders are willing to share their power and resources, they will multiply both their individual power and resources and those of the organization and their self-directed teams.* True shared leadership will unleash creativity and innovation and increase positive organizational outcomes and impacts. The power of top leaders to which we refer is not positional power but the power to influence the organization's growth and the multiplication of its positive impact. Quaker Oats, TIGR, and MSU Extension offer excellent examples of this lesson.

⑲ *Empowerment of teams is vital to achieve high performance.* The teams analyzed were empowered within their shared leadership environment and/or by the external associations they developed. In most instances, the parent organization provided information and resource support in combination with shared authority, responsibility, and accountability for team empowerment. In a few instances, the team and leaders drew heavily on their external associations for information and financial and/or other resources in self-empowering actions. The Ohio State University Extension team and the women's interest group provide very good examples of the latter approach.

⑳ *To reinforce the value and importance of teams and team performance, both the parent organization and the teams should establish team recognition and awards.* TIGR, Quaker Oats, and MSU Extension had arrangements for team recognitions and financial awards. In each instance, the recognitions and awards involved a financial dimension as well as meaningful nonmonetary recognitions and team benefits. Teams indicated that awards and recognitions did not constitute a major direct factor but were indirectly quite important for motivation and pride.

㉑ *Do not expect self-directed teams to flourish under a command-and-control or top-down administrative environment unless they are protected by a supervisor who is a shared leader and who understands the need to buffer the team from administrative interventions.* A self-directed team can readily be disempowered through administrative intrusions. None of these high-performing teams (interdependent and involving joint products or services and joint actions with mutual responsibility and accountability) reported directly to an intrusive administrator. All of the high-performing teams reported to a supportive leader within the team or one immediately beyond the team in a supportive supervisory leadership role. The Bosch team provides a very good example of supportive leaders, as do the teams of TIGR and the Ohio State University and MSU Extension teams.

Some Final Observations

Possibly the single-most important insight is to approach each team and its organizational context with a truly open mind, recognizing that it is a special case of complex conditions and relationships. While many basic team and organizational conditions are important for effective self-directed teams, we know of no standard approach to achieving unusually high performance in teams that must produce joint products or provide joint services or both.

The dynamics that the teams in chapters 3–7 portrayed in moving from formation to increasing performance differed substantially. How they were initially designed, the conditions under which they were initially implemented, and how they proceeded in their operation toward unusually high performance showed some similarities as well as marked differences. Teams also evidenced synergism as they progressed. They combined new knowledge, enhanced skill sets, divergent thought and approaches, analytical and problem-solving capabilities, broadened leadership actions, increased zeal, and spirited enthusiasm for increasingly greater team, organization, and/or community benefits.

For these reasons, the place to begin in forming or transforming teams and their broader organizational context is with a careful diagnosis of the conditions that exist, the challenges to be confronted, and the processes and other actions that are possible in obtaining the performance sought. We believe that the lessons identified in the five selected cases and the broader lessons shared in this chapter hold important and useful insights about how to begin and how to proceed. We hope that the observations we have shared will benefit those seeking to enhance or transform current teams or to design and implement new teams in providing supportive organizational contexts within which the teams can flourish.

We believe team members, team leaders, and their organizations can indeed increase the odds that their teams will become unusually high performing. We hope that what we have shared will help along the way.

NOTE

1. Russ S. Moxley, *Leadership and Spirit: Breathing New Vitality and Energy into Individuals and Organizations* (San Francisco: Jossey-Bass and the Center for Creative Leadership, 2000).

ABOUT THE AUTHORS

Mary Andrews is director of International Extension Programs, Michigan State University Extension, and leader of MSU Extension's education programs in India.

Margaret Bethel served as Michigan State University Extension regional director when she contributed to this research.

Ken Brochu served as engineering manager of ABS/TCS/ESC Application, Bosch Braking Systems, when he contributed to this research.

James Chatfield is an Ohio State University Extension specialist.

Tamara Feldblyum is DNA sequencing facility director at the Institute for Genomic Research.

James Kells is a Michigan State University professor and extension specialist in Crop and Soil Sciences.

Arlen Leholm is dean and director of University of Wisconsin Extension, Cooperative Extension.

William Nierman is vice president for research at the Institute for Genomic Research.

Kevin O'Keefe served as engineering manager and technical platform manager of XYZ, Bosch Braking Systems, when he contributed to this research.

Ashok Kumar Seth is a rural development consultant for the World Bank and previously served as lead agriculturalist for the World Bank in India and the South Asia Region.

Justin Shields served as president of Retail Wholesale and Department Store Union Local 110 when he contributed to this research.

Terrance Stone is at Northeastern University.

Roger Vincent served as plant manager of Quaker Oats, Cedar Rapids, when he contributed to this research.

Ray Vlasin is a Michigan State University Distinguished Professor Emeritus.